PINCKERT'S PRACTICAL GRAMMAR

A
Lively,
Unintimidating
Guide to Usage,
Punctuation,
and Style

Cincinnati, Ohio

ROBERT C. PINCKERT

94 93 92 91   7 6 5 4

Library of Congress Cataloging in Publication Data

Pinckert, Robert C.
  Pinckert's practical grammar.
  Includes index.
  1. English language—Rhetoric. 2. English language—Grammar—1950-
I. Title. II. Title: Practical grammar.
PE1408.P5348   1986   808'.042   85-29618
ISBN 0-89879-441-2

Book design by Alice Mauro.

Contents

———————— *Chapter Eight* ————————

Pleasing

Preface

Sixty years ago H.L. Mencken wrote: "The schoolma'am to this day clings to the doctrine that there is such a thing as 'correct English.' " She clung and still clings to it because language is as deep as the ocean. You can't tell what it will do next: Meanings erode from words, language levels blur, class distinctions fade. If English goes down, we'll go down with it.

Today you'll find editors, publishers, and agents clinging along with the schoolma'am to this long discredited notion of "correct English." Make a lot of mistakes, no matter how talented a writer you are, and you are not likely to be taken seriously. Everyone has something to say, but no completely safe or satisfactory way to say it can be found. Writers are well advised to doubt their English. Few writers feel they have been properly prepared for writing, so they turn for help to dictionaries, handbooks, and guides to usage.

Writing is hard enough without having to be reminded by omniscient books of the depths of one's ignorance. Here, though, is an encouraging book on this heavily overworked subject, a book that can actually be read and digested. Everything you never wanted to know about English and were always being told is supplied here in brief essays. The rules are all here with the excuses for breaking them. There are no maxims to memorize, and the puzzles and exercises are completely voluntary.

About the Author

Robert C. Pinckert studied at Cambridge University in England, on a Kellett fellowship, then earned his Ph.D. at Columbia University. He has taught his specialties, Shakespeare and writing, at Columbia and John Jay College in New York City, and has conducted special writing seminars for soldiers, nurses, firefighters, police officers, businesspeople and convicts.

Chapter One

Levels
of the Game

The Game of English

Language is so clearly a blessing and a curse that we hardly know what to think of it, any more than we know what to think of its sole possessors, human beings. We start learning it the day we're born, and never learn it completely. No one knows where it comes from, no one can explain the meaning of meaning, or define a sentence, or even say what a word is. But somehow it has to be mastered, because so much—perhaps everything—depends on it. The American philosopher Charles Sanders Peirce said: "My language is the sum total of myself." Communicating well with others is essential to our happiness, but we can't quite get it right. The political order depends on open, truthful communications, but where are they? Do truth and speech have anything in common? A heavy sense of how difficult language is causes shyness, stammering, stage fright, page fright (the inability to read), and pen fright (the inability to write). Why must we be judged by the way we wag our tongues?

People are competitive, to put it mildly, and play many games to see where they stand; their pecking order is established by talking, by using words that assert, probe, silence. All of us must play this game, and whoever cannot express himself, as an old saying has it, will be a slave. We compete to say things better than others and call upon special language to distinguish ourselves. We tell others what we know and they don't. Max Beerbohm said that

1

every kind of writing was hypocritical. That is true, since writing always has hidden purposes, some of them hidden from the writer herself. Of course, there are messages as well as motives for all communication, but the presence of content should not obscure the fact that we talk and write primarily for the same reasons that dogs bark and birds sing.

Everywhere people can be heard barking—talking *down* to others, teaching them, enjoying being *up*. Let's imagine you get into a taxi, you say, "Good morning," and the driver says, "What's good about it?" He begins grumbling to you about the traffic and then about the price of groceries. You find this boring, and start telling him about food preservatives—sodium nitrite, for example. He doesn't know anything about sodium nitrite and shuts up.

He jabbed you first, you took the round. Neither of you realizes just what you were up to. An opponent can be done in by a single word or even by a sound, yet we pretend that our use of language has nothing whatsoever to do with us. Either the language is being used correctly or it isn't. A master strategy in the Game is to make our opponent doubt his equipment. We find mistakes in his language and avoid them in our own. We go to school to learn more about these mistakes.

We take the Game too seriously, correcting our children for every mistake, laughing when someone says *He do*, pretending to be annoyed by accents. Sadistic Englishmen sneer at Yank words, masochistic Yanks kneel in awe of English intonations. Bernard Shaw said the two peoples were separated by the same language. Everyone is separated from everyone by language. Language may well have been invented for lying. What was the caveman up to when he said *mammoth* and the mammoth wasn't even there? Doubletalk may be worth more than talk. Jargon and slang are developed as secret languages. Class accents are cultivated to keep up class distinctions. Advertisers are those who master Blurbese, professors master Bookish. A reason there are so many languages in the world—tens of thousands—is that people work to thwart communication and to limit the number of those who can speak their language.

Instead of thinking about language in the old way—you against English— try to see it in a new light—you and English against the others. If you think you're fighting the language, you're going to lose. The language belongs to you; don't let anyone claim a bigger share in it than your own or try in any way to muzzle you.

Winning Attitude

The first step in becoming a winner is to realize you're in a Game, a tough one. No matter how sharp your Game gets, you will always have tougher competition to face. You must play all the time, and have suffered many defeats already. You may have been put off your Game by a late start or by teachers who loved to tell you when you were wrong. Some of the rules they hit you with from their moth-eaten rulebooks were pretty silly. Many of your supposed mistakes weren't mistakes at all, but attempts to use perfect Informal English. Why must you use Formal? Why can't you say *ain't*? No one seems to know. Who teaches Formal? They do.

You shouldn't assume that any teacher wants you to win. They don't want your English to be better than theirs. They became professors to prevent that. We others want you to lose. Those in charge of spelling, the publishers, have not reformed spelling because it's such a wonderful test for players. The point of the Spelling Bee, which exists only in America, is not to produce a better speller than the teacher, but to produce a classroom of losers.

If you're ever going to do well in this Game, see it as a Game, see that you need the will to win, and learn the Rules of the Game so that you can plan strategy and spot cheating. Then play to win, and play in your own style. You don't look like George Washington; why did your teachers want you to write like him? The secret of winning is not taking the Game so seriously. While your grim-faced opponents continue to believe that the game is serious, you can run circles around them if you're relaxed and know where the mine fields are.

Your opponents in the Game think that Good English exists and that they have mastered it, but they can always be done in by players who know more English than they do. Wilson Follett, for example, has twenty-two pages on the distinction between *shall* and *will* in his *Modern American Usage*. That's a world record. But somewhere, deep in the hills, is growing up a young challenger who will break that record.

Since no player can ever feel confident of his skill, there's no reason to remain in awe of your opponents. They may be more afraid of errors than you are. You can't play well if you're afraid. Shakespeare wasn't afraid. He never took English, he gave it. The best writers are the bravest.

Children see things clearly and are delighted by language, before the teachers take it away and chop it into ABCs. Think of jump rope rhymes, pig Latin, word puzzles, riddles, puns, wisecracks. How did we get this wonderful toy, our favorite toy? The mystery of the gift is not likely to be solved. Any human being can learn any language, but a machine can't, and an ape won't, maybe because it doesn't want to be mistaken for one of us.

Language is handled best by those who aren't afraid to play with it. Be curious and sassy, find out what's really going on. Nonchalance helps your game and throws your opponents off theirs. Are you afraid of the paragraph? Why? No one knows what a paragraph is. Having trouble with transitions? A bag of tricks.

Loosen up. Practice. Read aloud. To talk well, talk a lot. To write well, write a lot and do it fast. Let the pen flow. Don't agonize and rewrite and rewrite. In times past, writers wrote well by writing naturally and fast, by writing the way they wanted to, and they seldom rewrote.

However expert the pros, no one's game is perfect. Everyone errs, frequently in speaking, occasionally in writing. When you make a mistake, pooh pooh it and tell yourself everyone does it. If you want, join in happily when the fogies start talking about how the Game has gone downhill, how the language is being debased. But don't take such talk seriously. When they talk about keeping English up, they don't mean it's sinking, they mean keeping it out of the reach of the wrong people. Those who know a lot about the history of the Game do not get upset over changes. They do not have fits over clever ungrammatical ads, they are not scornful when people can't bring themselves to speak plainly and directly. (Few things are more difficult.) They do not foam at the mouth when someone says *due to* instead of *because of* or uses the word *quote* as a noun.

Don't think about rules, think about you. Golfers work on their swing and try to ignore the water, trees, and sandtraps. Success in the Game depends on attitude and practice rather than on knowledge and analysis. The Game can't be fully known. There are different sets of rules for different levels of play, just as in a video game; and the rules are always changing. At the top, the level of *Superformal*, things are rough: A misused word or a dangling participle is greeted with glares that would wither the president of General Motors. Luckily for us, scarcely anybody uses Superformal anymore but academics of the more rarefied sort and funeral directors. *Formal* flourishes in business, journalism, and government, and is played by the rules you learned in seventh grade. Editors, teachers, and bosses of all sorts tend to like Formal: it makes them feel secure. *Informal*'s rules are looser and encourage personal style. It's conversational, lively, and individual—as comfortable as a cut-off sweatshirt, and often about as stylish. *Superinformal*'s only rule is to make yourself understood somehow. "I ain't got no pen" is Superinformal. You know what it means; but do you want to be caught saying it?

Winning writers know the rules of Formal well enough to bend them, every once in a while, with the quirky personal vividness of Informal, like a pitcher with a sneaky curve that just nicks the corner of the plate. They mainly play by the rules, but cheat just enough to get away with it and earn the envy of less daring and more traditional players.

So learn the rules well enough to forget about them, the way you learned to ride a bike. When you no longer have to think about balancing, you're less likely to take a spill. If you think only of what has been done or what you're *supposed* to do, you're not thinking of what *you* want to do. Remember—in the war of words, *they* may make the rules, but *you* get to choose the weapons.

Formal and Informal English

We have two kinds of clothes—everyday and dress-up—and these correspond in language to Informal and Formal. When people talk about "correct" English, they mean Formal.

Informal	Formal
She got mad.	She became angry.
This is different than that.	This is different from that.
Easier said than done.	More easily said than done.

Now put your hand over the column of Formal versions below and see if you can guess what they are. Remember that I'm using Formal to mean dressy, not black tie.

Loan me your keys.	Lend me your keys.
I can't find them anyplace.	I can't find them anywhere.
They're laying on the table.	They're lying on the table.
This one key is kind of bent.	This key is a little bent.

Informal	Formal
Leave the dishes soak.	Let the dishes soak.
You almost ran over the cat.	You nearly ran over the cat.
Bob's throwing the party.	Bob's giving the party.
I'm anxious to go.	I'm eager to go.
I thought about wearing red.	I thought of wearing red.
It goes either with black or white.	It goes with either black or white.
Can I fix you a drink?	May I make you a drink?
Soda helps you digest.	Soda helps you to digest.
I didn't eat.	I haven't eaten.
I guess I better.	I suppose I had better.
That tasted real good.	That was very good.
This has less calories.	This has fewer calories.
Have you got any matches?	Do you have a match?
She's taking her shoes off.	She's taking off her shoes.
I haven't ever done that.	I have never done that.
If I was her, I'd ask him.	If I were she, I'd ask him.
She's asking if he wants to.	She's asking whether he wants to.
They're liable to leave.	They're likely to leave.
My philosophy is live and let live.	I believe in live and let live.
I'd like for us to go too.	I'd like us to go too.
Take care. Have a nice day.	Good-bye.

There are thousands of distinctions like these, some subtle, some obvious, that mark different language levels. The word *whom*, for a prize example, is almost dead in Informal but gets around fast in Formal. How many secretaries are allowed to say, "Who did you want to talk to?" These distinctions were not invented by language teachers to torture you, but by the English-speaking people who want to preserve different levels of usage. How you and I feel about this affects nothing. Anyone is free to say that *whom* is pompous or that if you can't use *whom* you should go back to school. Opinions of this sort are like noses—everybody has one.

If Formal did not exist, there would be no fun in being Informal. Having different levels of language (linguists prefer to call them *varieties* or *registers*) allows us to express ourselves when we switch from one to another. We can add emphasis in Formal writing, for example, by switching to contractions: *We'll do it, They can't do that.* Or by using clipped sentences, like this one. We can add emphasis in Informal by spelling the contractions out: *Do not run, I have had my dinner, I do not doubt it.* A bold writer can have fun shifting between language levels, keeping her reader off balance—though the novice who tries too many monkeyshines may only confuse her reader about the tone of her piece.

Formal may go against your grain, but it is still very much in demand. Mencken said, "Standard English must always strike an American as a bit stilted." True, but we often get up on stilts. When we seek to make a good impression, as when we talk to superiors, older people, attractive people, our language becomes more cautious and Formal. A man meeting a pretty girl will lower the tone of his voice, refrain from saying *ain't*, and try not to drop his final *g*s (talkin' 'n' list'nin'). Much of what is published is Formal. People require Formality, and are not so open and chummy as is often pretended (*Hoowee! how does that grab you?*). Business correspondence is Formal, as are reports, presentations, résumés, instructions, examinations. A talk is Informal, a speech Formal.

If you didn't worry about Formal, you wouldn't need this book. You should be a *little* nervous on Formal occasions, to avoid making mistakes. When linguists, who take a scientific approach to language, advise you to leave your language alone, they are not helping you to face the world. They say that distinctions between Formal and Informal are disappearing. Some are, but those that remain take on more significance than ever. You have to know these distinctions. You have to use *whom* correctly, and to do it, you have to be able to take a sentence apart with a handy old tool, traditional grammar.

Though our society is said to be getting more casual and Informal, whenever a new slob appears, a stuffed shirt pops up to put him down. A steady increase in years of education has led more people to expect to rise socially, but at the same time there has been a steady decline in mastery of Formal. Increasing education, strangely, has been accompanied by increasing illiteracy—maybe from the deleterious effect of TV on the left side of the brain. In a society growing less literate and less articulate, the expert in Formal has a real advantage in looking for a job.

It would be silly to argue that Formal is *better* than Informal, or vice versa. Each can be effective; each can be precise. Formal tries hard not to waste any words and to avoid clichés. Informal is talkative, friendly, easy, and has a huge vocabulary—though a speaker may not draw on very much of it. There are hundreds of Informal words for *complain*, for example. Some ideas call for Formal *(I love you, I'm sorry)* and some for Informal *(cough it up, what's the catch?, knock it off)* but most ideas can be handled well in either. Informal is more colorful, lively, and poetic than Formal. Formal is quieter, cooler, suggesting that you know good manners and are trying to express yourself carefully and considerately.

Some people learn Formal at home, but others acquire it more slowly and laboriously at school and through reading. They thus come to believe that Formal is "correct" and that writing is Formal. These beliefs may hold them back: They may never analyze this notion of "correct" and choose to be correct rather than effective, or they may be incapable of many kinds of writing that are not Formal. The sense that writing is terribly Formal holds people back when they're learning to write. The hope that the spoken language is always Informal, relaxed and loose, leads people to make a poor impression when they talk.

Speech should not babble, and writing should not be puffy and artificial; it needs ballast, the sound of a person talking. You need to know and love Informal to keep from soaring into excessive Formality *(Not the least fascinating aspect of these letters is the ladder they provide to the window of their author's study.)* and you need to master Formal so people won't assume you have no manners and have never read anything *(How long did you get that dress?)*. The pitfalls in expression lie in Superformal and Superinformal. Compare: *Man, I was real torn up to hear your aunt died, I'm sorry that your aunt died, I was grieved to hear of the passing over of your aunt. The doorbell's broke, The doorbell is broken, I believe that the bell is not functioning. Fantastic, remarkable, superior.*

The safest way to express an idea is always the way that attracts no attention to itself. The most common style in writing today might be called a natural Formal or a literate Informal, a comfortable middle level that avoids slang and clichés, but uses colloquialisms and contractions, follows all the rules and conventions of grammar and spelling, and avoids stuffiness. Studies have shown that Informal instruction is much better remembered than Formal, so I'll instruct you in Formal Informally.

Surprise Quiz

Let's have a little quiz to see if you know Formal. I'll give you a Formal and an Informal version of the same sentence and you tell me which is which. Ready?

> Everyone at the party had a smile on their face.
> Everyone at the party had a smile on his face.

Which is Formal? *Everyone had a smile on his face.* In Formal, everyone is followed by *he, his, him,* and in Informal by *they, their, them.* Formal *man* still embraces Formal *woman,* so you never say *he or she,* and you never write *he/she,* you just use *he.* Or, as in this example, *his.* Next question.

> She is taller than me.
> She is taller than I.

Which is Formal? *She is taller than I.* Few people still say this, so it is very Formal and close to stuffy. Next.

> She is one of the doctors who work in the clinic.
> She is one of the doctors who works in the clinic.

Which is formal? *She is one of the* doctors *who* work *in the clinic.*

> For you and me to say *ain't* would be wrong.
> For you and I to say *ain't* would be wrong.

For you and me to say ain't is Formal. This choice of the *objective pronoun (me, us, him, them)* is explained on pages 99-101.

> Those sort of people always win.
> That sort of person always wins.

That sort of person always wins is Formal. You couldn't say *Those sort;* Formally, you'd say *Those sorts.*

> Bob and Carol each has a bike.
> Bob and Carol each have a bike.

Each has a bike is Formal. The fashionable rule is that the subject closer to the verb *(each)* decides the verb form.

> None of the characters in the movie are likeable.
> None of the characters in the movie is likeable.

You can say *None is* or *None are* as you like. *None* means *no one* (singular) or *not any* (plural). Here's a rare situation where you can choose without making a mistake.

> Let's you and me dance.
> Let's you and I dance.

That was a trick. Neither of them is or are Formal. *Let's you and I* is ungrammatical. *Let us* would have to be followed by *me*, not *I*. *Let's you and me* is grammatically correct but sounds wrong, sounds Informal. A Formal person would avoid the problem and say *Let's dance* or *Shall we dance?*

If you got half right on this quiz you show lots of promise. You see how hard some apparently simple questions of usage can be. But most questions of usage aren't hard, and they seldom present themselves. When we have something to say, we generally say it right. When we worry about *how* to say it, we're probably worried about *what* we're saying.

When Is a Mistake?

Life would be simpler if we didn't have to know different kinds of English and could rely on what the Authorities told us to do. But what is correct always *depends*. An audience decides what's correct, not a set of rules, and whenever we express ourselves it's to a *particular* audience in both senses of the word. They expect language at a certain level of usage. This level can be generally Formal or Informal or, more specifically, technical, elegant, breezy, obscene—anything. What teachers and books tell us about Correct and Incorrect English may actually hamper us as we try to adjust to the many different audiences we face. We talk to people to get something, and seldom do we just want them to acknowledge that our language is correct. To make them give us what we want, we avoid language that upsets, distracts, or annoys—unless of course that's what we want. We don't always aim to please. If a friend phones you and says *Hi* and you say *Hello* you've probably made a mistake in English. If someone says *I'm pleased to meet you* and you say *How do you do* you've made a mistake in English. If you say *It is I* you've made a mistake; if you write *It is me* you've made a mistake. In general, talking is Informal and writing is Formal. If you correct your mom when she says *I laid on the couch,* you've both made a mistake and you've hurt her feelings.

Mistakes are only mistakes if they produce unintended results. They are of two kinds: the careless mistake, the slip of the tongue or pen that you didn't mean, and the misunderstanding or miscalculation of what the audience expects. A mistake is saying something you did not want to say or something the audience does not want to hear. The audience never makes mistakes. If you're doing the talking or writing you're making the mistakes. It may not matter how many in the audience catch a mistake, because if you make a few people very upset, that's as bad as making many people a little upset. The Game is much trickier and more interesting than the one Miss Thistlebottom tried to teach you in the seventh grade.

Can you get a list of mistakes? Yes, in any drugstore. But if you look up a supposed mistake in a guide to usage and find it there, that means lots of people make the mistake. Maybe it's no longer a mistake. How old is this guide or handbook? You can only rely on a few mistakes that have stood the test of time, like *ain't,* to be reliably wrong all the time—except when they're used for fun, on purpose, to startle your reader. I told you, it *depends.*

The choice of correct language is like the choice of clothes. Clothes and speech have a lot in common—they distinguish us from animals, and we hide behind both. It's good to have a large wardrobe; no one should want to wear jeans all the time or have one way of talking. In Formal we have to wear a uniform of some kind. Though people devote much time and effort to improving their looks, spend a bundle on clothes—they're even alert to crude means of expression called *clothes language* and *body language*— they tend to neglect their language, and fail to study it and practice it as they should. The time they spend in front of a mirror would be better spent in reading aloud. Some people give up too soon in the effort to improve their English, believing that they can't do it unless they suddenly become more intelligent. That's not so. The ability to talk and write is connected with native intelligence, but big improvements come through instruction and effort.

Arbitrary Rules

Using the language would be easier if we could rely on what was logical to say. But language isn't always logical. Logically, we would say *this friend of him*, not *this friend of his*. You can *unloosen* a knot but you're not allowed to *unmelt* the ice. *Idioms* are illogical in that they can't be translated. *Sleep over* does not mean *oversleep*. Spelling and punctuation swarm with illogicalities. A word should logically have only one meaning, but many words have a number of established meanings. Grammarians always concede that language isn't logical, and then go on to tell us what we shouldn't say.

English is alive and wriggling. New words and expressions—some good, some destined for short lives—enter the language, and old words and expressions die. New ways of using the language, whatever their merits, are liked by Informal people for a bad reason (they are fashionable) and disliked by Formal people for a bad reason (they are fashionable).

Some new ways do seem unreasonable. Reason or logic tells us to say *between you and me*. *Between you and I* is a mistake as old as the language itself, and is now what most Americans say. Should you try to correct most Americans? Go ahead, that's part of the Game. What would you say? If you want to be logical, say *between you and me*, and if you want to be normal (do you?) say *between you and I*. You should have a choice. It's boring to be the same every time.

Because language is not logical, it's hard to decide on what is correct, hard to learn it, and hard to use it. Most Americans say *I seen him, leave go the handle, I didn't do nothing*, and *I laid down*. If you question them about these usages, some will admit they knew all along the usages were wrong. Then why did they say them?

Take some supposed mistakes from Black English. Many blacks use old features of the language now referred to as Black English. *It ain't been no rain, it gonna rain, I sayin it be good.* To white ears these verb forms are so unusual as to seem foreign or perverted. They are only unconscious attempts to remove useless inflections and streamline the language in the way that, say, Chinese is streamlined. *He do* conveys its meaning and (to me) sounds more forceful and less buzzing than *he does*. Old Man River, he keep on rollin along, and so do English. Formal don't.

He do can't be objected to on grounds that most Americans say *he does*, for that would mean that most Americans were right. *He do* can't be objected to as a novelty—it's been used for centuries. The only objection to *he do* is irrational: white people don't like it because it's not the way they say it. That's why blacks shouldn't use it among whites. If one doesn't care what the audience likes, why talk? Why not just hit them? Should blacks say *he does* among whites? Sure. Should whites say *he do* among blacks? Sure, unless blacks want it for themselves.

Be Your Own Professor

Before you went to school, you loved language, loved to learn new words, and maybe laughed when you misused one. Let me try to rekindle your former interest in language with some questions. How do you know when you're misusing a word? Your supposed misuse may now be the common use. Does *status quo* mean the way things are? It used to mean the way things *were*. *Verbal* now means *oral*, as in *verbal agreement*, and it also means *talkative*. Formal people insist it can only mean *having to do with words*. Is *data* singular now, or plural? If you say *the data are in*, you may feel you're correct, but your audience may feel you're peculiar.

Many questions of usage can be settled by consulting a dictionary. But dictionaries are seldom consulted. And not all questions of usage can be settled by them, since they differ in their advice, some being strict and others tolerant. Your problems may be solved by relying on a dictionary, but what about the poor souls who write the dictionary—do they rely on you? They mainly rely on the printed word and on the usage of educated people. But linguists say that uneducated speakers are closer to the spirit of the language and are more willing to invent. In our society, celebrities are considered important, and they are often polled about their use of the language.

You can argue that the educated should decide matters of usage. That is the conservative approach—an understandable one, though it leads to irritability and tries to stop the language from changing even when the changes would be beneficial. Too much conservatism is responsible for the international scandal of our

English spelling and punctuation. You can take the position that the majority should decide. The majority ultimately *does* decide, of course. In the meantime, the educated have strong veto powers. They are the ones who have kept *ain't* in the Siberia of illiteracies for hundreds of years.

If the dictionary doesn't decide usage, if the majority doesn't, if the educated do not, if famous writers do not, who does? English teachers? They'd be the last to decide. No one is in charge. You must decide questions of usage yourself, on the basis of who you are, the situation you are in, and what your audience expects. Rather than asking whether a usage is good or bad, you must ask, good or bad for *what?* Like it or not, you have much more freedom in these matters than you perhaps know.

Although no one is in charge of the language, someone may be in charge of you—a boss, an editor, a teacher. But don't let him push you around: you can always find someone to help you. If you're jumped on for using *escalate* in the sense of *increase*, find a new dictionary that recognizes this usage.

Here are some real puzzles about usage: When others are slanging or swearing, should you join in? If you're a professional, should you use the jargon of your profession or plain English? If you have an accent, should you soften it, stress it, or forget about it? In England, should you ask for a tomāto or a tomăto? Obviously, only you can answer such questions. I can't tell you how to live. To learn that, you must ask Ann Landers.

Slob and Snob Meanings

To be Formal is to be safe: to prefer three-inch-wide neckties and four-inch-wide lapels. When a word has two meanings, the Formal person chooses the older meaning, which is usually stricter or narrower than the newer meaning. But there's no cause to get serious about your Game and insist that any word has a "correct" meaning. Words don't have meanings; people have meanings for them. The meaning of a word is whatever the audience thinks it is. (Sometimes they confuse us by thinking different things, but we must never let on that we're confused.)

Take the word *etymology:* it means the study of the original meanings of words. This word is itself misused, since, according to its roots, it refers to the *true* meaning of words. The true meaning cannot be the original meaning; it can only be the present meaning. If words didn't change meaning, there would be no etymology. To be *personally* concerned about changes in the language is grandiose: you can fight changes, welcome them, discriminate among them, but whatever you do, it won't matter. Those who lament the language falling apart are only projecting.

Words struggle for survival. The fittest survive, not the best. Good words get old and die, their meanings decay. That's sad, but nothing can be done about it. One must look on the bright side—at the new words being born. Formal people get upset when old words are given new meanings, because these new meanings tend to be looser and vaguer than the old ones. But sometimes they only pretend to be upset, and are hoping to catch the other players making mistakes.

Many words have an older Formal meaning and a younger Informal meaning. Well-known examples are *smart* and *dumb*. *His clothes look smart but he is dumb with fatigue.* Words like this, those that have double meanings, are closely watched by mean players. I'll warn you about some of these words so you don't get caught misusing them—that is, using their Informal meaning in a Formal situation.

> *Aggravate* does not mean annoy, it means worsen.
>
> *Answer* does not mean reply. It means a reply that gives satisfaction. *The witness will answer the question.* Never tell people to answer you.
>
> *Cohort* does not mean buddy, it means a company of soldiers.
>
> *Continual* does not mean continuous, it means repeated. *The Army lost battles continually, the war went on continuously.*
>
> *Didactic* does not mean preachy, it means instructive.
>
> *Dilemma* does not mean problem, it means a choice between evils.
>
> *Disinterested* does not mean uninterested, it means impartial.
>
> *Each other* does not mean one another, it means each of two.
>
> *Fabulous* does not mean excellent, it means doubtful, like a fable.
>
> *Fulsome* does not mean full or generous, it means annoying.
>
> *Incredulous* does not mean incredible, it means disbelieving. Events are incredible, people are incredulous.

Infer does not mean imply or suggest, it means deduce.

Microcosm does not mean sample or miniature, it means a little world.

Nauseous does not mean nauseated, it means nauseating. If you're nauseous, don't admit it.

Optimistic does not mean hopeful, it means believing that all is for the best.

Personable does not mean affable or amiable, it means good-looking.

Protagonist does not mean enemy, it does not mean proponent, it means the hero in a play. There is only one protagonist in any group.

Reaction does not mean response, it means a passive and automatic action following upon an action. Don't ask anyone for his reaction, ask him for his response.

Technical does not mean specific, it means having to do with a science or technique.

Viable does not mean practicable, it means able to live.

Many more words than these are misused, and I've only listed some that have caused a lot of protest. These words are dangerous. If you use their Informal meanings in Formal expression you'll be in trouble, and vice versa. In ordinary circumstances, if you use *smart, cohort, protagonist, disinterested,* and so on in their earlier meanings, you will not be understood. If there's some problem about the meaning of a word, don't use it. There are plenty of words. Nobody is twisting your arm and making you use a word that could cause trouble. Whenever you express yourself you open yourself to attack from both the right and the left, so stay in the middle of the herd—unless you're a leader.

Slob and Snob Sounds

To prove that writers are allowed to digress, I will now say a few words about pronunciation. Let's see whether you know what correct pronunciation is. How do you pronounce *want to?* As *want to, won teh, wuh neh,* or *wuhnuh?* All are correct. Just as there are levels of usage, there are levels of pronunciation. What is correct depends on the situation. In an unstressed position in a sentence, *want to* would be incorrect, would be *over*pronounced. He said he *didn't* want *to* come. In a stressed position, *wuhnuh* would be incorrect, would be *under*pronounced. Do you really *wuhnuh?*

How do you pronounce the suffix -*ing?* Do you say *ing, in, en,* or just *n?* Here again, correctness depends on the situation. I'd like *something* to eat. I'd like a little somethi*n.* You have *somethen* for me? *Sumpn* wrong? Another: Please stop *pushing.* You're *pushin* too hard. I spent the *day* pushen *papers.* Mom, *he's* push*n* me. Dropping your final *g*s is supposed to get you into trouble, but not dropping them can be as bad, by sounding like you're putt*ing* on airs. The rain may keep fall*ing* on *your* head, but it keeps falli*n* on everyone else's.

We overstress our consonants to show we're angry, and understress them to show we're relaxed. But ordinarily, the care we take in pronunciation depends on what the words mean and also on what the audience expects. On Formal occasions they want us to at least seem to be careful. All audiences like us to be intelligible. Spoken and written words have to be clear.

Be alert to the need for the right level of pronunciation. Listen to this: I wa*nt to* remin*d* all of you *to* bri*ng* a pen*cil to thee* meet*ing.* And listen to this: Ah wuhnuh rmine ulluhyuh tuh bring uh pensl tuh thuh meetn. The first version is overpronounced, the second version, underpronounced. Safety lies in the middle. In Formal situations, we pronounce our words more carefully, without being aware of it, and if we're not aware of it, let's leave it that way: being too cautious in pronouncing draws attention to itself.

Fortunately, in speaking naturally, almost everyone avoids the two extremes of staccato and mumbling speech. Few people nowadays botch pronunciation. Americans are perfectly sensible in not caring a hoot about it. Inarticulateness, not mispronunciation, is what sends people to defeat in the Game. It used to be thought that a distinct and careful pronunciation was most desirable, but no one believes that anymore except a few speech teachers. In the days of radio, actors and announcers had to make an impression by means of their voice alone, and exact enunciation became a shibboleth. In these days of television, announcers charm the audience through the eyes and not the ears, and their pronunciation moves between relaxed and sloppy. They say *wuhnuh, guhnuh,* and *awduh* even in stressed positions, and some are guilty of *genuwine, durring, childern, hunderd, offten, kep, perty,* and *sparkeling. Fur* is often used for *for. Butter* and *letter* are *budder* and *ledder.*

These new relaxations need not be deplored. The only justification for an older and stricter pronunciation is that it prevents confusion. If a new pronunciation, like *genuwine, hunderd,* and *fur,* causes no confusion, it's mean to object to it. Seldom does a mispronunciation cause confusion. The only confusing pronunciations I can think of are negative contractions that sound positive: *can't* pronounced as *can*, *doesn't* as *does*(n), and *didn't* as *di*(n)*t*.

The dictionary often gives two or more pronunciations for words, and these variations are multiplied by the effect the context has on pronunciation as well as by accents. Take the following sentence: *The chocolate sundae was invented in St. Louis, Missouri.* You could pronounce *chocolate* as *choclit, choclut, chalklit, chalklut, chocuhlit, chocuhlut, chalkuhlit, chalkuhlut.* You could say *sunday* or *sunduh.* You could say *St. Louis* or *St. Louie.* You could say *Missouri, Missourah, Mizzourah, Mizzouri.* In view of this wide choice, one does well to avoid ever saying such-and-such is the *Right* pronunciation. Most people are well advised not to worry about a particular pronunciation. Say it the way you want and be proud of it. No party or parties decide the meaning of a word, and no one decides the pronunciation. Only in dead languages are things decided. In English, you have a piece of the action.

A while ago I said that when you choose your words you should not rely on what you think the word *ought* to mean. In pronouncing words you should not rely on how you think the word ought to be pronounced: pronounce the words as you hear them. Don't worry about how they're spelled. Spellings lead you into overcorrect pronunciations such as *offten, calm, Jehovah,* and *Xmas.*

In the old days, experts in the Game separated the sheep from the goats by determining whether they pronounced the long "u" sound as *oo* or *eeoo.* It was forbidden to say *nood, redooce,* and *stoopid.* One had to say *niude, rediuce,* and *stiupid.* Fancy people even said *siuit, siuper,* and *reciuperate.* This distinction has disappeared and we get along with each other better now. A few of us still say *niews* and *diew,* but no one lives forever.

A word now about accents: everyone is said to bear the burdens of a class accent and a regional accent, and some people have a whole flock of them. Because of travel, relocation, and the influence of the media, accents all over the country are being leveled, though it's unlikely they'll entirely disappear. Our society does have social classes, but luckily they are not separated from one another by pronunciation, which happens in less fortunate countries. Our ears are not attuned to subtle distinctions of class accents. Some people believe that membership in the upper class can be established by pronouncing the magic words *vahse, ahnt,* and *lahff.* Throughout the country people will be assigned to slob status, not by peculiar pronunciations, but by *lazy* speech: *something* and *nothing* become *sumn* and *nuhn,* consonants disappear, and vowels are neutralized to the mumbling *uh* sound or else drawled out. But careless speech, like careless diction, can be found anywhere. In the land of the free, even the upper classes can be slobs.

If you have a regional accent, should you soften it? People do soften their accents unconsciously when they're among those using another. Should you consciously soften your accent? Don't bother. Regional accents are not so offensive as is supposed. They're now heard on national television, they attract attention, and are a source of good clean fun. What has to be guarded against is the odd, glaring regionalism that suggests that the speaker is quite mistaken about a word. President Kennedy could say *Havvid* and *Bahston* as much as he wanted, but could not say *Havaner, Cuber. Cuba* is not *Cuber.* President Johnson could say *Amurricuns,* and *lot* and *tom* for *light* and *time* as much as he wanted, but could not say *nucular* and *inviduous.* He said that every time he opened his mouth, he lost money. If so, it wasn't because he came from Texas. When we don't like a speaker, his voice, manner, or matter, we pick on him for regionalisms. If he's otherwise likeable though, he can almost get away with *moider.* Mispronunciations are often suspected but hard to prove, and usually we give the speaker the benefit of the doubt. But if he's annoying us by being inarticulate, we'll find something wrong with him. As Proust so delicately put it: "We are always less at our ease in the company of one who is not of our station."

For people without a speech problem, pronunciation is only a minor aspect of speaking. More important are volume, pitch, tone, pace, and quality of the voice. But what always counts most is having something to say. When we have something, we generally manage to put it across, whether in speech or in writing. Only a few people gifted with eloquence manage to speak and write acceptably while saying nothing.

Having something important to say makes expression easy. But it's not always easy to find something important, so be content with finding something important for *you* to say. You can only discover what's important to you by being in touch with yourself. Ideas worth expressing are generated through talking and listening to yourself. No one becomes articulate without getting in the habit of listening to the voice of the self. Looking and not listening, reading and not listening, will leave a person dumb.

Spoken and Written

In the beginning was the Word—some say—and others say the Big Bang. *Sound* is the first perception. What is heard sticks in the brain. For nine months in the womb, before we ever look, we hear iambic heartbeats and the sound of the ocean. First we listen. Then, much later, we talk and read and write. No one learns to write without mastering the three preparatory skills. The three later skills all depend on listening. So valuable is listening that all you have to do is look as if you're listening and others will think you are a wonderful person.

I have taught writers who could not read aloud and understand what they had written, and who were surprised to be asked to do so. And there are many professionals who would not care to read their own prose aloud. Writing, they believe, is a thing to be looked at: it's slow, careful, artificial. Why claim that it has anything in common with speech? Because, to have merit, it must have *spoken tone*. Writing meant for the eye alone is never as lively and persuasive as writing that sounds like speech. Before the time of print, no reader thought of reading silently; everyone read aloud. The great works of literature are meant to be heard.

Many good writers do not talk well, preferring to do their talking through the written word, and many good talkers never write, preferring the immediate response of their listeners. One may choose between the two means of expression, but one must never forget the primacy of speech. The more writing there is, after all, the more it resembles other writing and the less important it becomes. Homer, Buddha, Socrates, and Jesus never wrote a word. Shakespeare never published one. They did not spend their time looking at a box, listening to noise, or turning pages. They listened to themselves making sentences.

To forget that writing is meant to be heard is a fatal, though understandable, mistake for a writer. In school we're taught to remove all traces of speech from our writing and sound like a proper book. So thorough is this training that some writers remain forever shy about using colloquialisms, slang, and other natural and common expressions. But these authentic terms and syntactical shortcuts are needed for spoken tone. Even clichés can ease the reader along. Reinforcing the error is the preponderance of bad writing models: little of what appears in print can stand the test of being read aloud.

As people read more and more, or pretend to, the spoken language weakens. When lively new expressions are not spread by word of mouth, they fail to enter the language. Unusual tricks like inversions disappear from speech: instead of saying *so thorough is this training* and *remain forever shy* one can only say *this training is so thorough* and *remain shy forever;* instead of putting subordination at the front of the sentence as is done in written style, one can only tack it on to the end; *e.g.*, one can only tack subordination on to the end of the sentence instead of putting it at the front as is done in written style. Meanwhile, the writers are pouring out long, weird sentences that no person would ever say. Written language is constantly degenerating into nonspeech, and needs to be rebarbarized by writers brave enough, like Twain and Joyce, to speak.

The two languages are not the same—they can't be. In speech we can emphasize or de-emphasize whatever we please, just by changing the volume, pitch, tone, and pace of our voice. In writing we fall back on punctuation, underlining, parentheses. We turn to inversions and interruptions of normal word order, and make a studied choice of words, rejecting the ones that are too lively or too common. To remedy the loss of the living voice we use as many tricks as we can. The spoken *lousy* turns into the written *miserable, nice* turns into *pleasant, pretty,* or *tasty, awesome* into *excellent, nauseating* into *repulsive.* We don't translate piecemeal or consciously; we simply enter into speech mode when speaking and writing mode when writing, and forget that the two forms of expression should try to be close to each other.

Why is there always a tradeoff? If writing tried to mirror speech it would be incoherent, slack, repetitious, and bombastic. It would seem to have an impoverished vocabulary. It would go too fast and be unintelligible, or go too slow and be boring. In writing, we get to use words we might never say: *encapsulate, haunch, implausible, flummery, trivial, ameliorate*—thousands of lovely words. But if we use too many unusual words and too many long sentences the writing seems insincere: it won't appeal to the ear and the reader won't hear anyone telling him anything. The great work in writing is to find something to say; the great trick is to make it sound like someone said it.

So there shouldn't be anything odd about writing. It's pretending, yes, but pretending to be a person. *Person* comes from the Latin *persona,* a mask. Oscar Wilde said, "Given a mask, we'll tell the truth." Try it. To write, you never have to be yourself, but you have to be able to hear yourself speaking in someone's voice. Just as children improve their speech by constantly playing roles, so will writers improve their writing by pretending to be fashion models, derelicts, millionaires, fetuses about to be aborted, fish, or hot water bottles. In Virginia Woolf's best story, "Fluff," she's a dog. So remember to read your own stuff aloud if you can stand it, and write often in spoken style—monologues, dialogues, tirades, prayers. Do speeches for voices you are familiar with: Howard Cosell, Bugs Bunny, Henry Kissinger, Barbara Walters. You and your writing will be rejuvenated. Why sit at the grownups' table? They're so Formal.

Spelling

That people are playing language games is clearly shown by their refusal to reform English spelling. The English language has the worst system of spelling of any major language. It could easily be simplified, but the publishers refuse to do it. What do they care? They'd just as soon everyone toed the mark. The silly apostrophe could be removed from the language if typewriter manufacturers stopped making apostrophe keys. They'd never be missed. Think of the billions of hours wasted in erasing apostrophes from *it's.*

A wholesale reform of spelling is probably impossible, but little reforms could be made every year. While the publishers are stalling and having a big laugh, and while students are suffering, you can do your bit by refusing to put in apostrophes and hyphens and by using spellings like *lite, thru, ment, frend*—whatever you feel strongly about. You could also spell all the *-ant* and *-ance* word endings with an *e* instead of an *a* and all the *-ible* word endings as *-able.* Do it, and use me as your authority. Of course, if you misspell, you're only allowed to do it on purpose. If you misspell unintentionally and get caught, say you did it intentionally. If you misspell intentionally and your boss or editor doesn't like it, blame it on me and show her this page. Then change the spelling—until the next time.

There's no easy way to become a good speller. You're lucky if you're born with a good visual memory for how words look. Spellings of most words can be figured out from the way they sound, but there are still hundreds of important words whose spelling has to be memorized, such as those with double consonants—*recommend, transferred, committee*—those where the *y* and the *i* keep changing on you—*mercy, merciful, pay, paid*—and the great army of words that end with -*ent* or -*ant*, and -*ence* or -*ance*, such as *dependent, significance, prominent.* Some brilliant people go through their whole lives without ever figuring out how a word like *ocurrance* is spelled.

Punctuation is important and involves the mind; spelling is unimportant and involves the mind's eye. Many famous writers were poor spellers. But they probably could spell correctly if they had to take it seriously. Today, until things change, we have to take it seriously, since it has a crazy symbolic importance for the public. Since English spelling is so hard, it is used as a test, a rather unfair test, of a person's carefulness and literacy. If one can hardly spell anything, chances are he is illiterate; that's what the word means, unlettered. Most spelling mistakes do come from being unfamiliar with the *written* words, e.g., *I could of died.*

An occasional misspelling should not be a terrible offense, but it is. Misspellings have to be caught by careful proofreading. Too many people do not proofread, being afraid of what they might find. No matter how much you trust your own spelling, there will still be words you ought to check in a dictionary. This dictionary for spelling should be small and handy, and should be kept open at your fingertips, reminding you of the importance of spelling, and comforting you in your hour of need. The ability to catch your own misspellings is seen by others as a sample of your accuracy in all other matters. Check every word that looks phunny.

If you read a lot and are still a poor speller, you have a fate worse than you deserve. Maybe there's a vision problem. If you transpose letters, experts in eye training can help you. If that's not your problem, do this: keep a list of the words you misspell and see what kind of mistakes you make. Do you compulsively misspell the same few words? Do you confuse homonyms like *to* and *too*, *than* and *then*, *accept* and *except*? These confusions count for most of the mistakes in spelling. The three most frequently misspelled words are *to*, *their*, *its*, and their soundalikes. Are you misspelling words because you speak a minority dialect? Are you leaving the final *s* or final *d* off verbs? Do you write down pronunciations like *alot*, *enviorment*, *hunderd*, *perfer*, and *athalete?* If you misspell common words, you tell the world you don't read. Since verbs are so important, any misspelled verb equals ten ordinary misspellings. The reader assumes you're an illegal alien with his own verbs, like *drownded, murderd, layed, hitted, hurted, choosed, chosed, meaned, knowed, lead* (led), and *use* (used).

Looking at the kind of mistakes you make helps you get to the root of the problem. Maybe you didn't learn phonics in school and need practice in spelling the sounds in the word, syllable by syllable. Maybe you go too fast when writing the word, not proceeding syllable by syllable. Don't try to visualize the word. Sound it out. Maybe you don't proofread. Proofreading must be laborious, letter by letter, syllable by syllable, until you get faster at it. When you proofread, do it slowly *out loud.* Poor spellers get help from proofreading backwards, since there are many more misspellings near the end of words than near the front. With long words, the speller focuses on the outline of the word and botches the middle.

Whenever you hear a mnemonic (memory device) for spelling a word, learn it. Remember that your princi*pal* was a *pal*, there is a *rat* in sep*arat*e, defend*ants* have *ants*, there are three *e*s in depen*dent, al*ready is *not all* right, *we* are *we*ird. When *full* is added to another word, it has to spill one of its *l*s: grate*ful*, hope*ful*, spoon*ful*. Exaggerate the word's tricky syllables to help you remember the spelling: pro *nun* ciation, cal *en* dar, con ver *ti* ble, def *i* nite, exis *tence*, prom *i* nent. When you have a hunch a letter should be doubled, follow your hunch: co*mmitt*ee, su*cc*eed, ra*cc*oon, o*pp*ressed. Conceive of prefixes and suffixes separately: open ness, com plete ly, love ly, lone ly, dis appoint, re commend.

In the past, dictionaries offered a page or two of spelling rules. They don't anymore. There are no useful rules except the famous "I before E except after C, or when sounded as A as in n*ei*ghbor and w*ei*gh." Following is a typical spelling rule from a popular handbook:

> Double a final single consonant before a suffix beginning with a vowel (a) if the consonant ends an accented syllable or a word of one syllable, and (b) if the consonant is preceded by a single vowel. Otherwise, do not double the consonant.

If you can remember that, you can probably spell any word. This rule explains why you write *permitted* with two *t*s and *blooming* with one *m*. That's not much help, since you're not tempted to write *permited* and *bloomming*, or are you?

So good luck in spelling; remember, it's all a Game, and this time, they really are trying to get you.

Is Formal Dying?

If Formal's the standard, you may ask why I don't treat it with more respect and just say, "Do this, Do that." I believe you have to think about questions of usage for yourself rather than rely on advice, and develop confidence in your own ear. If you tried writing for the *New York Daily News* in the style of the *Times*, you would be out on your tin ear. If you write advertising copy as though it were a formal obituary notice, they'll find somebody else to sing the praises of whiter whites and fat-free calories. *Style* means *appropriate, effective* style—and what's appropriate? It depends on what you're trying to do, why you're trying to do it, and who your audience is. *It depends.*

You'll handle Formal much better if you're not looking up to it or looking it up. And finally, you *should* be confused, since confusion foments thought. Attacking or defending Formal language is not a particularly thoughtful thing to do.

The movement toward informality is accelerating. Formal is opening up and relaxing. Contractions, colloquialisms, and slang are showing up in surprising places. A few simplified spellings are gaining acceptance. Pronunciations based on spellings are losing their hold. Ancient battles between *who* and *whom*, *like* and *as*, *lie* and *lay*, *loan* and *lend* are being fought by fewer zealots every year. *The New York Times* encourages its writers to use slang, though not in the sacred news items. There, hot dogs are still called *frankfurters*, but who knows how long the *Times* can keep that up.

These are good developments. Whatever brings the two languages closer improves them. Pointless Formalities should be removed from the path of people struggling to become articulate. Struggling, I might add, against strong cultural pressures on them to remain silent and docile. The gulf between the inexpressive citizen and the expert, like the gulf between the poor and the rich, ought to be narrowed, not widened. We must love one another or die. Language should be used in a loving, not in a putdown, way.

Linguists, lexicographers, and the savvier English teachers have long deplored the excessive Formality of English as it is taught by the schools, and some of us have wondered whether it should be taught at all. Composition courses never seem to work—they're always being removed, restored, renamed, and revised. Everyone believes in them—except the students and the teachers. In advising writers, I spend much more time correcting defects caused by fear than mistakes caused by ignorance.

I don't believe that people have a right to their own language—we should try to share—but I believe they need much more encouragement in having their say. If students balk at writing professorese and plagiarize instead, they may only be trying to protect themselves. If they refuse to learn certain distinctions (*its* and *it's*), maybe they're saying life is more serious than that, or it isn't *that* serious.

It's hard to know what they're saying since they're so unused to saying anything. They're used to looking, used to being told, and not listening when they are told. Schools blame the TV monster for the literacy crisis. TV blames the schools. Others blame the culture of capitalism for the TV and the schools. Does anyone blame himself?

The new illiteracy is confused in the public mind with the welcome new relaxations of Formal language. That written English is becoming suppler and more personal, more like the spoken language, is a great blessing. The use of contractions, for instance, is acceptable in almost all Formal settings; you can begin a sentence with *and* or *but*, split reasonable infinitives, and end a sentence with a preposition like *with* or *for* without being judged a barbarian. But this loosening of written English still has a long way to go. That many people today do not read or write is a great curse, and the language should be made easier for them. But they should also be told they are accursed, that Circe's drugs turn people into swine.

Those who have an investment in Formal language—editors, teachers, lawyers, or anyone who has painfully mastered it—are for the most part upset by the movement toward Informality. They shouldn't worry. Formal is not about to disappear. The defenders of Formal remain powerful, and send to defeat any player in the Game who is ignorant or defiant of the rules. But the player who knows Informal as well as Formal will be better at Formal. Besides, it's plain unAmerican to be Formal.

══ Chapter Two ══

Choosing Words

Finding the Tone

This chapter is on diction, the choice of words. Diction also means pronunciation, but I'm using the word in its older, Formal meaning. To build good sentences you need proper raw materials—well-chosen words. Most complaints about how badly people express themselves and most books on expression focus on matters of diction: Don't use that word! That word gives me fits! Use short words! Use clear words! Omit unnecessary words!

Of course words are important. Gerald Ford probably lost the presidency when he said that Eastern Europe was not *dominated* by the Soviet Union. But if you concentrate on diction, that distracts you from the main problems in expression. Words are badly chosen and misused when one has little or nothing to say. With something to say, the right words come, and come in sentences. To write well you want something to say. You can know all the words in the dictionary without knowing how to put them together.

When finding something to say, you first work on the problem of tone. Tone involves three things: you, your subject, and your audience. What do *you* want to tell *them* about *it?* In expression, you always have a you, an it, and a them, so you might as well admit it, and begin negotiations. If you concentrate on *you* (what do I think? what do I want? what can I say?), you get nowhere. If you concentrate on *it*, your subject (what is it? why is it?), you won't get very far, because our knowledge is strictly limited, and much of what we know is useless or boring. If you concentrate on *them*, your audience (how can I please them? will they like this?), you won't come up with anything *you* want to say.

Let's imagine you're called upon to write a piece on littering. The subject is dear to you because you're fed up with having cans and bottles thrown into your front yard. You think about how much you hate litterbugs and plan to write a piece heaping abuse on them. This approach goes nowhere: no one cares whether or not you hate litterbugs.

You should think about the subject, too: What is litter? Garbage. Do I want to talk about different kinds of garbage? Not much. What is littering? Not easy to say. Is it conscious or unconscious? Does it involve carelessness or defiance or both? How much of each? How can I find out? Can a litterbug tell me why he does it? I may question a few, but it's not likely they'll know. So I'll do a heavy think piece on the reasons for litter. Is that what's needed?

You should also think about the audience: What are they willing to listen to? Do they hate litterbugs, too? As much as me? Less than me? Some of them might be litterbugs. Can I reform them? Fat chance. Do they want a pop psychology treatment of why people litter? Maybe some of that. How to solve the litter problem, is that what they'd like? Probably. Work on that. I like that. How to prevent litter. How to clean it up. There's a lot to say. How should I say it—serious, witty, angry, cautiously hopeful? Maybe I better see first what I have to work with, then decide how to say it.

You see from this example how you can get well into your work by thinking of what *you* want to tell *them* about *it*. Each of the three has its rights and must not be slighted. Finding the tone of the piece may sound to you like a new and difficult business, but it's not. It's not artificial, since the mind works on it automatically whenever you express yourself. I'm only urging you to think about the tone. You communicate well when you have some notion of what you're up to, some grasp of the subject, and some sense of what the audience wants. The chief fault of the amateur writer is an obliviousness to her audience; she can become too absorbed in her subject or in herself, especially when the two coincide.

A keynote in music determines the scale to be used. In writing, the tone determines the vocabulary to use. If you're writing swift narrative, you can't use fancy words. If you're reporting, you use transparent language and stay out of the picture yourself. Choosing the right words has nothing to do with avoiding those few words said to be taboo, has nothing to do with knowing a huge vocabulary. The right words are right for the job and have the right tone. An audience decides which words are acceptable, as it decides which statements are acceptable. You wouldn't use slang during a job interview or write a piece for a gay publication on why boys like girls. You need passwords, not just words. Lord Chesterfield advised his son: "Learn to shrink yourself to the size of the company you are in. Take their tone, whatever it may be." You don't always have to shrink—sometimes you can expand. Usually, the writer knows who her audience is, though she may forget about them when in the throes. The *creative* writer often proceeds in the dark, trying to create her audience and herself.

Finding the tone limits your choices, but you want that. With half a million words in English to choose from and an infinite number of sentences possible, if you don't start with a tone, as a musician does, you're lost.

Your Vocabulary

Most words are technical and of no importance. Four out of five are nouns. You should know as many words as you'd like. You don't need to know many. A study showed that 96 percent of the conversations on the telephone confined themselves to a vocabulary of about 700 words (which can lead you to think that people are twice as smart as gorillas who know 350 words, or else that people should stop talking over the phone). Most people use only a few thousand words, though they recognize five to ten times that number when they read.

The Bible has only several thousand different words. The Basic English vocabulary of 850 words allows you to express yourself very well. As a matter of fact, trying to limit your vocabulary is a way to purify your style: you should aim at the simplest, most common vocabulary that gets the job done. Aristotle said that the writer should use the language of common men (though he should try to think like a wise man). You're better off knowing and using a small number of words well than knowing a great number and using them badly. In fact, the vocabulary that is available to writers today, if jargon is excluded, is smaller than it has been in the past four hundred years. We live in serious times and are not allowed to show off with words that are made up, old, learned, or foreign.

Why, then, would you want to increase your vocabulary? Because that helps you in reading, makes it easier and more enjoyable. The more words you know, the easier you read and the more fun you have when you find a new word. A new word tells us what other people are interested in. Also, enlarging your reading vocabulary increases your ready vocabulary.

New words are acquired, not from lists in magazines, but by seeing them in contexts that make you want to figure out their meaning. Say the word aloud. Words that are heard are much more easily acquired, so prick up your ears when you hear a new one. Make a habit of referring to the dictionary, which should be handy as you read. No book, not even the Bible, contains more surprises. As writers gain experience, they come to rely on dictionaries less and love them more.

People buy vocabulary-building books thinking them to be shortcuts to literacy, but there are no shortcuts. There's no substitute for the years of reading that lead to mastery of Formal. Formal takes practice. People who are tired won't practice: they'll turn on the TV rather than read a book, telephone rather than write. Often they're not so much tired as bored, and mistakenly avoid making an effort that would release them from boredom. It's not boring to read and write; it's a challenge. Two out of three people in the world can't do either one. Twenty-five million Americans can't read, and countless millions don't. TV has made reading unnecessary, as motors have made walking unnecessary and intravenous feeding has made eating unnecessary. Think about the word Tube.

What should we read? Books that engage the mind and require a personal and thoughtful response. Any book that can be read in less than a week is an entertainment. The longer you spend on a book the better it is. What reads fast is not worth the eyestrain. You learn about language by reading slowly and critically. Reading fast is a modern disease. We got into Vietnam because President Kennedy took a speed reading course. That slow you down? Good.

Fluency

Some people avoid reading in the belief they read too slow, some remain silent in the belief they speak too slow, some avoid writing in the belief they write too slow. Even Moses thought he was a poor, slow speaker. But speed is not important. Reading talking and writing are often done too fast, much more often than too slow. If one is convinced that she is too slow and can't be persuaded otherwise, then there's only one thing for her to do—it's not to give up, but to practice. Like piano keys, words get easier to use through practice. No one learns to play a piano by looking at it. And the point in playing is not to hit the keys fast, but make them sing. If you make one sentence that sings, that's worth a shelf of books that mumble and drone.

There are two problems in diction—choosing the right words, and choosing them without taking all day to do it. People are more concerned about the latter, and seek to increase their vocabulary in order to seem more fluent and articulate, not because they want to go around sounding like a dictionary.

One becomes more fluent through practice, listening, talking, reading, and writing. So stop *looking* at books, magazines, and TV and start *listening* to them. There are plenty of things to look at, if you just want to look, but there's not a lot worth listening to. You have to go out and find it. You may even have to say it yourself. When you look you only want to look more, but when you listen, you think.

Read out loud. If that turns out to be boring, what you're reading is not worth listening to. Talk to yourself: get better at this by keeping a journal. Or talk to anyone by writing a letter: write to editors, politicians, dead people. Hang around the library until you hear a book talking to you. Recite your creed: I believe that nothing can be more important than a book. Someday the book I am looking for will be written. Maybe I will write it. Deliver speeches to the mirror. Say to it: My best feature is not my smile, my eyes, my hair; it's this, my tongue. You, tongue, are my instrument. I wag you, you don't wag me. My ten fingers speak—with a pen or on a keyboard.

If you practice in this way for years you'll become fast and fluent. But no matter how fast you get, you must not break the Formal speed limit. Whether you are speaking or writing, Formal requires you to walk, *andante*. You don't want to dally (chatting, dithering, wool gathering) and you don't want to rush (gushing, babbling). Joe Louis said, "When a man's got something to say he don't need all week to say it." Experience also tells us that when someone has something to say, she takes her time to say it right.

A reader always assumes that when you write you have time. Therefore you can't be hasty or doubtful in your choice of words. You can't offer alternatives and corrections, you can't hold out a handful of synonyms. You can't submit *notes* or *remarks*, for what you submit is assumed to be in final form. Any slip of the pen is a more serious matter than a slip of the tongue.

Audiences are lenient with a speaker, because they know she's under pressure of time. Even serious slips are forgiven, so happy is the audience that someone is talking to them. Good speakers know this and derive their confidence from it. (They also know that few people are listening: the audience is looking, catching words and phrases rather than sentences.)

In view of the audience's tolerance, there's no excuse for being tongue-tied. The secret of speaking well is an air of confidence. Slow careful speech is effective speech, and marks the quick mind. You must show your listeners you care about what you're saying, that you're weighing the words, and that some weigh more than others. Pauses convey meaning. There are pauses at the ends of sentences, and pauses before verbs and direct objects that bring out these words in the sentence. Cancelling these pauses by blurting *uh uh uh* wrecks your speech.

These audible pauses sometimes pop in when we find ourselves embarked on a sentence with no idea where it's going. Since we use the *uh* when we're in trouble, using it frequently suggests we're having lots of trouble. As we become more articulate, we find ourselves less frequently caught in sentences we have to fight our way out of. We gradually acquire the skill of framing the whole sentence in our mind before saying or writing it. Some people even learn to think in paragraphs. Cheer up: it gets easier.

Wordiness

What's wrong with these? *I'll see you at 10 A.M. in the morning. It's over and done with. My tardiness was due to the fact that I was late. Kills bugs dead!* The fault is obviously wordiness, because that's what the heading says. But wordiness is not obvious. In Informal it's used all the time for emphasis and clarity, and then it ceases to be wordiness. Make sense? Multiple negatives are common examples, and are found in all languages: *I didn't ask for nothing, no, no, I don't want none.* These are no more objectionable than reflexive pronouns: *He cooks himself.* But in Formal they are wordy. Formal tries to be brief and achieves emphasis not by repetition but by omitting the unemphatic.

The sin of wordiness takes two forms. When expression is dull and long-winded, the sin is mortal and called verbosity. When some apparently useless words creep in, we have the lesser sin of redundancy. Redundancy is seldom detected, but when it is, the audience resents having their priceless possession, their time, taken from them. An audience can be killed with a joke or a redundancy.

Deliberate repetition for heavy emphasis is sometimes allowed. The device grabs attention because it is annoying—a fact to which advertisers seem oblivious. Though an effective speech has often been described as one in which the speaker tells you what she's going to say, says it, and then tells you what she said, she shouldn't get caught. Amplifying the message, or saying it in different ways, hides the repetition. To amplify, you need lots of material. That's covered in Chapter Six.

Redundancy is hard to detect because we allow it in Informal. Simple English sentences teem with unnecessary letters and words. Words could be abbreviated and many modifiers and most inflections left out, but this isn't done, since people don't want language to be too dense and streamlined. Curt messages, though complete and logical, are often misunderstood. Much that seems redundant helps make the meaning clear and allows the audience to get away with being inattentive, which is their normal state.

Before swearing never to repeat ourselves, let's know a little more about why we do it. Why do we say, *At this point in time my answer is affirmative, and in the month of June you'll have my promise for the future,* instead of saying, *Now my answer is yes, and in June you'll have my promise?* Maybe we love to hear the sound of our own voices. (Did you catch my wordiness—*hear the sound?*) Sometimes we use a lot of words when stalling for time. *(Stalling for time?)* Sometimes we use a lot to appear to be helpful or humble. *(Appear to be?)* But usually, we're just careless and say things twice over again because we don't recall the less familiar shorter expressions.

The following is a bore of phrases not to be used in Formal. Boiling them down makes for instant elegance.

Normal	Elegant
appear on the scene	appear
bring to a conclusion	conclude
bring with you	bring
enclosed herewith	enclosed
explicitly state	state
make a motion	move
substitute in their place	substitute

Normal	Elegant
will leave tomorrow	leave tomorrow
whether or not	whether
more preferable	preferable
well off financially	well off
inside of, outside of, off of	inside, outside, off
where to, where at	where
one and the same	the same
each and every, each one	each
any and all	any
and etcetera	et cetera
as compared to	compared to
in this day and age	today
satisfactory enough	satisfactory
round in form, square in shape,	round, square
many in number, blue in color,	many, blue
two acres in area, small-sized	two acres, small
in spite of the fact that	although
due to the fact that	because
the time now	the time

For practice, why not remove these Laurel helpers from these Hardy nouns? early beginnings, end result, existing problem, free gift, general consensus of opinion, hard question to answer, important essentials, mutual cooperation, other alternative, overall length, pair of twins, past history, potential danger, reason why, self will, separate groups, tangible sales, widow woman.

Then, cut the tails off these verbs: explain about, follow after, include in, mix together, penetrate into, proceed onward, protrude out, recall back, repeat again, rock back and forth.

In English, you have to watch for little adverbs—*off, in, with, together*—drawn to the verb like a magnet. In Formal, don't say *rest up, rise up, burn up, eat up, drink up, start up, settle up, hurry up, write up, open up*. Listen up now: the *up* is seldom needed (it *is*, though, in expressions such as *put up, hold up*, and *let up*).

However natural the redundancies, they are not allowed in Formal. You are to be as brief as possible without being obscure. You shouldn't be *terse*, though, moving so fast the message has no time to sink in. Tight-lipped, laconic style is for New Hampshire farmers and tombstones.

What Are the Right Words?

The first requirement of a right word is that it not be *used* wrong. The user understands what the word means among her audience, not what it means in Heaven. The right word conveys its meaning and does the job you want it to do. If you want a flowery word, it will be flowery; if you want a vague word, it will be vague; if you want a shocking word, it will shock. Should you be flowery, vague, or shocking? Informally, be what you want. Formally, behave or get spanked.

A right word can be right on target, not just suited, but delightfully suited to the purpose. No better word could be imagined. The word is suited not just in its denotation, or dictionary meaning, but in its connotations, its flavor, its tone. Knowledge of denotations and sensitivity to connotations—neither is easy to acquire. Neither can be taught to you, because there are far too many words. Word meanings soak in through hearing and reading the words over a long period of time. You discover the more mysterious qualities of words by falling in love with them. Reading poetry and learning new languages will make you fall in love.

A dictionary can tell you that *children* is standard and *kids* is slang, it can tell you that the experts frown at *downplay* and *input*, but it can never tell you what word you should choose. The choice of words is never an impersonal matter, nor an indifferent one. Even when words seem to have the same meaning, they have different sound and rhythm. In a business letter, should you *ask*, *beg*, or *request*? Do you drink *cheap* or *inexpensive* wine? Should a highway sign read, *Watch out for falling rocks*, or *fallen rocks?* Is your neighbor an *officer, policeman, cop*, or *fuzz?* He may *have* his faults but he *possesses* his good qualities. *Did* he *leave* or *has* he *left?* If he *has left* maybe you can catch him. Often, when you're torn between two words, neither is right. Should a highway sign read *Reduce Speed* (no matter how fast you're going) or *Reduced Speed?* Actually, it should tell you what the speed limit is. When you're stumped for the right word, rethink the thought or state what the problem is.

The right word looks right, feels right, and sounds right. If it doesn't, it draws attention to itself, and draws attention to the user. Sometimes you want that, but usually you don't. Good expression swallows up its words. A word here and there may sparkle, but when many do, the style is flashy.

The right word often appeals to the senses. Vivid words stir the senses—*shiny, leaden, square, hoists, shoves.* Diction is dull when it's too abstract and no longer refers to what is seen, heard, and felt. As a rule, avoid abstract words and choose vivid ones, avoid general words and choose specific ones. Be as precise, as specific as you can without being distracting. Instead of saying that something is *pretty,* say why it's pretty—it's well made, smooth, colorful, bright, balanced.

Say *mother,* not *parent; laughter,* not *amusement; illness,* not *reasons of health; quiet,* not *peace; taut,* not *tensioned.*

Abstract words are usually longer than concrete ones: that's why it's a good idea to look for shorter words. You use short words not because people are busy, but because short words are more forceful. Instead of saying, *This is antagonistic to our interests,* say *this hurts us.* Instead of *There are differences between the two,* say *They differ.* English is basically a language of one-syllable words, and these words, being more common and natural, are more forceful than the longer ones. *He departed, He left. I'm secure, I'm safe. She telephoned, She called. He accepted the bribe in this manner, He took the bribe this way. We located the vehicle, We found the car. Our society is male dominated, Men run things.* English is a snappy, forceful language of little words that are the devil to put together right. Come off, come into, come across, come up with, come down on, come over, overcome—good grief!

Suppose you're thinking of choosing the word *overweight.* Should you use that word, or say *plump, stout, well-fed, gross, enormous, like a hippo?* What would a doctor say? *Obese.* What would a retailer say? *Portly.* A teenager? *Chubby.* A journalist? *Gargantuan.* A thin person? *Fat.* You might want to stick with the neutral word *overweight.* Usually the right words come to you when you first form the thought. The more practice you get in writing, the more you trust the words that come right away without your hunting for them. If you agonize over diction you get bogged down.

It's easy to go too far in hunting for specific and vivid language. Journalese, written by those who are paid by the word, has the words jumping off the page. People never *eat,* they *nibble* or *gobble;* they never wear *clothes,* they wear *Guccis* and *Puccis.* Much advertising copy and magazine writing is overstimulated, and the hysterical words wipe each other out. When everyone is using the language of the blurb, the cool understatement stands out. Classy language is cold language. Snappy diction is sloppy diction—*a rash of delays on the subways, an explosion in higher education, desperate for some coffee, heavenly mousse, Macy's sofa riot.*

Language doesn't have to be precise; in fact, it can't be, but if it's too hyped, it doesn't say anything. The exactly right word need not be an exact or narrow word at all. Amateur writers root around in the thesaurus and come up with unnatural words. Words are not ornaments to hang on the writing. Concentrate on the idea, and the right words come. Effort is better spent in studying the problem of tone and in strengthening the sentences.

In Formal diction you try to be natural and avoid the extremes of too abstract or too vivid. You don't make your language picturesque; you shouldn't seem to be painting, you're revealing. You don't make your language musical either, because that would mean you weren't serious about what you're saying. These are serious times. Haven't you heard that the Russians have 40,000 tanks?

Wrong Words

There aren't any. There are wrong *uses* of words. Every word accepted into the language has lovable features. I've never met a word I didn't like. Words can be wrongly used in two ways: when they're chosen from an inappropriate level—naughty words at a tea party—and when they're given meanings that don't belong to them. When a word is badly misused it's funny, and it's called a *malapropism:* the crutch of the matter, penny larceny, you misconscrew me to the upmost, your multifauceted talents wet my appetite, my mother is psychosomatic, my wife runs the househole. Malapropisms are words used in ignorance of their meanings. When words are used without remembering their meanings, we have *fuzziness.* Though fuzziness is a more common and less glaring fault than a malapropism, it can be as amusing to the connoisseur, as when a Harvard professor says *This fills a much-needed gap,* or when Professor Chomsky talks about the *concrete steps the Israeli government has taken,* or when the weather forecaster says it will be *clearly cloudy* and *fairly rainy.*

Among the delights of misused words are mixed metaphors: With one foot planted firmly in the Middle Ages, with the other Dante salutes the dawn of the Renaissance. There's something fishy here that has to be stamped out. She was putty in his hands and he got his fingers burned.

We've all been guilty of such mistakes. Misused words are much commoner than people suppose, since language is by its nature incorrect and funny. All language is figurative; all words are metaphors, inadequate signs and sounds trying to represent what's in the real world. Language cannot mean exactly what it says. Nothing ever *is* another thing. Mathematical language is more precise and reassuring. But if one gets too worried about the shortcomings of words, he may wind up like the professors whom Gulliver visits, who reject words and hold up in their hands the objects they want to talk about. The thought that no one chooses words perfectly should not be upsetting, but comforting.

Smart people try to avoid using words whose meaning they're unsure of. But even they err in choosing words that *sound* like the right ones. (These misuses are as often misspellings as mistakes in meaning.) Examples: *accept except, affect effect, allusion illusion, all together altogether, any way anyway, born borne, complementary complimentary, council counsel, eminent imminent, ever so often every so often, felicitous fortuitous, flaunt flout, flounder founder, past passed, prophecy prophesy, raise rise, respectfully respectively.*

A common and well-intentioned mistake occurs when people stretch a word out. Feeling that big words are better than small, that the air should be filled with syllables, they are guilty of stretching the following words:

determine becomes determinate	standard, standardized
history, historiography	use, utilize
life, lifespan	view, viewpoint, overview
mingle, intermingle	visit, visitation
method, methodology	
oblige, obligate	
often, oftentimes	
regardless, irregardless	
readers, readership	

If you love short words, you won't want to stretch them.

Vagueness

When the exact word is found, a better cannot be imagined. When a poor word is used, a better is easily imagined. A word can be faulted on a number of grounds: it's vague, ambiguous, fancy, phony, old, or new. Vagueness is the worst and most common fault in diction. For every word used wrongly, dozens are used vaguely. As pride is the underlying sin of sins, so vagueness is the underlying fault in poor words.

Vague words are useful, certainly. If they weren't, they wouldn't be called on so often. They let us talk without thinking. In Formal we have to appear to be thinking. It takes effort to choose among words that have clear meanings, and we have to show we're making the effort. Laziness is resented even more than vagueness. What happens when you hear someone talk like this? *I got bored so I got my coat on and I got into my car and when I got to the bowling alley I got there too late so I got drunk instead.* The words convey their meaning, but the lazy reliance on *got* and *and* suggests that the speaker is not trying to sharpen her diction and please her listeners. It also suggests that maybe she couldn't sharpen her diction if she tried. The words haven't been chosen, they emerged.

In Formal, each word must look as if it has been chosen. Words that come easily are resented. Frequent colloquialisms, no matter how natural they are, are resented. Overused words like *got, case, thing, very,* and *great* are resented. Audible pauses—*er, like, you know, man, I mean*—are resented. The speaker is telling her audience she's not about to knock herself out for the likes of them.

Vague and Wordy are the inseparable Laziness twins. We say *in the case of a layoff* instead of *in a layoff, in the line of retailing* instead of *in retailing, in the field of economics, in economics, from the point of view of safety, for safety.* Vagueness leads us into annoying novelties. Though it's clear English to say *clockwise* and *crosswise,* it's not to say *methodwise* or *legalwise. Filmwise* is vague, *taxwise* is OK. Lacking energy to search for the precise language we want, we fall back on cloudy words like *relationship, tendency, climate, situation, atmosphere, area, data, phenomenon.*

Vagueness allows us to hold onto vague ideas that we like. We know from experience that when we try to make an idea clear it often disappears, leaving us speechless. But we owe it to others, if they owe it to us, to try to be clear and to stick our neck out and say something. It can generally be said in our defense that we're vague from laziness and not from intent, but sometimes we do intend to be vague. For example, we would *want* to say *deal with* if we didn't know how a thing should be dealt with, or say *contact the mayor's office* if we didn't care whether the contact was by phone, letter, or in person, or say *we are processing your application* if we were stalling the applicant.

Sometimes the vagueness is just downright cowardly, and we may not be able to get away with it. What's being said here?

> I want a meaningful job and an employer I can relate to.
>
> We want an aggressive manager who can grow with the organization.
>
> With quick and certain punishment I will bring back law and order in the streets.
>
> I pledge allegiance.
>
> She's a ballbreaker.

Vagueness allows us to say one thing and mean another. Doing this on purpose is called equivocating, and despite the fancy name, it's common as dirt.

When trying to be vague we need to avoid slipping into ambiguity. The word *anxious* causes a furor because it's ambiguous. Vagueness is soothing but ambiguity is upsetting—unless it's in poetry, where some people say they like it. Vagueness suggests a cloudy meaning; ambiguity presents a puzzle of meanings to choose from: I have nothing on. Your figure is wrong. I am the furrier. My, you've grown another foot. Let me back into the bed. You've taken the part for the whole. Do you hate homos like me? No more than small farmers, frozen food managers, or photos of photographers.

Can you open the door? is objected to because it means *Will you?* and *Are you able to open the door? Would you pass the sugar?* means *Please pass me* and *Are you willing to* pass me the sugar? A common ambiguous construction that should be avoided is the negative statement followed by *because. He's not angry because he knows the truth.* (He's angry for some other reason, or knowing the truth keeps him from being angry: in one reading, he's angry—in the other, he's not.) *She couldn't leave him because he's rich.* (His wealth was such an attraction that she stayed, or he's not rich, he's poor, so his wealth certainly couldn't be the reason she left him: in one reading, she leaves—in the other, she doesn't.) Turn these sentences around, beginning with the *because* clause, for a clearer, less ambiguous reading. *With* phrases cause many ambiguities too: *I am not going with her.* Are you going at all?

Many words have different meanings, but with most of them the context clears up the meaning. Some words, though, have different meanings that are close to each other, and when these words fail to make their meaning clear, they flunk the ambiguity test. *Brainwash* means persuade, train, torture. Are brains washable? *Finalize* means end, prepare to end, officially end. *Verbalize* means talk, talk for relief, talk too much. *Togetherness* means being together or liking to be together. Such words, doomed to be ambiguous all their lives, will therefore have short ones.

So never pick an ambiguous word when you're only groping for a vague one. Whatever you think you're doing, Formal audiences will get mad at you if they catch you being ambiguous or too vague. They'll think you're tricky, or what's worse, that you have a loose grip on words and are not able to manipulate them properly. When people object to your words, they're objecting to you.

People are not rational about words, they love and hate. The *American Heritage Dictionary* tells us that our dear little friend *etc.* is banned from Formal. People follow the winds of change, but their devotion to the Really Bad Words never varies.

Old Words

Nobody knows why a good old word dies. The words *kin* and *gotten* are dead now in England, though alive and well in the U.S. Only a few old-timers in the Middle West still say *bidden* and *dassn't*, which are fine words. Sometimes a new word kicks an old one out, but often a good word dies without being replaced. I cry over the loss of *weep* and *lest* and the adjective *cross*. Once a word starts to slow down, more people stop using it, and then it goes fast. Words are now slipping from the language at an unbelievable rate, owing to the triumph of TV over print.

Dead words are called *archaic* or *antique*. Many people have the notion that antiques, such as *yon, tarry, thence, whence, deem,* and *amidst*, can be used in Formal. The opposite is the case: you can use antiques all you want Informally—to show off or have fun—but you cannot use them in Formal. Though there are hundreds of antiques, I'll only warn you about the following, which still show up and are tempting: alas, albeit, amidst, aught and naught, aye and yea, beauteous, behoove, betwixt, deem, delve, ere, erstwhile, fraught, goodly, hither, impudent, joyous, morn, nether, nigh, oft, save (meaning *except*), swoon, tarry, unbeknownst, wax (meaning *to grow*), whereon, and wondrous. You can't even use the handy words *whence* and *thence*. *Hence, henceforth, drunken*, and *sunken* are going fast. It's now chancy to start a sentence with *yet*. The IRS has killed the word *spouse* through its tax forms.

In the past, poets enjoyed use of the grand vocabulary of antiques; today we're serious and can't use antiques even in light verse. Not long ago Kipling could say *East is East, and West is West, and never the twain shall meet*. Try using *twain* today and see how far you get. Try using *shall*. The mass media have brought about a standardization and shrinking of the usable vocabulary. On the whole, this has benefited the language, by helping to protect it from jargon and by removing distinctions among the language levels. But many lovable old words have been lost forever. Today, only bold or important writers dare try oddities in their diction. Formal expression, remember, requires a certain squelching of personality.

We'll now turn to the huge category of words and expressions that are so feeble they'd be better off dead. Familiar phrases are called *shopworn, threadbare, flyblown, ready-made, secondhand, hackneyed, trite, clichés, stereotypes, catchphrases, stock phrases*, and *commonplaces*. From all these bad names you can see how much they're disliked.

> Jack, the picture of health and the spitting image of his old man, was as honest as the day is long, but he swore like a trooper. Far be it from me to criticize his way with words, but it goes without saying and it's plain as the nose on your face his use of the King's English made him stick out like a sore thumb and got him into hot water.

Clichés look lively, but are often vague and wordy: *heave a sigh, sleep like a top, sustain an injury, mount a massive assault, token of our esteem, water over the dam*. There are so many clichés, certain people use them for a language. Dictionaries of clichés have been compiled, but you don't have to look up phrases in a dictionary to see if they're clichés. All ready-made phrases except ones like *How do you do* should be avoided in Formal. You must choose the words one by one and they must be yours. Whenever you compare, using *like* or *as*, watch out for a cliché. Instead of saying that someone is happy as a lark or happy as a clam at high tide, say happy as a bride, as a poodle, as a chicken with an egg, or payday happy, Friday night happy, or just say happy. What's wrong with *happy?* Trust the words. In a fruit store you don't have to squeeze all the fruits, and in writing you don't have to squeeze all the words.

Informally, you can use all the clichés you want. In fact they're needed for the relaxed tone. Some clichés manage to preserve a charge of meaning. When they work, they're no longer called clichés, but proverbs or idioms. Here are oldies but goodies: Keep your shirt on. Out of the frying pan. On the warpath. Up to his ears. Barking up the wrong tree. Best thing since popcorn. Drink him under the table. After my scalp. Crying over spilt milk. Butter side down. You can think of many others. It's hard to avoid such common expressions, but in Formal you must.

There's a special category of clichés known as "rubber stamps," that let us know what is Very Good and what is No Good. VG is expressed by *nice, natural, terrific, dynamic, fantastic, amazing, phenomenal, exciting, significant, creative.* Some bizarre new terms of approval are: *operative, relevant, sensual, luxe, executive, organic, meaningful, fulfilling, aggressive, hard-nosed, hard-driving, vibrant, staggering,* and *mind-blowing.*

NG is expressed by *insecure, negative, bureaucratic, liberal, reactionary, imperialist, populist. Ists* and *isms* are bad news. *Scientists* and *capitalism* are OK, though.

Smart people try to avoid rubber stamps, especially in Formal. These words shed no light on the subject, but only signal that the user, who has the right ideas, is purring or snarling. To avoid vague adjectives, kick the adjective habit. Instead of using a linking verb and a VG or NG adjective, tell what the subject does, and make clear why it's good or bad. If someone is *uptight*, is he worried, priggish, or inhibited? If something is a *ripoff*, is it a gyp, clever profit taking, or theft? If a society is *permissive*, what does it permit?

Our emotions are vague, and any word that calls for an emotional response has to be vague, too. *Sexist, democracy, rights, free enterprise, exploitation* are all grand words, vague words. The more powerful the word—take *love* and *death* for examples—the vaguer it is. Vague suggestive words are the meat and potatoes of politics and advertising. One can get somewhere by clever use of these words, but maybe it's not a place one would like when there.

Fancy Words

A former authority, H.W. Fowler, said: "There is nothing to be ashamed of in *buy* or *see* that they should need translating into *purchase* and *observe*." He might have added that there's nothing to be ashamed of in *purchase* or *observe*, either. If *buy* is as good as *purchase* and saves five letters every time you use it, why not stamp out *purchase* altogether? I'll answer that one. Variety is the spice of life. *Purchase* may offer no improvement over *buy*, but it does offer a change. If you choose to use *purchase*, you're saying, For one reason or another I like *purchase*. In expressing yourself you're allowed to express yourself, if only a little. Even in Formal you can kick up your heels now and then and show off your diction without having to be questioned about every word, just as musicians are allowed their *rubato*. You don't know rubato? Get smart; play the Game.

Unless you're aiming at an unusually simple style, you do well to slip in a fancy word from time to time, to wake people up and show how confident you are. You add sparkle to what you're saying, and you may flatter the audience. A two-dollar word might be worth two thousand dollars.

A fancy word is like a fancy tie, expressive and bold. Fancy writing, though, is like being overdressed or wearing too much perfume; it's egotistical and rather pathetic. You'd be surprised at how many fancy words you use, usually to be funny. Here are common ones: abode, attire, citizenry, communication, consume, converse, crave, dwell, edifice, evince, facility (meaning building or toilet), garment, missive, remuneration, repast, reside, trice, thrice, transpire, vanquish, veritable, visage, and weep.

These words are well known, and people understand why you might be tempted to use them. Such is not the case with foreign words, which are not so well known and which have to be used with extra caution. If they are well known they are not fancy, but clichés like *savoir faire, femme fatale, bon vivant, joie de vivre, idée fixe, raison d'être, bête noire*. If they are not well known, your audience may be embarrassed by its ignorance and resent your putting on airs. The Formal rule is: Don't use a foreign word or phrase if there is a good English equivalent.

If speaking, you have to decide whether you're quoting the word from the foreign language or whether you're trying to use it as a regular word in English. This affects tone and pronunciation. How should you pronounce *timbre?* As *timber, tamber,* or *tamb?* Do you say *Gesstapo* or *Geshtapo, lawn jeray* or *lingerie, chaúffeur* or *chauffeúr, haute quizzine* or *la ote cuisíne?* The pronunciation depends on what your audience expects, not on whether you know the foreign language. As a rule, try to anglicize the pronunciations, since the foreign sounds are resented and since you may stumble in shifting languages. Of course, if you give the words English pronunciation you don't get credit for being able to speak in tongues. But you may get credit for English. And, as teachers love to say, you should know at least two languages—English and your own.

To sum up, fancy words, whether rare, foreign, or a foot long, must be used sparingly. Modern styles are seldom showy and pointed; they are generally verbose, chatty, and flat. In the past, writers could use fancy words like *ablutions, obsequies, repine, impecunious,* and *Weltschmerz,* but you can't anymore because of our shrunken vocabulary.

Only one kind of fancy word is still flourishing, and that is the *euphemism.* The term means speaking *favorably.* Euphemisms enable cars to become automobiles, drinks to become beverages, persons to become individuals. This is the Age of the Euphemism, and advertisers and PR people make money as euphemists. Euphemisms, like works of art or facelifts, protect us from the harshness of the world: we have hundreds of euphemisms for bodily functions, drunkenness, madness, and death. A horse sweats, a man perspires, a woman glows. Since euphemisms are such an important, permanent feature of language, they cannot all be thrown out as dishonest or evasive. They are objectionable only when they don't work, because they are unnecessary or too fraudulent. Here's a little quiz on euphemisms.

What's a prison?	a penitentiary
a penitentiary?	a correctional institution
a correctional institution?	a rehabilitation center
a bombing raid?	a retaliation, an interdiction
What's firing people called?	rationalization, termination
What happens when a museum sells a painting?	It deaccessions it.
Where do you kill germs?	on environmental surfaces in your home
What's a hospital?	a health care institution

a store?	a supermarket
a supermarket?	a savings center
Then what's a bank?	an earnings center
What's a gym?	a physical fitness center
What isn't a center?	a comfort station
What's a slow student?	a slow advancer
a bribe?	a campaign contribution
a payoff?	an honorarium

If euphemism is allowed, so is *dysphemism*, or using bad names.

What's a homosexual?	a queer
a woman?	a broad
a person with standards?	rigid, elitist, a dinosaur
What's his class?	patrician, mandarin

Nothing happens to the language when words are used this way. They don't lose their meanings; the people who use such words may lose their meanings, that is, may deceive themselves. For every one who tells lies, there are countless sincere people who deceive themselves with their own words.

Formal is not squeamish, and avoids euphemisms when it can. It avoids dirty words, too. Of course there are no dirty words, only dirty minds. To the pure all things are pure. But who's pure? People are weak, worried, repressed, and that's why dirty words should not be flung about. The only free speech is a madman's. Use dirty words with discretion.

Fad Words

If a newly invented or imported word is a good one, it will make its way into the language, and no amount of protest from those who don't like the look or sound of it will prevent its final triumph. The English-speaking people, and Americans especially, do not show so much prejudice as speakers of other languages do against new and imported words. In fact, we welcome neologisms too warmly. Most of them are not useful, and lack the clarity and wealth of associations enjoyed by the old words they threaten to displace.

A new word may be a good one, but it has to prove itself over a period of time, has to clarify its meaning before being used in Formal.

To be Formal is to be conservative, and you should avoid new words no matter how much you dote on them. New words are often used aggressively, and may make the audience feel behind the times. Because new words are resented we like to use them with friends—to affirm our closeness by saying we're not afraid to use this new jargon or slang with each other.

There are three kinds of new words: fashionable words, jargon, and slang. Let's see why and how they are used, and try to decide if they should be banned from Formal.

Occasionally, fashionable words are new words for new things that everyone's talking about, but usually they are ordinary words that suddenly leap into the spotlight, like *guidelines, thrust, establishment, liberation, ongoing, overview, hopefully, escalate, image,* or *lifestyle.* People object to fad words without knowing why. This is why: the words are echoing through the air and are easy to catch. Since they're easy to use, using them marks the user as lazy. Also, the more a word is used, the more it's misused and the vaguer it gets. Fad words are new words or new uses of old words, and many people love the old and hate the new. *Health reasons* is no worse than *reasons of health, normalcy* is no worse than *normality,* but people object to them merely as novelties. The media, of course, love what's new, but that doesn't mean your audience does. So when an old word suddenly starts running around fast, stay away from it; it has a disease.

The usual objection to fad words is to their being faddish, but the proper objection is to their vagueness. A word on everyone's lips has to be vague to be well liked. Vagueness is the underlying fault when nouns are used as verbs. Just what is done when you *update, upgrade, or implement,* when you *customize* your car, *winterize* your house, *destabilize* a government, *concretize* a value, or *audibilize* your signals? Do you *doctor,* or treat? Do you *lawyer,* or counsel? Do you ever *author, parent, eyeball, dialogue, birth,* or *impact?* Are you *conflicted* and *problemed* about English? Using such verbs deprives you of the old verbs, which are the jewels of a language.

To believe that most new words are no good is not being stuffy. They aren't. Clear the mind of modern cant. Here's the rule to follow: If the word stands for a new reality—IUD, DNA, PVC, aerosols, polymers—don't hesitate to use it. If the new word stands for a new concept, don't use it. The experts who invent new concepts may not be illuminating your mind so much as blowing smoke in your eyes. We could well do without words and expressions such as: open marriage, affirmative action, behavior modification, child production, cognitive dissonance, counterculture, death instinct, double-bind, dry skin, greening of America, halitosis, image management, ethnicity, ethology, sociobiology, parapsychology, future shock, futurism, structuralism, male chauvinism, modernism, orientalism, imperialism, Caesarism, sexual politics, the work ethic, neoconservatism, the new hedonism, the new taurine excrement. Stick with the older categories of thought represented by the older words. Remember that nothing fails like success. New words should not be embraced, much less trusted. The philosopher Hobbes said, "Words are wise men's counters—they do but reckon with them, but they are the money of fools." In short, new words and new fads in using words must be inspected. Let us not follow P.T. Barnum's sign: This Way to the Egress.

Jargon

The word *jargon* used to mean the song of birds, and now it means the song of doctors, lawyers, coaches, psychologists, dope addicts, and professors of English. (Not all of them.) Jargon is special language used by a group. Its main purpose is to save time, to enable the group to speak of its own concerns in a swift, precise way. Another purpose, a fishy one, is to promote the solidarity and interests of the group by means of secret language. Any group has a right to all the jargon it wants, but they all seem to produce more than they need. Jargon becomes a problem when it escapes from the group and other people start using it. When that happens, the words begin to lose whatever meaning they had. And outsiders prefer the jargon that has little meaning to start with.

Many new terms escape or are sent out from the academic disciplines (especially the social sciences) and find a wider popularity. Fortunately, academic jargon won't live very long, but since it is written as well as spoken, it lives longer than slang. The following jargon is objectionable because it is vague. Adjectives: counterproductive, creative, culture-bound, diametrical, interpersonal, preemptive, substantive, unilateral. Nouns: complex, conditioning, cooptation, dialectic, dichotomy, empathy, fixation, frame of reference, ideology, interaction, interface, interlink, interiorizing, mandate, module, trauma, value judgment. Don't bother to look these up.

If you look over the list, you will see that most of the words are NG and VG rubber stamps. The more popular the jargon, the likelier it is to be some kind of stamp. *You're a revisionist. You're a teleologist. You're an epiphenomenalist. You're an anal retentive.* Anytime we label a person's thought or character, we resort to jargon. It's all right to say that someone's a *leftie*, but it's not all right to say that he's a *leftist*.

I'm not being fussy in warning you away from jargon. A good writer never touches it. If one can't come up with a better word than *feedback, in-depth, ongoing,* or *meaningful,* he should aim for a career in which jargon is rewarded and leave English to her poor but honest lovers. The trouble with technical-sounding terms is that they aren't technical: plain English is more precise. The trick in technical writing is to use plain language.

When you're tempted to use an expert's word, welcome that as a warning: the poor word veils a fuzzy idea. Clarify the idea and the special word won't be needed. Back off and rethink the whole sentence or paragraph if you have to. If you're running short of time, consult a thesaurus. Be patient; remember, there's always a way out. You can't paint yourself into a corner, since there are infinite ways to express your ideas.

Slang

Slang and jargon are similar in being special languages for special occasions. The jargon of golfing would include: *drive, slice, hook, birdie, bogey.* Golf slang would include: *hacker, sky shot, duffer's side, big mouth, rain bringer, smother, killing snakes, yips, voodoo ball.* Slang is jargon with feeling.

The impulses to use slang are admirable: the desire to say things in a fresh way, to wake up the language, to be witty, youthful, exuberant, to increase one's intimacy with friends. The actual words produced by these good impulses are almost always disappointing. Using slang well is even more difficult than using Formal well. Like jargon and bad words, slang is overused, and since it's overused, it suffers a loss of meaning and is then misused. Misused words make the user look foolish. One reason slang is loved is that its origins are unknown and its meanings cannot be deduced—the words merely sound appropriate: *nerd, gimmick, geek, the blahs.* But the lack of roots causes the word to wither up: slang usually dies after a few bright years of life, and anyone using outdated slang looks foolish: she's no longer the *cat's whiskers, cat's pajamas, cat's meow*, she's not a *cool cat*, nor is she *in the catbird seat*. Also, slang is for the young, and if you use it and aren't young, you'll look foolish.

The few slang terms that stand for new things—like *sneakers* and *jeans*—are likely to enter the language, but most slang substitutes for conventional words. Because it does, there's always the suggestion that the user of slang doesn't know the conventional words. The same stigma attaches to slang that attaches to all fad words: the words are so popular that picking them shows laziness rather than vigor. Most slang terms are rubber stamps. Gee. Wow. Crazy. Wild. Off the wall. Busted. Ice. She's getting off on doing a number on him and hitting on him for where he's coming from. Carl Sandburg said that " Slang is language that takes off its coat, spits on its hands, and goes to work." The truth is, most slang takes off its coat, spits on its hands, and lies down and falls asleep.

Only a small part of slang is attractive and clever. *Vibes*, for example. Flicks. Threads. Wheels. Bug. Smokies. Corn. Hun, thou, and mil. Tube steak for hot dog. Slammer. Oreo. Flaked out. Goofy. Short fuse. Fast idle. Spinning your wheels.

The slang of businessmen is falsely robust: hard-nosed, up front, in place, on the horn, on the blower, bite the bullet, ball of wax, bulls and bears, can of worms, witches' brew, stonewalling it, stroking, bottom line, take a bath, the crunch, gut reaction, off the top, ballpark figures, hardball, ground rules, windfall, shortfall, tradeoff, killing, thrust, three-pronged, trajectory. As you see, slang often has an aggressive tone. Using slang can be an assertive act, implying that the user is more in the know or more vigorous than his listener. If you're assertive, use lots of slang. If you're mild mannered, stay away from it. Don't hit your boss with it, let him hit you instead.

* * *

This chapter on diction was the least encouraging in the book, because I told you mainly what *not* to do. You've been warned against using so many words you're probably wondering if you have any left. Sure you do. A normal, simple vocabulary is what's wanted in Formal. You have to be careful if you use a common vocabulary, because people will understand what you're saying, and so will you. On the other hand, you don't have to work at showing off. Some writers advise using a *mixed* vocabulary of fancy and common words. An occasional word from a different language level will be allowed, but any real mixing of levels wrecks the tone. And the tone of what you say is a big part of what you say.

You *can* be successful in saying little or nothing, in using vague terms, generalities, jargon, and slang. What the others are doing, you can do, too. As they say, everything bows to success, even grammar. So don't fret and agonize over your choice of words, wondering whether they are "correct." Make sure you have the right tone, and the words select themselves. Everyone mischooses and misuses words. Diction is the basic step in expression, but not the crucial step. Diction is only naming things—animals can do that. The crucial step is predication, expressing yourself in sentences—nouns and verbs, things and actions.

Mark Twain said: "The difference between the right word and the almost right word is the difference between the lightning and the lightning bug." He did not think, Oh, I love the word *lightning bug*, I'll use it. He thought, The difference between the right word and the almost right word is the difference between *blank* and *blank*. Then he filled in the blanks.

Chapter Three

Punctuating by Sound

Eye versus Ear

Punctuating is our way of showing, in writing, certain pauses and sounds in our speech. Just as the letters of the alphabet are signs representing sounds, so are certain punctuation marks. In talking about spelling I argued that the letters should represent the sounds better than they do, and I'll argue now that punctuation should represent sounds better than it does. Punctuation tells us what writing is supposed to sound like when it's put back into speech. It's like notes on a sheet of music and, like musical notation, it must be exact.

Scarcely any punctuation is intended for the eye—it's intended for the ear and the voice. But, as in music, some people are tone deaf, or nearly so: they don't listen to the sounds their voices make, and read any piece of writing in a monotone, pausing every few words and making comma sounds, or else making full-stop period noises for every dot or curve of punctuation they come across. Some even ignore all punctuation and read word after word in a robot monotone until they run out of breath, using no emphasis at all. That's why we have handbooks on punctuation full of detailed rules—to tell your *eye* what your *ear* ought to be hearing and your voice ought to be saying.

With practice, you can learn to *hear* punctuation, just as you can learn or unlearn a regional accent. That's what the people who are comfortable with language do—punctuate the way they'd talk.

If you can learn to hear the cadences of speech, the rises and falls of your voice, you can skip most of the rules and punctuate by sound, falling back on the handbook method only for the odd or unusual case that you're not quite sure about. But if you're one of those whose voice insists on going flat and mechanical whenever your eye strikes words on a page, then reverse the method: rely primarily on the rules, and appeal the unusual cases to your ear. Either way, ask yourself: What do I want this to sound like? Then punctuate accordingly.

Punctuation marks were not invented by grammarians who laid down the rules for their use; the marks developed gradually over a long period, and became distinguished from each other as they became associated with distinctive sounds. Their purpose was not, and is not, to help people read faster by breaking up writing into pieces the eye can handle, but to help people read correctly and musically. The secret of punctuating well is to understand what sounds the marks really represent. You need to know what a comma and a period *sound* like.

You don't punctuate pauses. There are frequent pauses in any sentence—every few words, in fact, especially when you're reading aloud and sometimes have to take in a whole phrase before you know how to pace and pitch it. We've all heard newscasters getting into trouble by failing to prescan written copy, having to stop and try it again. No, what you punctuate is *sounds*. Your teachers used to tell you to put a comma where you had a strong pause and a period where your voice came to a complete stop. That was helpful, but not helpful enough, because of the way a lot of us read aloud.

I'll honor the rules, and tell you where the little marks go according to the rule books. Then I'll teach you to punctuate, not according to the pauses and the grammatical structure of the sentence, but according to the melody in your speech. You choose which method is best for you—sound first, or rules first.

The best way, if not the only way, to discover the sounds or melodies of speech is to practice reading aloud with feeling and with proper attention to the marks. Practice with prose, Informal prose—a movie review in *Newsweek*, the letters to the editor in your local newspaper. Try to make it sound like talking. Practice with metered verse, where rhythm and punctuation go hand in hand: *The cat is in the parlor the dog is in the lake the cow is in the hammock what difference does it make.* Did you put periods after *parlor, lake,* and *hammock?* You need more practice. You need to read some poems by e. e. cummings and Don Marquis and *hear* the invisible punctuation these poets use instead of the kind you can see. Also, read plays aloud: they were made for the voice, not the eye. Practice.

There's not a lot you need to learn about the rules of punctuation for the *eye*—the Formal rules. You're pretty confident about using periods: you know what misplacing one could do to your bank balance. You don't make many mistakes with question marks, and most of the use of quotation marks is just common sense—they go around the word, phrase, or sentence quoted, and single marks go inside of double marks if you have a quote within a quote. Parentheses, too, are pretty straightforward (here's all you need to know about them). Exclamation points speak for themselves (loudly!) and you shouldn't be using very many of them, anyway, unless you're writing romance novels or advertising copy. Dashes, the skidding interrupters, work like parentheses and often travel in pairs—are you still paying attention?—to add sudden thoughts and maybe wake up the reader. You can duck using semicolons altogether if you try hard enough. And even colons are generally avoidable. But commas are the most frequent mark of punctuation and the most troublesome, as well. So I'll talk a little about periods because their use, like the placement of other forms of punctuation, depends on what a sentence is. But it's commas, the unavoidable commas, that I'll spend the most time on, so you can learn the rules and use these little hookmarks to catch readers' attention and hold it tight.

All About Formal Commas

To paraphrase Kipling, there are nine-and-sixty ways of telling what a sentence is, and not a single one of them is right. You've been told a sentence is a complete thought. There is no such thing. There's always more to be said about any thought, and undoubtedly it will be. You've probably been told that a sentence makes sense in itself. Some do, and some don't. Heard any political speeches lately? It's a lot simpler, and Formally correct, to say that a sentence is a group of words containing one or more nouns and verbs in a special relationship. These nouns and verbs are what make the sentence go: What *verbs*, and what *gets* verbed— subject, predicate, and maybe object. What does or is, and what gets done to. Most punctuation, especially commas, serves to help a reader spot the noun and verb easily and not get lost among attached modifiers, like adjectives and adverbs (which I'll tell you about, along with the other parts of speech, in the next chapter). As long as that group of words doesn't have its independence knocked out by being introduced with some subordinating word like *when* or *because,* it's a sentence and should end with a period or other full stop (a question mark or exclamation point).

There are, of course, exceptions. Answers can be punctuated like sentences. *(Where did you go? Out. What did you do? None of your business.)* So can questions *(Why?)* and commands *(Go away!).* Once in a while, for emphasis, short phrases or clauses can be punctuated like sentences. *(Of course.)* Don't overdo this, even in Informal. In Formal, don't do it at all.

Because this subject/verb relationship is so important, most of the work commas do is to keep other parts of the sentence out of its way. Therefore, never put just one comma between a noun and its verb, or between a verb and its object or subject complement (part of the subject on the predicate side of the sentence). The subject, verb, and object or complement (if any) are the story the sentence is telling. Don't clutter it up with commercials, and especially not with a commercial that goes on and on and never ends. Put two commas, or none, between subject and verb, or verb and object or subject complement. That's the rule.

Since most sentences have the subject noun near the beginning, it can be confusing if a sentence starts with something other than the main idea. *Because it was raining that Thursday in the mountains near Steamboat Springs, we went inside.* When the introducer is long or might confuse the reader, i.e., in spotting where the introducer ends and the main sentence begins, follow it with a comma. If it's short, or there's no real chance of confusion, leave the comma out. That's the rule.

After introductory single adverbs, you can put in the comma or leave it out, depending on how you want the sentence to read. Either *Slowly, he turned* or *Slowly he turned* is OK. If you want to emphasize an adverb in some other position, you can treat it as parenthetical and enclose it in commas. *She fell, hard, and skinned both knees.* It's up to you.

If there are three or more items in a series, separate them by commas. Formal requires commas after each item. Informal allows you to skip the last comma or, in some circles, to leave out the commas completely if the items are single words and can't be misread. *The holiday cake was pink white and green.* Or, *He'd never seen a three-wheeled, gull-winged, pedal-driven bicycle before.* Using commas in a series can also be a matter of style—what you want the reader to hear.

Two or more words may modify one noun. Do you use a comma or not? Well, it depends. With the ear method, I tell you to put a comma whenever there's a comma sound. *He was a dirty old man.* But, *He was a dirty, wealthy old man.* Did you hear the comma? In the second sentence, did your voice lift after *dirty* and come back down on *wealthy?* That was the comma sound. *The wicked old president was replaced by the wicked new president.* But, *The wicked, old president was replaced by the wicked, new president.* Hear the commas? Hear how they emphasize *old* and *new?* This isn't grammar—it's style. There's a rule on this involving modifiers of equal importance, but who decides how important each modifier is? You do. So don't worry about the rule. If you want a comma sound in situations like this, put the comma in: style counts here.

When a sentence contains at least two complete independent clauses (that aren't introduced with subordinators like *because* or *although*), Formal requires you to use *both* a comma and a coordinating conjunction (for instance, *and, but,* or *or*) between the clauses. Informal lets you drop the comma between the two parts. *(He bought a Great Dane on impulse and the landlord didn't like it.)* If the clauses are very short or if they're short *and* are strongly connected or strongly contrasting in sense, you can drop the conjunction. *(Man proposes, God disposes.)* Even in Formal.

If you're introducing a short quote or bit of dialogue, use a comma. *He said, "Open the door." "Why," she inquired, "don't you open it yourself?"*

If you have a modifying phrase that *doesn't* limit or define the noun it's talking about, enclose it with commas. *My uncle, who owns a fast food restaurant, has been plagued with raccoons* means that there's just one uncle and that the information inside the commas is parenthetical: it could be lifted out by its comma handles and still leave a complete sentence, if one that is less detailed and maybe less interesting. (Remember, I told you that no sentence is a complete thought.) But *My sister who plays the piano got rid of the starlings for three blocks around* means you have more than one sister, and you're only talking about the one who plays the piano. *Who plays the piano* is a restrictive clause, restricting the meaning of the noun it modifies. Likewise, *Carol wore a wig which shocked us.* Restrictive clause, *which shocked us*—no comma. *Carol wore a wig, which shocked us.* Nonrestrictive clause, use a comma. In the first sentence, the wig itself is shocking; maybe it was pink with purple stripes. In the second, it's the fact that she wore any wig at all that's shocking. The wig itself might be relatively attractive, for a wig.

Finally, if somebody's being addressed in a sentence, put commas around the name or words of address. *(Did you know, Carol, that the Painted Desert is growing by four inches a year? Bob, who cares? Listen, readers, to the comma sounds.)* The same is true of other interrupters like *well, oh,* and *damn.* That's back to our two-commas-or-none rule, between subject and verb, or verb and object or subject complement.

The *overall rule* in either Formal or Informal is, if you can do without a comma, leave it out. Let the flow of the sentence, the way you string your words, phrases, and clauses together, do the work. Don't litter.

The Ear Method

Now it's time to *listen* to all the marks and hear what they have to say. There are three kinds. The first is the *full stop,* which takes in four punctuation marks—the period, question mark, exclamation point, and semicolon. The second kind is the *half stop,* which includes the comma and the other marks that can be considered variations on it—the colon, dash, and parentheses. The third kind of punctuation mark is the *spelling* mark, which is not really punctuation since it does not represent any sound and is intended only for the eye. These spelling marks are the apostrophe, quotation marks, the hyphen, and the slash; they are, in my opinion, more trouble than they are worth and most languages do without them.

Freedom to Punctuate

You've probably been taught many punctuation rules which you've forgotten. Here are typical rules taken from current grammar books: Use a comma after a long introductory phrase. Use a comma before a coordinating conjunction that joins main clauses. Use a semicolon between items in a series that have internal punctuation. Don't use a semicolon before *and* or *but.*

None of these rules needs to be honored. Rules provide no help in those cases where you have a choice between several possible marks, and these are the majority of cases. In Informal, and in Formal with little flashes of Informal—Formal with its jacket off—there's only one useful rule in punctuation: Choose the right mark for the sound you want the reader to hear.

Here's a typical sentence that can be punctuated in various ways: *I went to her apartment and I found him. I went to her apartment, and I found him.* You heard the comma? *I went to her apartment. And I found him.* You heard the period? Obviously, no one could help you punctuate this sentence. If you were speaking the sentence, you'd speak it in a certain way. Your job is to punctuate it the way you'd speak it.

If you say *I went to her apartment and I found him,* the sentence is flat. If you say *I went to her apartment, and I found him,* you're suggesting there is something odd; with the comma you've split the idea of the sentence into two ideas. If you say *I went to her apartment. And I found him,* you're showing surprise: the second idea is important and needs a sentence to itself. And if you don't like these choices, you try other punctuation or change the words.

Punctuation is sounds. The sounds make sense, and if they didn't there'd be no reason for them. Punctuation has meaning, and using it involves all your skill and judgment: it's not a mechanical matter like spelling. In times past, dictionaries provided rules of punctuation, but they've given up on that. Rules requiring us to analyze the sentence grammatically only distract us from listening.

You might want to protest at this point: if the ear method is so easy, why isn't it taught? Well, it's easy in one sense, but hard in another. If you know how your writing sounds, it's easy, because then you have no choice: you just put in the mark that represents the sound you want. If you don't know how your writing sounds, it's hard, because then you can't choose the right mark.

To convince you that you're free to punctuate, whether you like it or not, let's look at some well-known sentences; guess how these sentences were punctuated, and then I'll tell you what punctuation the original writers used.

1. Give us the tools and we will finish the job.
2. My father taught me to work he did not teach me to love it.
3. My theory is to enjoy life but my practice is against it.

4. Read over your compositions and wherever you meet with a passage which you think is particularly fine strike it out.

5. Better we lose the election than mislead the people and better we lose than misgovern the people.

Here are the answers.

1. Churchill, in this request for help during the war, did not say or write a comma after *tools*.

2. Abraham Lincoln wrote *My father taught me to work; he did not teach me to love it.*

3. Charles Lamb wrote *My theory is to enjoy life. But my practice is against it.*

4. Samuel Johnson wrote *Read over your compositions, and wherever you meet with a passage which you think is particularly fine, strike it out.*

5. Adlai Stevenson, a good loser, wrote *Better we lose the election than mislead the people; and better we lose than misgovern the people.*

This exercise should prove that no matter how much you know about punctuating, you can't punctuate someone's stuff for him. And if you can't do it for him, he can't do it for you.

But it's worth pointing out that Churchill *didn't* write, "Give us, the tools, and we will finish the job," and Samuel Johnson *didn't* write, "Read, over your compositions, and wherever you meet with a passage, which you think is particularly fine strike, it out." There's room for variation, but variation has limits if you want to be understood. Before you throw away the rules, be very sure you have an ear you can rely on to tell you where the marks should go.

A delightful aspect of punctuation is that it has meaning even when it is left out. In *The Waste Land,* T.S. Eliot wrote of *red sullen faces,* not *red, sullen faces,* because he wanted us to connect red and sullen. He also wrote HURRY UP PLEASE ITS TIME without punctuation. Oh, you say, but he is T.S. ELIOT. But he wasn't T.S. ELIOT then, only a writer who knew how to put down on paper what he heard.

Period

In discussing the marks' sounds, we'll first deal with the full stops: period, question mark, exclamation point, and semicolon. We start with the period, the most important of the marks.

You already have a general idea of what a sentence is—a group of words that can stand alone and has a subject and verb in a "thing/ does (or is)" or "thing/done to" relationship— and you know that you put a period at the end of it.

In school, your textbooks said that you had to have a sentence to use a period, but obviously you have to use a period to have a sentence. You have a sentence if you can get away with making a period sound, and, as I've explained before, you can always get away with more in Informal than in Formal. You have a sentence fragment when you write a period where no reasonable, educated person would make a period sound. The writer of sentence fragments doesn't know how to use the basic mark of punctuation. If you write a comma where others want a period, you've made the dread mistake called a *comma splice*. If you miss a period you're in trouble. OK: *Bob is cute, Carol is cute.* Comma splice: *Bob is cute, I love blonds.* Probably OK: *Bob is cute, he's a Leo.* Was Dr. Johnson guilty of a comma splice when he said: "The Irish are a fair people, they never speak well of one another"? No, he wasn't. The comma splice exists only in writing, and Boswell did the writing.

What is the period sound? You've been hearing it all your life without analyzing it. The final word in a sentence is generally stressed; that is, the voice becomes a little louder or rises in pitch or does both. (This prepares the listener for the end of the sentence. You don't want to shock him with a sudden silence.) And then the end of the sentence is signaled by a lowering of the voice, in pitch or volume or both, which is followed by a strong and complete pause. The voice doesn't just drop and stop; it distinctly drops and stops.

For practice in hearing the sound of the period, listen to a radio or TV announcer. Whenever he makes the sound, say Period, or scratch yourself. For practice in distinguishing pauses from commas and from periods, read the following aloud over and over, until you hear the melody. Read expressively.

> one two three four five
> one, two, three, four, five,
> One. Two. Three. Four. Five.

The *soundless period*, used to mark abbreviations (abbrevs.) and acronyms *(M.C.P.)*, is hardly useful, being soundless, and is vanishing from words like *Dr Ms Mt etc St Inc Me Mo Pa Ca Co*. If your boss or editor still requires that you put them in, you'll probably have to. But if you're your own boss and can choose whether you want a period after *Prof* or *Prot* or in *AA USA PCB UFO*, leave them out. Definitely leave them out from *SANE NOW FIAT* and *SMERSH*, since they're sounded just the way they're spelled.

Arguments about whether to put the periods in seldom arise in Formal because you're not supposed to abbreviate in Formal. Under cross-examination at his trial, Oscar Wilde was asked whether there was any crime of which he was not guilty, and he proudly claimed that he had never been guilty of abbreviation. You must follow him in this example.

Question Mark

Somewhere in a question the voice rises in pitch and usually increases in volume. The sound of a question means that things are up in the air and something must be done. Like a suspended chord in music, a question wakes people up.

Only real questions, not things that look like questions, have to be marked with a question mark. Looks are deceiving. You can't tell a question by the way it starts off or by the subject and verb being turned around. Any word or group of words can be a sentence, and any word or group of words can be a question.

> You were in her apartment, weren't you.
> You were in her apartment, weren't you?
> Pass the mustard.
> Pass the mustard?
> I wonder will it come.
> I wonder will it come?
> Why did he *do* it!
> *Why* did he do it?
> May we hear from you at your earliest convenience.
> Would you be so kind as to send the check by return mail.
> In the meantime what about her.

The writer decides whether any questions are being asked.

Sometimes the question sound occurs early in the sentence. *Will you please (?) get in bed before my feet get frozen.* You may forget to put a question mark at the end of the sentence, since that's nowhere near the question sound. Some languages solve this problem by putting a question mark before the sentence. If the question sound is miles away from the end of the sentence, it doesn't matter much if you use the question mark or not, but still, if there's a real question sound anywhere in the sentence, remember to put a question mark at the end.

People forget to put in their question marks because most questions reveal themselves by reversing subject and verb: *You do, do you?* This makes the question mark unimportant, but you must remember to put it in anyway. Indirectly quoted questions have no question sound: *She asked who Bob was.*

Though the question mark requires a full stop, you don't always use a capital letter after it. *Are you ready? she asked.* No capital *s* in *she*. *Will it rain? will it sleet? will it snow? Who knows. Who* starts the new sentence; therefore capitalize *w* in *who*. Little questions that are parts of a larger question do not begin with capitals.

Exclamation Point

To exclaim means to cry out. Whenever you write something that's cried out, use an exclamation point. An exclamation can't be whispered or muttered. The exclamation point comes after words like *phooey, ouch,* and *Holy Smoke* only if they have been exclaimed. Exclamations, like fortissimos in music, wear a person out, and you should never use more than a few.

Though the question mark is put at the end of the sentence, the exclamation point goes right after the exclamation. *No! No! No! A thousand times no!* Since an exclamation comes to so emphatic a stop, the sentence doesn't resume afterwards; start a new sentence with a capital letter, except in *quoted* exclamations. *"Drop dead!" she shouted.* Small *s* in *she*.

A writer should rarely have any problem in choosing between an exclamation point and another mark, but if she does, she should lean to the calmer mark. The question mark can suggest shock, but the exclamation point cannot suggest a question. Hear the differences in the following: *Why did he do it. Why did he do it? Why did he do it! What have I done. What have I done? What have I done!*

Almost every exclamation, by the way, is a quotation. The reason is clear: Other people exclaim, the writer doesn't, because she's sitting down and is not supposed to be yelling at the reader. Even when she exclaims, it sounds like she's quoting herself. When quotes are used, the exclamation point goes inside the quotes. Only once in a hundred years would you end a sentence with a quoted exclamation inside an exclamation, in which case you'd put an exclamation point either inside or outside the quotes, or else look up what to do in some wise book.

Semicolon

The semicolon, the last of our four full stops, is easily the most interesting of the lot. People think of it as a kind of heavy comma, but that's all wrong—it's a period. Think of it as a light period. It definitely represents the period sound. The difference between the semicolon and the period is that after the semicolon you don't pause as long as after the period. If the reader is going fast there's no distinction between periods and semicolons, and therefore no point in using semicolons.

Since the semicolon is a kind of period, you can't use it unless you have a sentence on either side of it. You use semicolons to put two or more sentences together to make one sentence. But that one sentence must be one sentence; all its parts have to add up to a single idea. You cannot link unrelated ideas with a semicolon. You can't say *I will arrive there tomorrow; I like to fly*, but you can say *I will arrive there tomorrow; I'm catching the midnight plane.*

Here are examples of correctly used semicolons. See if you don't hear them as brief periods.

> He hit the serve as hard as he could; she returned it easily.
> I need a vacation; I haven't had one in ages.
> Carol wore a dress; everyone else wore jeans.

What would happen if we didn't have the semicolon? Nothing much. The period can substitute for it, or in short sentences with closely related ideas, a comma can and should be used in its place. *Carol wore a dress, the others wore jeans.* The semicolon, a recently invented punctuation mark, shows its function by its appearance—it's a compromise between a period and a comma. It's used by those who can't decide between commas and periods. Good writers are decisive and stay away from semicolons. Amateurs and professors use far too many. Fiorello LaGuardia called lawyers "the semicolon boys." The sound of the semicolon often appears in speech; some period pauses are brief. But the distinction between a brief period pause and a longer one is not important. The semicolon is not much needed, if it's needed at all, and it seldom appears outside of Formal writing. Since it's a sign of Formality, use it, but don't become addicted.

It's a tempting device for making longer sentences. If your readers want longer sentences, use semicolons, and if they want shorter sentences, don't. The temptation to make sentences longer should be examined. Stretching the sentence out may be a way of covering up a weakness in the idea. Sometimes the writer figures that if she makes the sentence impressively long, no one will notice anything missing. If you find yourself resorting frequently to semicolons, that probably means the ideas are weak. A semicolon allows you to pack a sentence, but a sentence is not a bag. It's more like a stroke or blow, and you want it to be a sharp one.

Some handbooks say not to use a semicolon before *and* or *but*. But you can, of course, just as you can use a period before *and* and *but*.

> Bob left his wallet in the car; but he didn't worry about it.
>
> I thought it would be a headache; and I was right.

Some people who have never been told about the sound of the semicolon put it in the wrong place. They associate it with words like *however, meanwhile, instead, nevertheless*, and when they see one of these words they toss a semicolon in, half the time on the right side of the word, which is the wrong side to use it. The semicolon, as a period sound, can't come after words that are joining new thoughts to the sentence. Do not write *He was tone-deaf, however; he liked disco.* Use a period or semicolon *before* words like *however, furthermore, likewise* and a comma after. Test by their sounds. Semicolons are not commas. Writers are misled by teachers who tell them to use a semicolon if they can't decide between a comma and a period. A writer should know whether she's tacking things together with commas or separating them with periods. Fudging by using a semicolon is not smart.

There's one minor use of the semicolon that has caused people to get a wrong notion of what the semicolon is. This is the *semicolon for the eye only.* In long sentences with many phrases and clauses, semicolons are often used to separate the major items from the minor items—even though these semicolons could be commas.

> Three uniformed men walked into the room: General Kachow, a graduate of West Point; Admiral Boom, a graduate of Annapolis; and Colonel Bang, a graduate of the Air Force Academy.

> These are my favorite recipes: beef with ginger, cooked in my wok; Peking Duck, which takes a day to make; and lasagna, the tasty Italian dish.

Comma

Now we move on to the half stops—the comma, and its three special variations—the colon, dash, and parenthesis. There is one "ear" rule for the use of the comma: When you have a comma sound, put a comma in. What is the sound? It's a lilt or lifting of the voice which is then followed by a pause. In pronouncing the word before the comma, the voice is stressed, it rises in pitch or volume or both, then falls down a little and comes up again. It goes *up down up.* By going *up* before the pause, the voice tells the listener that the sentence is not finished, that the pause is not a period, and that more is coming after the pause. The comma means *more coming.* It warns the listener that the approaching pause is not serious and that something will be added.

Let's listen now to the song of the comma. In the following sentence there is a clear pause but no comma sound. *My friend Lou watched TV.* There was a distinct pause before the verb *watched.* Now listen to the commas: *My friend Lou, who was ill, watched TV.* You sang *Lou* and *ill.* Now read the following sentences aloud.

Please move over.	Please, move over.
Our flag is red white and blue.	Our flag is red, white, and blue.
Look up Bob.	Look up, Bob.
Sometimes he does what he wants.	Sometimes, he does what he wants.
Her work is in fact excellent.	Her work is, in fact, excellent.
That night I did not expect the vampire.	That night, I did not expect the vampire.
Just think snow.	Just think, snow.

Oh phooey.	Oh, phooey.
I was born March eleventh at noon.	I was born March eleventh, 1960.
Pass me the jam.	"Pass me the jam," she said.
I haven't thought much of Lola since she went out with Bob.	I haven't thought much of Lola, since she went out with Bob.

You shouldn't need more evidence to convince you that commas have sound and meaning, and that you can't put them in or leave them out according to whim or according to a set of rules. My advice is to forget everything you've heard about commas, if you haven't already, and concentrate on listening for the comma sound. As I said at the start of the chapter, the way to learn punctuation is to practice reading aloud with feeling. You'll be surprised at how quickly you'll master punctuation by reading with feeling and melody. And occasionally read off the punctuation marks as you go, to help them sink in: *She said comma quotation marks I love submarine races exclamation point quotation marks.* If your own punctuation is really terrible, do not punctuate as you write, but do it afterwards, while you read it aloud slowly and expressively.

A word of warning now. There are two places in a sentence where commas are put in unnecessarily. There may be significant pauses before the verb and before the object of the verb, which emphasize these important words in the sentence. Don't mistake these strong pauses for the comma sound. The rule, you recall, is two commas or none between subject and verb, or verb and object. But sometimes it depends. Occasionally, when the subject of the sentence is a mile away from the verb, you can put a comma before the verb: *What I've always dreamed of and want more than anything in the whole world, is to learn to punctuate.* You heard the comma before *is.* If you heard it, you get to use it.

You're not in charge of spelling, but you *are* in charge of how you want your writing to be read. Using the comma is an art, and you are the artist. Punctuation is correct only when it correctly expresses your intention. If you write, *Today, the case is different,* someone might tell you that the comma after *Today* makes the punctuation heavy. Your answer should be that you want *Today* emphasized, and that he can jump in the lake with his theories of heavy and light punctuation. Another example: *I need to have my hair cut twice a year, for school.* By putting the comma between *year* and *for school* you're saying that both ideas are important. A different example: *In this cake I use butter eggs flour and sugar.* Someone might ask where your commas are. Answer by saying you wanted to go faster than *In this cake, I use butter, eggs, flour, and sugar.* I must warn you, though, that at the present time not many publishers in America will allow you to omit the commas from series constructions.

If you write *Hey Stevie, come here,* do you need a comma before *Stevie?* No, except in the most Formal writing. If you write *I made the sauce, and surprisingly enough, it was good,* do you need a comma before *surprisingly?* No, not even in Formal. The rule is that if a parenthetical phrase or clause (double commas) follows the comma-and-conjunction that connects two sentences, the first comma of the parenthetical pair drops out.

Here is an eye sentence from *The New York Times: America is shocked, bereft and, quite properly, worried.* A better ear sentence would be: *America is shocked, bereft, and quite properly worried.*

What were you taught about punctuating a series? *Buy me root beer, french fries, and a hamburger.* Do you put a comma after *french fries?* Most teachers say leave it out, most handbooks say put it in. What do you say? That you haven't been told the truth about commas, that they represent comma sounds. If you're asking for root beer french fries and a hamburger, ask for them your way. Of course, you have to figure out what your way is. What's your way here? *Women should stay home to cook, clean and raise children.* And here? *I have a large wooden platform bed.* Do the rulebooks want you to set off interjections? *Oh, hell, yes.*

A final reminder. Commas often come in pairs, acting as handles to show that parenthetical elements of one sort or another can be lifted out of a sentence without destroying its sense—that is, taking away the subject or its verb. *Csonka, the fullback, is strong.* The basic meaning of the sentence is that Csonka is strong. Subject, verb, subject complement. The parenthetical or removable idea is that he's a fullback. That's important information, but it's not absolutely necessary for the sentence to be a sentence. *Put that bomb down, Achmed, before you get hurt.* Although it's important that you're talking to Achmed and not Stanislaus if Achmed's the one holding the bomb, *Achmed* is still parenthetical and should be enclosed by commas.

What's parenthetical? In everything but the most Formal writing, *you* decide—by listening. You know a piece is parenthetical if your tone drops when you say it, telling the listener you're interrupting the main message for lesser stuff. If you can read the sentence in a flat monotone, with no emphasis and no pauses—like a robot or the mechanical voice on the phone that tells you the time—and if the sense still comes out the way you want it, then the piece isn't parenthetical and you should leave the commas out.

Parenthetical elements are set off by commas, dashes, or parentheses. If the parenthetical element comes in the middle of the sentence make sure you enclose it in a pair of marks. Don't forget one of the pair, even though the sound is not so strong at one end as at the other. If the parenthetical element comes at the start or the end of the sentence, of course, you need only one comma or one dash. Unfortunately, you always have to use a pair of parentheses; you can't get by with one, which causes a problem about whether to put punctuation inside or outside the closing parenthesis. This problem arises because it may result in double punctuation, which is an impossibility, since no one can make two sounds at once, at least not with the voice.

Using commas well is a difficult and often unappreciated art. Since not everyone will master the ear method or care to, and since not everyone knows exactly how she wants every sentence to sound, here's a summary of the comma *rules*. In Formal, use commas:

— between items in a series.
— after many adverbs, phrases, and clauses that introduce a sentence. *Opening her eyes, Carol looked at the alarm clock.*
— to enclose nonrestrictive clauses. *Bob, who was awake, yawned.*
— before a coordinating conjunction introducing a main clause. *She blew him a kiss, and he caught it.* (Only in America is the comma *expected* here.)
— to set off direct address and other parenthetical interrupters. *"Carol, will you fix breakfast?"*
— to introduce or interrupt short quotations. *"Not," she said, "on your life."*
— to prevent misreading. *Not long after, he saw Carol.* . . . or *Let's talk about Bob, and good writers.*

Then there are the style commas you can always make your own choices about:

— to emphasize an adverb. *She snored, heavily.*

— to give extra emphasis to modifiers of equal importance. *The snarling dog had sharp, hungry-looking teeth.*

Commas are generally not expected or used after every adverb, before the verb, before the direct object, with restrictive clauses *(The dog on the porch bit the mail carrier)*, or before a coordinating conjunction connecting short main clauses that have either strongly related ideas *(I wash the car and it pours for hours)* or strongly contrasting ideas *(I get all the seeds in the ground but we don't get a drop)*.

Dash

The dash looks like a stretched-out hyphen. In fact, when you type a dash you type two hyphens. But the dash does the opposite of the hyphen. The hyphen holds two pieces together, the dash pushes two things apart. The dash marks a sudden and dramatic break in thought or a sharp change in tone. Whatever is set off by dashes is emphasized. The dash has a distinctive sound almost impossible to mistake: the word before the dash is heavily stressed, for the break in thought must be sharp. The pause that follows is an unusually long one. The dash pictures its sound.

> I knew nothing about men—until I met Reggie.
> I knew nothing about men until I met—Reggie.
> I never said he stole—rubber bands?
> Then he sat down—on the Pekingese.
> I like English—muffins.

The dash is such a useful punctuation mark, conveying excitement or surprise, setting up jokes, indicating long pauses, that writers are tempted to overuse it, thinking it makes their writing livelier. You may have received—or may have written—letters gushing with dashes. Did you hear the dashes in that sentence? Were they justified?

The dash is overused for another bad reason: to substitute for other punctuation marks. Unsure writers trust in the dash because they think they can use it anywhere. Unfortunately, dashes slow sentences down.

If overusing the dash makes it less dashing, it should be reserved for special occasions. If you're writing Formally, you're supposed to be calm, not gasping. Some English professors say that when a writer is born she is given only a certain number of dashes to use in her lifetime—and shouldn't waste them.

Parentheses, Brackets, Ellipses

You can tell when you have parenthetical or nonessential parts in a sentence as it's read because the voice drops down distinctly. It does so even when the parenthetical matter is important or exciting and set off by dashes. Listen: *He asked her—he couldn't resist—for a date. She gave him one—from the box on the table.*

Commas are used to set off parenthetical matter that is *close to the meaning* of the sentence. By contrast, dashes *emphasize* and parentheses *minimize* what they set off. Parentheses look like arcs trying to encircle what's between them. That's a good way to think about them: as the writer's attempt to draw a circle around stuff she's not happy about putting in the sentence. Parentheses confess the writer's embarrassment at having to insert what doesn't really belong. Dashes introduce something dramatic, parentheses, something dull. Both devices tempt the writer to dodge the work of arranging the thoughts and working them in properly.

Note how the voice drops way down and almost disappears to read what's within parentheses here:

> William Shakespeare (1564 to 1616) was a middle class heterosexual. He married Anne Hathaway (a shotgun wedding) when she was three months pregnant. He had three children (Judy, Susy, and Hamnet) before he was twenty-one. In his sonnets (written around 1595) he talks about an affair with a Dark Lady (dark meaning brunette and also unknown).

As you see, these afterthoughts are just sneaked into the sentences. A writer with a lot of parentheses is goofing off. Interruptions are annoying, especially when unimportant. Try not to write an entire sentence that must be within parentheses. (If you do, naturally the period goes inside the closing parenthesis.) Punctuation never appears before the opening parenthesis. (This takes note of the fact that the parenthesis has a sound.) Additional punctuation follows the closing parenthesis (if needed). Did you hear your voice drop for those parentheses of mine?

Similar to parentheses are *brackets*, a highly specialized form of punctuation. They are sometimes used in place of double parentheses, or parentheses within parentheses, but most publishers find these brackets within parentheses ugly and have stopped using them. That suits me; there's no need for a sentence to look like a tool rack. Brackets are still used to enclose comments and corrections in quoted material. If you have to interrupt or explain while you're quoting, what *you* say is put within brackets.

The *ellipsis* is another rare but useful sign. It's easier to use an ellipsis than to remember its name. The ellipsis is a row of three periods that shows that something has been omitted from a quotation. A three-dot ellipsis has no sound. A four-dot ellipsis, or a period plus an ellipsis, has the sound of a period. Brackets are used to put something into a quotation, ellipses to leave something out. *This damned sole* [sic] *was guilty . . . of the sin of average* [sic].

Use the hyphen or dash to show missing letters *(Dear M—,)* and the ellipsis to show missing words. Informally, the ellipsis, also called suspension dots, is used like a dash to mark interruptions and thus has the sound of the dash: *"Oh Bob . . . ," she said, as they sank . . . slowly . . . to the couch. . . .*

Colon

At the end of my treatment of useful punctuation is the colon. Not so long ago, the colon was used interchangeably with the semicolon; it used to be a light period. Today it's distinguished from the semicolon, though some people still confuse them. The colon looks like a double period, but it represents a comma sound or a dash sound. Ladies use it instead of the dash. The comma is a hurdle, the dash a springboard, the colon an opening door.

When used as a mark of punctuation within the sentence, the colon means *as follows, here's the explanation or list,* or *here's what he said.* It tells the reader to pay attention to what's coming. It catches his eye and brings the sentence to a pregnant pause, as if it were a heavy comma or a light dash. It should be used only when exactly suited to the situation, only to introduce an explanation or restatement, or a longish list or quotation. With a short explanation, short list, or short quotation, do not use a colon—use a comma or dash. Examples of proper colons: *Here is the weather report for tomorrow: increasing winds, small craft warnings on the Sound, fol-*

lowed by rain and possible hailstorms. There are four basic nutritional groups: meat and fish, milk and eggs, cereals, and fruits and vegetables.

Here are examples of improper colons: *The weather report says: fair and windy. This is what people want: bread, love, and dreams.* The colon is too strong in these sentences. It usually is when it comes right after a verb. Don't say *All he could think about was:* or *My theory is:* There's a good test for whether you're justified in using a colon. If you can insert the words *as follows* before the colon without making the sentence too heavy, the colon is justified. You wouldn't say *This is what people want, as follows: bread, love, and dreams.*

Now let's learn for all time the difference between the semicolon and the colon. If you're making a new point in your sentence, use a semicolon to fasten it on. If you're restating or explaining what you just said, use a colon. Whatever follows a colon refers back to what immediately preceded it.

> Look at the rising sun; we have gotten through another night.
> Look at the rising sun: it has turned the clouds pink.
> Two years ago there was a happy event; and they named him Bruce.
> Two years ago there was a happy event: Bob and Carol had Bruce.
> The meeting had little business; it was swiftly done.
> The meeting had little business: they had to decide on buying a widget.

Some people love to use a capital letter after the colon if a complete sentence follows. This newfangled usage confuses some readers who can't see the point in starting a new sentence inside an old one. Of course, if the colon introduces a quotation or something that sounds like a quotation, then follow the colon with a capital letter.

> She proposed a solution to the arms race: Armies should fight with their fists.
> He was a man of principle: So many women and so little time.

The colon is also used conventionally and soundlessly in giving chapter and verse *(Matthew 5:7)* and in writing time *(6:15).*

Apostrophe

Now for the last and least of the punctuation marks, the spelling marks meant primarily for the eye. These are the apostrophe, quotation marks, hyphen, and slash. If you ever become a big shot in the literary world, do us all a favor and refuse to use the spelling marks. The sooner these jots and tittles disappear from the language the happier we'll be and the more time we'll have for fishing. I would rather leave out these marks, but I use them because my editor tells me to. Writing is very much a give-and-take affair.

The apostrophe is used to show contractions and possessives. *There's the boys' gym.* You didn't hear those apostrophes, did you? I hope not. Apostrophes are sprinkled all over or neglected entirely because no one can hear where they belong. They are misused not because writers are stupid but because apostrophes are useless. Strong players in the Game of English love to find misused apostrophes and then laugh or scowl, as the mood strikes them, at the weaker players. You must learn about apostrophes, not because they're worth knowing, but to protect yourself. Handbooks have whole chapters on the apostrophe, discussing where to stick it in cases like *Bess's, bosses', Jack and Jill's, Jack's and Jill's, Cortez'* and so on.

The possessive apostrophe originated a few centuries ago as a mistake: some printers thought that *Bobs book* was a contraction of *Bob his book,* and since they used an apostrophe in contractions, they stuck one in *Bob's,* and it's been there ever since. You must perpetuate this error and indicate possession by putting in an apostrophe and an *s.* If the word already ends in *s,* you need to decide whether to add another *s* after the apostrophe. *Decide first how to spell the word before inserting the apostrophe.* (This is easy advice for those who write by hand but hard for those who are typing and have to leave a space for the apostrophe.) Think whether you have a singular or a plural. If you're writing about the *executives john* or the *drivers side,* think whether it belongs to one executive or driver or more than one. If *a lady* has *gloves,* write *lady* and then add the apostrophe and the *s.* If you're thinking of *ladies gloves,* write *ladies* and then add the apostrophe.

Another question arises: you've put the apostrophe after *ladies,* do you need another *s* after the apostrophe? Whether you need one depends on you, not on rules. No rules cover all the possibilities. If you want the reader to pronounce another *s,* put another *s* in. It's unlikely you want the reader to say *ladieses.* But you have a real choice with quandaries like *Jesus' Jesus's, Hess' Hess's, Jones' Jones's, Davis' Davis's. This is Jesse James' Cave.* Or, *This is Jesse James's Cave.* Or, *This is Frank and Jesse Jameses' Cave.* Simple, isn't it? The constructions are logical and can be figured out, if you have the time. Decide how many *bosses* or *Moses* you're talking about, and write down the singular or plural form. (Where you can avoid a special plural form, do it: write *the Roberts' dog* instead of going crazy over *the Roberts's dog* or *the Robertses'* or *Robertses's dog*.) In short, if you have a word that does *not* end with an *s* or *z* sound, add apostrophe *s*. If you have a word that ends with an *s* or *z* sound already, add an apostrophe, and then another *s* if you *want* an extra *s* for a zizzizz sound. (In England the rules are different: you can't write *Mrs. Jukes' knickers*, you *have* to write *Mrs. Jukes's knickers.*)

Remember: never, never use an apostrophe with the pronouns its, his, hers, ours, yours, theirs, and *oneself.* These pronouns show possession, the apostrophe shows possession, and if you show possession twice you will be fired. Washington, Jefferson, and others with wigs used apostrophes with these pronouns, but they were confused. Leaving apostrophes out shows your careless, putting them in wrong shows you're incompetence. (Did you catch these?) You only use an apostrophe with a pronoun when you have a *contraction.* Test whether you're having contractions by letting them relax. When tempted to write *it's*, try *it is* and see if that works; for *they're* try *they are*, and for *who's* try *who is*. This rule isn't much help, since the misspellings are usually the other way around: *you are* is spelled *your*, *they are* is spelled *there*.

Only a few words in English are contracted, since we have such short words already, and they cause few problems. You should take note of when you're using contractions, since they're poison in *very* Formal situations. In Informal you regularly use contractions unless you want to emphasize the words by using their full form. The distinction between contracted words and their full forms is important: *I am* versus *I'm, I will not* versus *I won't, I'd* versus *I had* and *I would*. Do not avoid contractions because you're puzzled about apostrophes. From time to time you will balk at writing contractions that you would otherwise say, such as *One of you's lying, That girl over there's done it.*

Though the apostrophe used for contractions is older than the apostrophe used for possessives, the former is disappearing first, from headlines and *Dont Walk* signs and so on. Bernard Shaw did not use the apostrophe in contractions, and got away with it, but foolishly continued to use it with possessives.

Some people who don't have to teach apostrophes find them amusing, like these: *the president's wife's secretary's daughter's boyfriend's cat*. Have you ever used the double apostrophe—*Tony's's the best pizza in town?*

To be fair, I must admit that I can think of an instance in which the apostrophe is useful: *These hamsters look like my parents'*. If I've told you more about the apostrophe than you want to know, it's more than I want to know, too.

Quotation Marks

The next pitfall is the most difficult punctuation mark of all, quotation marks. Correct use of these marks, which always come in pairs, have no sound, and are used inside and outside of real punctuation marks, is incredibly complicated, and that's why they play a grand role in the Game of English. As a test, why don't you send in your solutions to this question: how do you punctuate a quoted exclamation appearing at the end of a quoted question? For example, *Did Bob ask, Did she really say* Yes? Anyone sending in the right answer will receive a large prize. *Did Bob ask, "Did she really say* 'Yes!'?"?(?)

Luckily, the use of quotation marks is now becoming confused, which may bring about the collapse of the system. Some publishers, at the insistence of writers, are starting to leave the marks out, and some are using single quotes, dashes, angles, or odd marks where they used to use the standard double quotation marks, our little old handwritten friends, 66 and 99.

We'll now run through some current conventions in quoting. Quotation marks are not used with long quotations, which are set off by being single spaced and indented. A long quote is more than four or five lines of prose or more than two lines of poetry.

In an *indirect* quote quotation marks are not used, even though some of the words are directly quoted. Indirect quotes read faster than direct quotes and cause no punctuation problems. *Groucho said he would never join a club that would have him as a member. Nixon said he was not a crook.*

Quotation marks are used with direct quotations after a verb of saying, as in *he said, they asked.* A verb of saying is followed by a comma if needed and if the quote is going to be short, or a colon, if the quote is going to be long. *He said "damn." He said, "Damn." He said: "Damn the torpedoes! Full speed ahead!"* After the comma or the colon comes the open quote mark, then comes the quote, starting with a capital letter. At the close of the quote, period and comma go *inside* the closing quote mark. Colon and semicolon go *outside.* Putting the colon and the semicolon outside the marks is logical enough (though ugly) because the sentence is being resumed. Putting the comma inside the marks is an illogicality in the present system, if the colon and the semicolon go outside; but that's the way it's done, and that's the way to do it. When the quote is an exclamation or a question, the exclamation point or question mark goes *inside* the quotation marks. When the whole sentence in which the quote appears is an exclamation or a question, the exclamation point or question mark goes at the very end of the sentence. In England these rules are different—so don't go.

Words, thoughts, and questions *in the mind* are not put into quotes. *Should I say Thank you? She's asked herself time and again: Will I ever learn to punctuate?* In writing dialogue, what each person says is normally a separate paragraph. Sometimes two people can speak in one paragraph if a mix of direct quotation and paraphrase is used, so long as the speakers are kept clear. *(He said he didn't want to go. "Why?" she demanded. He mumbled something.)*

Put single quotation marks around a quote within a quote. When single and double quotation marks coincide, questions arise about where to put the real punctuation marks. Such questions can often be solved. Be patient and sort everything out. (Problems of quotes within quotes are avoided by making one of the quotes indirect, thus getting rid of one set of marks.) Here's a quote within a quote: *Did he ask, "Why did she say, 'What's in it for me' "?*

In Formal do not use quotation marks to be funny or sarcastic or because you're ashamed of a certain word. In Formal you're responsible for the words you write, and putting some wretched words in quotes won't excuse you. You can't write: *This swimsuit is "sensuous,"* or *This food is "organic."* Formal people do not sneer. Don't use quotation marks for emphasis—*underline.*

Titles of small pieces—stories, essays, articles, and poems—are put inside quotation marks. *Everyone loved Pinckert's essay, "Quotation Marks."*

Hyphen and Slash

The style book for the Oxford University Press says that if you take hyphens seriously you will surely go mad. We won't worry about that. Unfortunately, others take hyphens seriously, and to placate them we must constantly check in the dictionary for hyphenated words. Is it *hell fire, hell-fire,* or *hellfire?* I will try to spare you those trips to the dictionary.

The hyphen used to be a small mark at the right-hand margin of the page to show that a word was being split. This little bar was invented to hold together the broken pieces of a word. Once having used the hyphen this way, people extended its use to join two words together that looked like they might be one word or ought to be one word. *Mail-man* finally did turn into *mailman, volley-ball* turned into *volleyball, sun-bathing* into *sunbathing.* The hyphen seems to be a useful way of bringing words together, but it actually delays acceptance of new compounds. Some people in England still write *to-morrow.* The writer is saying, I'm chicken, I want to write these two words together as one word but I'm afraid.

If you want to combine words, do it! All of us have a sense that certain words should not be combined: *pocket billiards, racing car, ice cream, split level, putting green.* Do you like *diningroom* or *warthog?* If you don't want to combine two words, don't combine them and don't use a hyphen either. Test by sound. The *secret of the hyphen* is that it is used between words that we want to sound together without pause as one word. We say *She looks like a million dollars,* but we also say *She's a million-dollar baby. The move was well organized, It was a well-organized move. I eat mashed potatoes, I eat mashed-potato sandwiches. She gave me a don't-give-me-that-stuff look. Her look was Don't give me that stuff. I ate leg of mutton in my leg-of-mutton blouse. Eat Dirt Cheap, Eat Dirt-Cheap. Believe this little, used grammar book. Believe this little-used grammar book.*

We use hyphens with compound numbers and fractions because we want to say these groups of numbers as one. *Give me twenty-two bagels. Use three and three-quarters cups,* or *Use three-and-three-quarters cups.*

Nowadays we can fashion lots of new words without timidly inserting hyphens and nobody stops us: *semicolon, reentry, cooperative, selfserving, microphysics, psychodocudrama.*

The *slash* can be dismissed in a few words. It has become fashionable as a shorthand mark that means *and/or* or *both*, as in *his/her*, *country/western*, *social/political*. As shorthand it's welcome, but the ambiguity it stands for is unwelcome. The writer doesn't know whether to push the two words apart or pull them together, and draws a picture of her problem. But she should conquer her neuroses and make choices, not present ambiguities. If the slash means *and/or* and if you can't use the slash, you can't use *and/or* either. Instead say . . . *or* . . . *or both. In Formal* you want to avoid anything that cannot be pronounced, *e.g., your idea(s) is (are)*. The slash is also used to show where lines of verse end when verse is written as prose. Roses are red,/ Violets are blue;/ If you insist on these dumb slashes,/ I'll put them in for you./

Underlining

There is one other kind of punctuation I've saved till the end—underlining. It's not generally thought of as punctuation because it's not a point but a line; it's a tone, the tone of emphasis. Underlining (or in print, italicizing) directs the reader to stress the words in saying them. In most written sentences the important words are naturally stressed and do not have to be pointed out to the reader. But sometimes you *must* underline: a seven-word sentence like *I never said Nixon authorized that burglary* can have seven different meanings depending on which word is emphasized.

Like any device to achieve emphasis—exclamations, questions, dashes, abrupt sentences—underlining loses its effectiveness when used too often. But the device is not forbidden to you, no matter how Formal the occasion. You may have been taught *not* to underline for emphasis, but that's one of those rules intended to dampen your spirits. Here are examples of legitimate underlining: *You may write a check, but I prefer <u>cash</u>. The duchess said it was a <u>damn</u> shame.*

Anything you offer as an *example* should be underlined. *Dot your <u>i</u>'s and cross your <u>t</u>'s.* Really foreign-sounding foreign words should be underlined. *I sang it <u>con amore</u> after I ate chile con carne.* See if you can underline the following correctly.

> Ain't you got no onions? I ain't said I ain't. I ain't ast you is you ain't, I ast you ain't you ain't. Now is you or ain't you got no onions?

Today, almost everyone follows the convention of underlining the names of books, publications, ships, operas, and other works of art. This convention, which directs attention unnecessarily to these words, arose from the need to distinguish real names from the names of works of art. For example, if you write *in Hamlet*, the reader is supposed to be confused whether you're talking about the man or the play. This is hardly a problem. If you wrote without underlining that you loved Madame Butterfly and went aboard Queen Elizabeth no one is likely to be confused. But since everyone does it, you too should remember to underline book titles, names of newspapers and magazines, and names of works of art. Small works of art—songs, poems, and articles—are put into quotation marks.

* * *

We're now finished with punctuation. Remember that the marks belong to you, they're your way of conducting the reader. But you must know how they sound. Allow no one to fool with your punctuation. When you want your reader to go slowly or dramatically you provide the cues, lots of them. If you want him to go fast, use a quicker, lighter punctuation.

If you're having trouble punctuating while you're writing, that's a tipoff the ideas are a mess. You haven't gotten the ideas clear, and they're not making clear sounds. You'll remember what I said before, I hope, that when you struggle for words the ideas are defective. When you have good ideas, sentences you want to say, the right words come and the sentences punctuate themselves. Where there's bad punctuation, there's bad prose. When Oscar Wilde said he spent the morning putting in a comma and the afternoon taking it out, he was kidding. A good writer never worries about punctuation, she just listens to it.

Read over these sentences now to pick out the one you'd use for the most laughs.

> Take my wife, please.
> Take my wife. Please.
> Take my wife—please!
> Take my wife—please?

I tested you to see whether you read the sentences loud enough for you to hear the punctuation. Did you? I myself prefer the second version, the way Henny Youngman says it.

Here's a tough passage for you to punctuate. Don't peek at the answer, which follows.

> Is Here come the judge your joke he shouted
> No came the answer it is Sammy Davis Jrs

The answer.

> "Is 'Here come the judge!' your joke?" he shouted.
> "No," came the answer, "it is Sammy Davis, Jr.'s."

If I were in charge, I would drop seventeen of those punctuation marks!

> Is Here come the judge! your joke? he shouted.
> No, came the answer, it is Sammy Davis Jrs.

You'll be delighted that grammar can be handled in just one chapter, the next.

Chapter Four

Rules of the Game: Grammar

Rules of the Game

In a sentence, all the words are related to each other; grammar is the attempt to explain the relationships. It's the study of sentences, or human speech. Obviously, speech can be studied from many points of view—how it develops, how it's learned, what it is, what it should be. Grammar is a huge subject and the term itself is quite vague.

It wasn't always so vague. The word is related to *graphic*, *autograph*, *graffiti*—having to do with things scratched or written. Grammar originally meant the study of writing. Writing, since it can be corrected, has fewer mistakes than spoken language, and thus the idea of grammar includes the idea of correctness, or so-called good grammar. Grammar began as the study of what should be done in writing, not in speaking. When Latin was no longer spoken but written, it had lots of grammar. English was spoken and had no grammar. In an English grammar school, students studied Latin. How could English be studied? It wasn't even dead.

The way English is taught in schools today, it might as well be dead. It's taught as if it were a written language. The children are taught not only that writing is different from speech but superior to it. This idea has to strike them as weird; they begin to suspect that their teachers are trying to push them around. They're bombarded with terms. Do this, don't do that. Don't you want to get ahead? Don't you know objective from subjective? Dangle one more participle and I'll scream! Students hate this bottomless subject. It's so tricky, even the teacher is confused. She talks about sentences, sentence fragments, and comma splices as if she knew what they were, but no one knows what they are. She doesn't teach English, she teaches mistakes in English, and she doesn't know what a mistake is. The students catch her confusion, become anxious about using their mother tongue, and some of them decide never to dare to write again, not even letters.

Maybe I can help you change an old attitude toward grammar and writing, and help you see that they are not so threatening as all those rules suggest. I'll try to show that there aren't so many useful rules as you may have supposed. The good rules, the basic rules, you learned in your crib, and needn't worry about. The not-so-good rules, the arbitrary ones always being changed by the mysterious Rules Committee, have to be followed, but there aren't many of them, and there's no reason ever to be scared of them. If someone accuses you of syllepsis, zeugma, or anantapodoton, laugh and say the construction is common in Shakespeare.

There are as many rules as anyone wants to find. Luckily, only a relatively small number of them can be enforced. If few people have heard of a rule, it's not much of a rule. On the other hand, if many people have heard of a rule, it's not much of a rule either: you don't get much credit for not saying *ain't*, but you get a lot of credit for not dangling a participle—from those who know a dangling participle when they see one.

An honest discussion of English grammar, grammar in the sense of what has been done and what can be done in the language, would require many volumes. But a description of the language is not what people are looking for. They want a prescription of what should be done. They want someone to speak with authority and clear up the mess. They're looking for a miracle. Any treatment of grammar that tries to be honest as well as useful has to strike a balance between describing and prescribing. I am not honest. I prescribe Formal (and use Informal). I did not invent this Game.

To prove it's a game, look at just one well-known rule. Where's the mistake in these sentences? *No one loves her like he does. She treats me like I was her mother.* The supposed mistake is, of course, the use of *like* as a conjunction, i.e., using *like* to begin a clause. These sentences are forceful and cannot be improved, but they are taboo—and have been ever since the poet Tennyson told

Prince Albert that using *like* as a conjunction was vulgar. Since then, those who hate vulgarity have refrained from using *like* as a conjunction. Where did the rule come from? The Committee invented it. Is it a good rule? No. Must it be followed? Yes.

A mistake in grammar is an infraction of a rule, and it makes no difference whether the rule is defensible or whether you like it. Your audience decides when you've broken a rule. Just as any utterance can be a sentence, depending on whether the listener hears a sentence, so any utterance can be a mistake. Since you are at the mercy of your audience, you had better think about what they expect, and forget about what is Right and Wrong under the Eye of Eternity or the eye of Miss Thistlebottom.

A home run in one ballpark is an easy out in another. If you say to the delivery boy *I wish it were time for lunch* and *These frankfurters are for whom?* and *I am a better tipper than she,* he will think you sound pretty funny. If you say to the Duchess of Exurb *I wish it was lunchtime* and *Who are these hot dogs for?* and *I'm a bigger tipper than her,* she may never invite you back.

In this chapter on mistakes, I'll be talking about mistakes that will be discovered by the wrong people, who are in this case the Right People. There won't be any point in my trying to sort out big mistakes from little ones: all mistakes are big. According to one way of thinking, if you say *I brang the beer* or *I brung the beer* that would be a little mistake, because you did not offend against meaning and you got your point across. But most audiences would consider that a much worse mistake than if you said *I have conveyed to this place the carbonated, slightly alcoholic malt beverages.* A mistake is a mistake, whatever it is.

If mistakes are something that others think you're guilty of, it's not likely that you'll be able to avoid them. But the point of writing is not to avoid mistakes. I've made a thousand mistakes in these pages, mistakes in English—I'm writing in English. It's good to make mistakes. Everyone should be willing to take his lumps. It's not good to go around thinking you're safe from mistakes. Pity poor Disraeli, desperately correcting proofs on his deathbed and saying, "I will not go down to posterity talking bad grammar." So don't get all upset by the uncertainties of grammar. I wouldn't want, and I don't think you would want, a situation in which certain people made no mistakes and others made all of them. A person who really knew grammar would not be fit to talk to.

What Good is Grammar?

Not much. Grammar is largely negative and analytical. Some enlightened teachers of composition refuse to spend one minute talking about questions of grammar. Composition is putting things together, and is hard to teach. Grammar is taking them apart, and is easy to teach. Grammar goes on forever. Teaching it has always offered job security. The demand for grammar, like the demand for medical attention, is unlimited. Grammar is the perfect subject, since anyone can teach it and no one can master it. It is even being taught to a large number of apes, who have in fact been getting good marks. Though there are apparently no slow learners among these anthropoids, none has yet come up with a striking sentence, much less a good essay.

I'm not giving you a grammar lesson because it's easy for me. I think you have to know a little grammar and from time to time have to review that knowledge if you're going to catch mistakes when you revise and proofread. It's hard to know what a mistake is if you have no idea of its name or why it's thought to be a mistake. A piece of advice like *Cut modifiers, conjunctions, and articles* isn't much help if you don't know what they are. Questions of usage focus on words, questions of grammar on categories. For some people, the categories of grammar are too abstract, and they don't want to learn them or they soon forget them. We walk, but we don't have to name the muscles we use. Why must we name the parts of speech? As a rebel in Shakespeare's *Henry VI* says: "It will be proved to thy face that thou hast men about thee that usually talk of a noun and a verb and such abominable words as no Christian ear can endure to hear."

If you asked a graduate student in English to name the parts of speech and the parts of a sentence it's unlikely he could do it. But this minimum of grammar is needed; these terms are your tools for taking a sentence apart. Everyone must be able to explain what each word is doing in a sentence. Analyzing sentences used to be called *parsing*, but few know this word, since parsing is not regularly done in schools anymore. Even *syntax* is dead, the thought of a tax on sin being too depressing. The poet e.e. cummings says: "Who pays any attention to the syntax of things will never wholly kiss you."

If a sentence can't be analyzed, questions of correctness can't be solved. You can generally trust what *looks* or *sounds* right, but not always. What you're used to may not be correct, especially in Formal. Some people are lucky and without knowing much grammar seldom fall into mistakes. They don't know it, but their subjects and verbs agree, their pronouns have clear reference and are in the proper case. Some people don't even know they're speaking prose. But almost everyone, including me, will benefit from the following review. I promise to hold technical terms to a minimum.

Grammar Quiz

To find out if you can skip this grammar review, why don't you take a little quiz and see how you do? Each of the following sentences is unacceptable in Formal. I'll bet that if you can pick out the error in each sentence you can name it or explain why it's an error, and if you can't name it or explain it, you can't pick it out.

1. As far as time, we have a whole hour.
2. Jim told Bob he was wrong.
3. I have more trouble with spelling than grammar.
4. Bob approved of Carol going.
5. I do not care whom she said did it.
6. For we women to back down would be silly.
7. He was in the Marines, and his son wants to be one too.
8. Is this enough questions for now?
9. Standing on the bridge the island looked dark.
10. The Senate along with the House of Representatives have adjourned.
11. I wrote to RSVP on the invitation.
12. I wish I were born in England.
13. He manages to occasionally change the oil.
14. First lie on the floor, and then you should jump up.
15. To shut the dog in, the gate should be closed.
16. Dress warm when you go out.
17. He was late so I left.
18. New York's Governor Cuomo is cute.
19. I should have planned to have gone to the party.
20. It shouldn't take only ten minutes.
21. If one can't stand the heat, stay out of the kitchen.
22. The chances of the car skidding or you losing control of the steering is great.

Now I'll give you the answers, using a few technical terms which will be explained later.

1. *As far as time, we have a whole hour.* A mistake in *diction.* The conjunction *as far as* has been confused with the preposition *as for.*

2. *Jim told Bob he was wrong.* The mistake is in the *reference* of the pronoun *he.* The reference is *ambiguous.* The sentence should be *Jim told Bob that Bob was wrong* or *Jim told Bob that Jim was wrong.*

3. *I have more trouble with spelling than grammar.* It should be *I have more trouble with spelling than with grammar.* This fault is a lack of *parallel structure;* the preposition *with* should be repeated to make the parallel clear. Similarly, the famous ad should be *Winston tastes good as a cigarette should taste.*

4. *Bob approved of Carol going.* This should be *Bob approved of Carol's going.* A mistake in the noun's *case;* the possessive case, *Carol's* should be used before the emphasized noun, *going.* Sometimes you want the possessive, sometimes the objective: *I hate your being sick, I hate you being sick.*

5. *I do not care whom she said did it.* This should be *I do not care who she said did it.* Another mistake in *case. Who,* the *subjective* case, should be used, since *who* is the subject of the verb *did.* In choosing the pronoun, see how it's used in its own clause.

6. *For we women to back down would be silly.* Again, a mistake in *case.* This should be *For us women. Us,* the *objective* case, is the object of the preposition *For.* Pronouns in the front of the sentence may look like subjects but often aren't.

7. *He was in the Marines, and his son wants to be one too.* This should be *He was in the Marines, and his son wants to be a Marine too.* A mistake in the *reference* of a pronoun; *one* cannot refer to the plural *Marines.*

8. *Is this enough questions for now?* That should be *Are these enough questions for now?* This mistake is a lack of *agreement,* between a plural subject *questions* and a singular verb *is.*

9. *Standing on the bridge the island looked dark.* Should be *Standing on the bridge, we thought the island looked dark* or *As we were standing on the bridge, the island looked dark.* The mistake is a *dangling participle, standing.* Participles, like verbs, require subjects. The island isn't standing on the bridge; someone has to be standing. Hemingway wrote this sentence, but he knew what he was doing.

10. *The Senate along with the House of Representatives have adjourned.* It should be *has adjourned.* A mistake in *agreement* between subject and verb. *Senate* is the subject. Similarly: *The ham-*

mer along with three thousand tacks is over here. Carol with her dog runs to work. Convention, not logic, requires you to detach the *with* and the *as well as* phrases from the subject.

11. *I wrote to RSVP on the invitation.* Should be *I wrote on the invitation to RSVP.* The fault is a *misplaced modifier.* The modifier, the phrase *on the invitation,* should be closer to the word it modifies— in this case, *wrote.*

12. *I wish I were born in England.* Should be *I wish I had been born in England.* A mistake in the *tense* of the verb.

13. *He manages to occasionally change the oil.* Should be *He occasionally manages to change the oil.* The fault is a *misplaced modifier.* The adverb *occasionally* modifies the verb *manages,* not the infinitive *to change.* You *can* split an infinitive with an adverb, but not with one that belongs elsewhere.

14. *First lie on the floor, and then you should jump up.* Should be *First lie on the floor and then jump up.* The fault is a *shift* in the verbs, from the imperative *lie* to the declarative *should jump up.*

15. *To shut the dog in, the gate should be closed.* That should be *To shut the dog in, close the gate. To shut the dog in* is a *dangling* phrase. This *infinitive* phrase needs a subject which follows it immediately.

16. *Dress warm when you go out.* Should be *Dress warmly when you go out.* A word usually considered to be an *adjective* has been used in place of an *adverb.* Here you want an adverb to modify the stressed verb *Dress.* (You could probably get away with saying *I am dressed warm.*)

17. *He was late so I left.* Should be *He was late and so I left.* A mistake in *usage.* In Formal *so* is not permitted as a conjunction. *And so* is OK.

18. *New York's Governor Cuomo is cute.* Should be *Governor Cuomo of New York is attractive.* New York doesn't own Cuomo, so the *genitive* form *of New York* is better than the *possessive* form *New York's.* (And *cute* isn't Formal.)

19. *I should have planned to have gone to the party.* Should be *I should have planned to go to the party.* A mistake in the *tense* of the infinitive *to go.* You need the present tense after a verb like *plan.*

20. *It shouldn't take only ten minutes.* Should be *It should take only ten minutes.* The *should not* and *only* are a *double negative,* thought of as an offense against logic.

21. *If one can't stand the heat, stay out of the kitchen.* Should be *If you . . .* A *shift* in the pronoun, from *one* to *you* (understood).

22. *The chances of the car skidding or you losing control of the steering is great.* Should be *The chances of the car's skidding or of your losing control of the steering are great.* This sentence had three mis-

takes. *Car skidding* and *you losing* are *fused participles*. The subject of the sentence, *chances*, should *agree* with the verb—*chances are*.

If you caught all the mistakes, skip this chapter, unless you love grammar. I hope you got a kick out of spotting the mistakes. What could be more enjoyable than the mistakes of others? In Informal, every one of these sentences, with the possible exception of *Jim told Bob he was wrong*, is perfectly acceptable. If you were alarmed by some of the terms I used, don't be, because I'll explain them all shortly.

Eight Parts of Speech

Nouns are words that name persons, places, and things. Whatever exists or can be said to exist is a noun (or *substantive*, as it used to be called). Nouns can express action, like walking, swimming, thinking, but express it abstractly. Verbs call for an agent to perform the action.

For some reason *pronouns* are always named as a separate part of speech even though they're nouns. A pronoun is a noun that stands for another noun. There aren't many pronouns—*we, they, mine, hers, each, myself, which, that, another*, etc.—but they cause a lot of trouble.

An *adjective* modifies nouns and other adjectives (leaves with *late fall* colors). Modifying means describing, qualifying, telling something about another word. Modifying is not a good term, since no word is actually changed by a modifier; another idea is simply added to it. Consider the phrase *a silk dress*. *Silk* is a descriptive adjective that modifies the noun *dress*. *A* is a limiting adjective, a special kind known as an *article*. It limits the number of dresses being talked about.

The *verb* is the most important part of speech. It's the word that allows us to make a sentence. It's needed for the predicate, or what is being said about the subject. A verb expresses action (he *ran*) or a state of being (he *is*). Verbs have tense and tell what happens in time. Nouns exist independently of time. Only humans are aware of time, only humans know verbs. When an ape makes a sign for a verb, like *eat*, he is really thinking about the noun, *eating*, and if you don't believe me, ask him.

Many words refer to action without being verbs. How would you tell if the word *swimming* is being used as a noun or as a verb? Use this guideline: If it's a noun you can put an adjective in front of it (*good* swimming) and if it's a verb you can put an adverb after it (I'm swimming *well*).

The *adverb* is a versatile part of speech, since it can modify verbs, adverbs, and adjectives. Like a pair of pliers, it does a lot of jobs and is overused. Any modifier that's not modifying a noun or adjective has to be an adverb. *Slowly, Freudianly, very, too*—these are adverbs. An adverb tells where, when, how, or how much.

The *preposition* is a word that's placed in front of a noun (*preposed*), and shows the relationship of this noun to other words in the sentence: *for* a ride, *into* the river, *behind* bars, *off* the top, *in* the way, *with* pleasure. Prepositions are these familiar little words indicating direction that are placed before nouns. The noun that follows the preposition is called the *object* of the preposition, and the two words form a *prepositional phrase*.

The *conjunction* is used to join one word with another, one phrase with another, or one clause with another. Coordinating conjunctions are *and, but, or, nor, for,* and *so*. Coordinating conjunctions do not join similar things, they join similar structures. You can say *bacon and eggs*, you can say *bacon and motorcycles*, but you can't say *bacon and after breakfast*. You can't say *My car gets poor mileage or like it burns money*.

Coordinating conjunctions join words, phrases, or clauses. Subordinating conjunctions only join clauses of unequal importance. A phrase is a group of words doing one job. A clause is a phrase that contains a subject and predicate. Subordinate clauses such as *after I left, who she was, because he snores* begin with a subordinating conjunction and have to be joined to a main clause in order to make sense.

The last and least part of speech is the *interjection: ah, well, gee, ouch, um*. Interjections aren't at all interesting, since they have no relationship to anything in the sentence and are just thrown in.

Now you remember the parts of speech: noun, pronoun, adjective, verb, adverb, preposition, conjunction, and interjection. These terms from Latin sound a bit obscure, but they're easy to understand. Everything in a sentence, whether a word, phrase, or subordinate clause, is being *used as* one of the eight parts of speech. The subject of a sentence has to be something being *used as* a noun. The predicate has to contain a verb.

Sentences would be easy to analyze if words were used as only one part of speech. But many words function as different parts of speech. *Round*, for example, is used as a noun *(a round of drinks)*, verb *(she rounds the turn)*, adjective *(round table)*, adverb *(all year 'round)*, or preposition *('round the clock)*. Usually it's easy to figure out what part of speech a word is acting as, but sometimes it's impossible. In the term *dress designer* is *dress* a noun or adjective? Is the possessive form of a noun *(Bob's)* a noun or an adjective? In *It cost a dollar*, is *dollar* a noun or an adverb? If you can answer these questions, you don't need this review. But then, no one can answer these questions.

Parts of a Sentence

Every sentence has to have a subject, both in the ordinary and the grammatical sense of the word. A sentence has to be about something, and some thing has to be a noun. When you're looking for the subject of a sentence, don't just hunt for nouns—the sentence may have lots of fascinating nouns. Look for the noun the predicate is about. What is being said about the subject is called the predicate; the fancy word means *what is being said*. Therefore, you can't pick out the subject unless you've been all the way to the predicate. You can't start at the front of the sentence.

The predicate contains the verb. To find the subject and its verb you look for them together. If you can't find the subject until you've found the verb and if you can't find the verb unless you know the subject, you had better find them both at the same time. You should hear or feel that collision of subject and verb. In good sentences this is easy to do, but in some it's difficult because the predication is so feeble. Some sentences are a bust because the speaker forgets the subject. This accounts for the frequency of faults in *agreement* between subject and verb. The worst fault in grammar is to fail to make a sentence with a subject and verb, and the second worst fault is to have a subject and verb disagree. In the good old days we had missing verbs *(Kojak with his lollipops)*. Today we also have missing subjects *(In choosing a career calls for a lot of thought)*.

Sometimes a sentence has more than one subject and verb. Each separate subject and verb forms a clause. When a clause makes good sense by itself *(he laughed)*, it's a main or independent clause. When the clause is introduced by a subordinating conjunction like *before, because, although,* or *if,* it can't stand alone anymore and is called a *subordinate* or *dependent* clause. Once you've found the main subject and verb of the sentence, you look for phrases (groups of words that go together) and clauses (phrases that contain subjects and verbs). Page-long sentences are not hard to analyze; you just find the main clause or clauses and then take the lesser clauses one at a time and see what they're up to.

Subordinate clauses are used as nouns, adjectives, or adverbs. Here are noun clauses: I don't care *who said it.* I want to know *how he found out.* That is *why I'm angry. When he comes home* is no concern of mine. Here are adjective clauses: Here's the number *where you can reach him.* She's the one *who gave it to me.* Here are adverb clauses: *Since he left* I've been glad. *When he came back* I was furious. I took him back *because he's Bob.* You can't tell what kind of clause it is by looking at the first word. In fact, you can't tell what anything in a sentence is by looking at it: you have to find out what it's *doing.*

You want to recognize clauses right away, since many rules concern them. You're not supposed to string too many subordinate clauses together. Problems arise about where to put the clause in the sentence and about the tense of the verb in the clause. In Formal, noun clauses are not supposed to start off like adverb clauses, or vice versa: *I wonder whether* (not *if) she's going. The reason is that* (not *because) I'm going too. The best part comes when* (not *is when) she says yes.*

A verb can be one of several kinds. A *transitive* verb requires an object to complete the meaning: *I put . . . I laid . . . I sliced . . .* Transitive verbs require direct objects that receive the action named in the verb. (The object can be named or implied.) An *intransitive* verb doesn't have an object: *I danced, I sang, I read.* Most verbs can be transitive or intransitive, depending on the sentence. *I danced*—what?—*a solo. I sang*—what?—*a song.* The direct object answers the question *What?* The verb can also have an *indirect* object. I danced a solo for *him.* I sang *her* a song. A few verbs are always either transitive or intransitive. *Fall* is intransitive (you can't *fall* something) and *make* is transitive. Dictionaries tell whether verbs are transitive or intransitive so we can avoid mistakes in usage. *Lay, raise,* and *set* are transitive, but not *lie, rise,* and *sit. Hens rise after setting and laying.*

A special kind of intransitive verb is the linking verb: *am, is, were, have been*—all forms of the verb *to be.* They link the subject to the part of the predicate called the *subject complement: The dinner was* beancurds. *I will be* an evangelist. After the linking verb, the predicate is *completed* with an adjective or a noun.

There are a few special linking verbs besides the forms of the verb *to be*. It's good to know them since they require the use of an adjective after them instead of an adverb. He *became* hungry. The lobster *looked* good. It *seemed* silly not to order it. The price *sounded* cheap. The lobster *tasted* good, but soon he *felt* sick.

However long and complicated a sentence is, its basic parts are simple: a subject and a predicate. The predicate contains a verb. The verb can be followed by nothing, by an object complement completing the sense of the verb, or by a subject complement referring back to the subject. Everything else in the sentence modifies some part of the basic sentence. All modifiers are either adjectives or adverbs.

Subject and Verb Agreement

A subject and verb have to agree, which means that a singular subject takes a singular verb, a plural subject a plural verb. Mistakes in agreement are common in speech but unforgivable in writing. Often the speaker is merely interested in naming her subject and then aborts the predicate, or gets so excited by the predicate she forgets her subject. If she remembered that both are needed and framed the sentence in her mind before saying or writing it, she wouldn't make faults in agreement. Examples of the fault: *The woman with all those cats* live *in that house. The value of these fine Victorian homes* keep *going up.* Check the following: *All we heard at night were crickets. There are five years' difference in our ages. What has been, the doctor asked, the results of the tests? This book as well as four others have fallen into the bathtub. One out of four adults are functional illiterates.* Whenever you write a sentence with an inch or more between subject and verb, you had better check whether the two agree.

If you can think of your subject as either a number of separate *items* or as a single *group*, then you decide whether the verb should be singular or plural.

> The arm and the hand (is, are) held out straight.
> Here (is, are) pencil and paper.

A variety of drinks (was, were) offered.

Two and two (is, are) four.

The memoranda (is, are) on the desk.

The family (is, are) sitting down.

Headquarters (is, are) there.

No one can guide you in these choices; you have to guide your audience. You don't often have this freedom. You can't say *they is* and *one are.* And, unfortunately, your options have been limited in some cases by the Rules Committee cracking down. In Formal you have to use a singular verb after *either, neither,* and *everyone.* You cannot say *Neither of them are there.* In Formal you must say *There are more than one,* not *There is more than one.* The Committee is trying to make *none* singular *(none is, none was),* but this pressure can still be resisted.

When you have a double subject separated by *or* or *nor,* and one of them is singular and the other plural, which verb do you choose? *Either the president or his advisers is—or are?—mistaken.* In these cases, use the subject closer to the verb to determine the verb. *Either the president or his advisers* are *mistaken.* You can do the same thing with different forms of the verb: *Either he or I am going crazy. I am the one who is going crazy.* (Don't say *I am the one who am going crazy.*) Say *Not only we but Carol is going crazy.* If that sounds clumsy try *Not only we are going crazy but Carol is too.* If you don't like that keep plugging away. You're expected to have lots of time to do things right.

Getting Tense

Only foreigners make serious mistakes in verbs, and they are forgiven because we understand how complicated our system of verbs are. (Catch that mistake?) Some supposed mistakes are made by dialect speakers using their standard forms. *He come, she fooling me, I be surprise.* Dialect speakers have to shift to the dialect of the ruling class, or become the rulers theirself.

Native speakers who are not burdened with a dialect cope miraculously with English verbs despite the language's unusually complicated system of tenses, moods, and voices. We can say such things as *If I were to have been being beaten, I would have had to protest* or *Bob, when Carol had had* had had, *had had* had; had had *had*

had the teacher's OK. (A rough translation: When Carol had written "had had," Bob had written "had"; but "had had" was what the teacher approved of.) No one can choose the right tense by looking in the rulebook. *I find I like English, I find I liked English, I found I like English, I found I liked English.* Rules tell us the right form for the right tense, but can't tell us what tense we want. We have to feel tense. When we're writing a sentence and have to think about the tense, there's something fishy. Simplify the thought to avoid an outlandish verb phrase.

We won't review the verb system but I will warn about two popular mistakes. The verb *would have* is threatening to replace *had* in current usage. *If he would have been there, this would not have happened.* (It should be *If he had been there . . .*) *Would* and *could* are sneaking in to replace *will* and *can. By proofreading we could* (should be *can*) *catch our mistakes. If you look closely, you would see* (should be *will see*) *why TV is called the Boob Tube.*

Here are some sentences that test your feeling for the right tense.

> The people had cheered when the Pope (had passed, passed) by.
>
> He (has made, made) so much money he bought a station wagon.
>
> (Finishing, Having finished) his writing, Bob collapsed.
>
> The market has been dropping because the buyers (have been, are) scared.
>
> If I (were, had been) living then, I would have been drafted.
>
> I'm exhausted, (being, having been) awake all night.
>
> We should have asked him to (have sponsored, sponsor) us.
>
> After she gave up Perrier, she (feels, felt, has felt) better.
>
> I (use, used) to like (popped, pop) corn but now I like (bake, baked) beans.

In each of these sentences, the first choice is wrong. You probably discovered that if you think about the tense you get confused and are tempted to pick the more complicated one. But the seat of your pants is right in telling you to choose the simplest, easiest verb. Check the tense by making sure that if one thing happens *before* another, it's put in an earlier tense; if it happens *at the same time*, the tenses agree; and if it happens *after*, it's put in a later tense. All tenses look good, so don't look at them—*say* them.

Shifts

When subjects or verbs are unexpectedly and unnecessarily changed inside the sentence, we have what's called a *shift* in the point of view. Shifts are very common—unnoticed in speech, but noticed in writing. They are borderline faults, since a writer is allowed to change subjects and verbs. It's only when she does it needlessly, jolting the reader, that she's committed a fault. Sentences with shifts *look* OK; to catch the mistake you must hear it.

> Everybody should wash your hands before eating.
> Catfish caught the ball and then throws it home.
> She was a polite girl, or so it had always seemed to me.

In the first sentence *Everybody* shifts to *you*. In the second, past tense *caught* shifts to present tense *throws*. In the third, the subject *she* shifts to *it*.

Shifts to the present tense are common, since thinking is always in the present. In the historical or literary present, past events are viewed as happening now or as always happening. *Hamlet picks up the skull. At the concert Mozart plays beautifully.* This literary present tense is not used so much in English as in other languages—which is fine, since it's confusing. Stay away from it, and use it only for a synopsis. Don't know *synopsis?* Where's your dictionary? Give me twenty push-ups.

The use of the present tense is also complicated by what's called the eternal present. *He believed all men* are *created equal.* In Formal, a truth is expressed in the eternal present and an untruth is put in the past. *He thought marriage* was *a trap. He thought the world* is *round.*

There are needless shifts in the *voice* of the verb. In the active voice: *Catfish caught the ball.* In the passive voice, a word that ordinarily would be a direct object is made the subject, and then receives, passively, the action of the verb. *The clock was wound. I'm being stung by a bumblebee.* Don't shift between the active and passive voices as some dope does here:

> Carol shopped all over, and the widget was finally purchased.
> I hate writing, and am made sick when I have to do it.
> The football was kicked and went seventy yards.

Also, don't shift between the moods of a verb:

> Give me a drink, and then you should read this sentence for me.
>
> Carol is offering the appetizers when she drops them.
>
> He takes a break when he is doing his homework.

Do not change the subject within a sentence unless you have to. You can change it, of course, if you can justify having different subjects in one sentence. Here are sentences which shift their subjects and consequently strip their gears.

> This medicine will help you, and you will feel better instantly.
>
> The hunter entered the clearing, and the leopard was spotted.
>
> I read science fiction; it's exciting to me.
>
> *Hamlet* will be read by each student; then you will write a report on it.
>
> Your hair should be shampooed and the shampoo should be rinsed thoroughly.

For practice you might like to repair these sentences. You say you have enough trouble with your own? I understand.

Dangling Verbals

Some words look like verbs, are made from verbs, have a couple of tenses, take subjects and objects like verbs, but really aren't verbs at all. They are not used as verbs, but as nouns, adjectives, and adverbs. They are *verbals*, and come in three kinds—gerund, participle, and infinitive. The gerund is the verb form that ends in *-ing* and is used as a noun. *Dancing is healthy.* The gerund *dancing* is the subject of the sentence. *I like dancing.* The gerund *dancing* is the object of the verb *like*.

The participle is a verbal used as an adjective. *Dancing too fast, I fell.* The participle *dancing* is an adjective that modifies the noun *I*. *I am happy dancing the tango.* Here the participle *dancing* trails the noun it modifies, *I*. The present participle, like the gerund, ends in *-ing*. A past participle uses—guess what? the past participle of the verb. *Having swum the channel, I am tired.*

Swum is the past participle. If it's not clear what noun the participle modifies, we have the hilarious dangling participle. *Born in 1564, his birthplace was Stratford. Born*, a past participle, cannot modify *birthplace. Being late to work, the boss fired me. Being late* does not modify *boss. Eating our lunch, the cow came toward us.* This is wrong, since the cow already had lunch. *In the bushes sighing softly, she felt the breeze. Lying in the hammock, it struck her that Bob was OK.* Headline writers are notorious for dangling participles: *Law Protecting Sailors Attacked by Admiral.*

The third kind of verbal is the infinitive. The infinitive is the word *to* plus the infinitive or timeless form of the verb. *I want to dance. To dance* is the infinitive used as a noun. *To dance is fun. To dance* is the subject. *That's a long time to dance.* Here the infinitive is used as an adjective modifying *time. To dance you need good shoes.* Here the infinitive is used as an adverb modifying *need*— need *how.* There's a past infinitive for prior action *(to have danced)*, but it's rarely used.

These verbals—gerunds, participles, and infinitives—often join with other words to form verbal phrases, as *walking to work fast, filled to the brim, to dance all night.* You'll recall that to exist, a verb needs a subject (named or understood), and the same is true of verbals. It must always be clear what subject is performing the action. If there's confusion, you have a *dangling* verbal. Here's a dangling gerund: *By walking to work, a half-dollar was saved.* A dangling participle: *Walking to work, a half-dollar was saved.* A dangling infinitive: *To save a half-dollar, work is in easy walking distance.*

You only have dangling verbals when you speak of actions to be performed by a particular agent. If the action is general or impersonal, the verbal doesn't dangle. *Considering the difficulties, the results aren't bad.* In that sentence, *considering* does not dangle, because no one in particular is supposed to do the considering. Similarly, the following are OK: *Speaking frankly, the Yankees can't win. Weight can be lost by eating only hot dogs. To be brief, grammar is duck soup.*

Similar to the verbal phrase is the elliptical clause. In an elliptical clause the subject is left out: *if awakened, once aroused, while on duty, until exhausted.* An elliptical clause dangles when its subject is not the same as the subject of the sentence. *While walking my dog, the fire alarm sounded. When tender, turn down the flame. Beer cannot be bought if under twenty-one.*

Prepositions: Problems of

A verbal phrase is used as a noun, adjective, or adverb, and so is a prepositional phrase. The prepositional phrase is almost always an adverb, telling us where, when, how, why, or how much. *I walked in the rain. In the rain* is a prepositional phrase used as an adverb, modifying *walked*. Walked where?——*in the rain. For coming in late, I got the sack. For coming in late* is a prepositional phrase used as an adverb modifying *got*—why was it you got the sack? *A man with a moustache rehired me. With a moustache* is used as an adjective modifying *man*—what kind of man? *In the lounge is not a safe place to hide. In the lounge* is used as a noun, the subject of the verb *is*.

You'll be pleased to know that the only mistake you'd make with the prepositional phrase is to misplace it. Since most of the phrases are adverbs, and since adverbs can easily be misplaced, you will, from time to time, misplace a phrase, as was done in the unsettling song lyric, *Throw mama from the train a kiss.* Here are other misplacements: *With his strength, the coach made Csonka the fullback. The teacher told us on Monday to do it. She served him in pajamas on paper plates. She kissed him in the narthex. She stuck her tongue out at him through the window. These cats have short tails with blue eyes.*

Phrases starting with *with* are often misplaced because it's hard to figure out what they modify. *I like swimming and tennis, with tennis my favorite.* What does the phrase *with tennis* modify? *With* can be a fuzzy word, expressing a fuzzy connection of ideas. *He goes swimming with a swimsuit. Think about Bob along with Carol.* In Formal watch out for loose *with* phrases, and never write a long *with* phrase.

Since a preposition indicates direction and implies movement, the noun in the prepositional phrase is thought of as an *object*. Don't say *For we to do that would be wrong*, say *For us. With Bob and I cooking* should be *With Bob and me cooking.* You want to recognize prepositional phrases right away in order to use *objective* pronouns with them.

That you shouldn't end a sentence with a preposition is one of those rules no one understands but everyone has heard about. There, I just ended a sentence with a preposition—*about.* Or did I? Actually, *about* is part of the verb, *heard about*, and not a preposition at all. People confuse prepositions with verbal particles. *What are you looking for?* In this case, *for* is not a preposition but part of the verb *are looking for. This is the kind of nonsense I won't put up with. Up* and *with* are part of the verb *put up with.*

So what's the fuss about ending sentences with prepositions? What's objectionable is the construction in which words that should be together are torn apart. In *What did you give me that book to be read to out of for?* the real objection is to the separation of *for* and *what.* Other examples: *This is the man whom I spoke to you on Tuesday about. I admired the ease which he wrote with.* These ugly sentences are easily repaired. *This is the man about whom I spoke to you on Tuesday. I admired the ease with which he wrote.* You get the idea. Instead of saying *whom blank blank about, which blank blank with,* say *about whom* or *with which.* Also, you run into no problems with witchy *which* or treacherous *whom* if you change the sentences to get rid of them altogether: *The man about whom I spoke* becomes *the man I spoke about, the ease with which* becomes *his ease in.* There are quite a few ways to skin a cat, and you keep trying until you find one you like or until you give up.

When you're ending a sentence with what looks like a preposition, think whether this forlorn word is needed. *I want the donut with the hole in* becomes *I want the donut with the hole. Which tree was it the cat climbed up?* becomes *Which tree did the cat climb? What did he want to say that to us for?* becomes *Why did he want to say that to us?* Or check whether the word does not actually belong where it is. *What are we supposed to talk about? About* belongs with *talk.* You wouldn't say *About what are we supposed to talk? Which steps did he walk up?* You wouldn't say *Up which steps did he walk?* Usage, whether Formal or Informal, should always sound like English. You don't want people to laugh at you just because you're obeying orders.

The Case of Six Pronouns

One of the blessings of English is that nouns are not inflected as they are in other languages; that is, the form of the noun is not always being changed according to the way it's used in the sentence. English plurals are formed regularly by adding *s,* with a few exceptions *(ox, oxen; leaf, leaves; sheep, sheep.)* Possessives are formed regularly by adding *s*—Carol's, Bob's. (We discussed the case for and against the use of the apostrophe in the last chapter.)

All these *s's* in plurals and possessives add to the geeselike hissing noises English makes.

With pronouns, which unfortunately play a major role in The Game of English, we run into a few problems of inflection. Nouns in a sentence are subjects, possessives, or objects; the three uses of the noun are called *cases:* subjective, possessive, and objective. The possessive case is no problem. And with the hundreds of thousands of nouns in English, there are no problems with the subjective and objective cases, since they take the same form. We're so unaccustomed to thinking about case we resent it in foreign languages and fall into frequent errors in using the few pronouns we have that show it.

Only six words in the whole language show the objective case. These six are *me, him, her, us, them,* and *whom (whom* includes *whomever,* which is nearly kaput). If you can use these six words without making a mistake, skip this chapter. Still with me? I thought so. Everyone is puzzled by *whom.* Wishful thinkers have been telling us for ages that *whom* is dying, but this is not the case. The faster it dies in Informal, the livelier it gets in Formal.

We'll get to *who* versus *whom* in a minute, but let's do the easy pronouns first. When a pronoun is an object—*direct, indirect,* or *prepositional*—for goodness sake, use the objective case. When it's a subject, use the subjective case. Even if you can't tell objects, you can tell subjects, because they have verbs.

Rule number one is to pay no attention to the position of the pronoun in the sentence. Just because it comes near the start of the sentence does not mean it's a subject, and just because it comes after the verb does not mean it's an object. Most Americans now say *Between you and* I and *With we girls* and *Among we students.* These errors arise partly from illiteracy, but mainly because the position of words in our sentences is so important for meaning.

Here are examples of the correct choice of the objective case: *Along with us taxpayers, he voted for the budget. Besides you and her, who is going? The teacher wanted Bob and us to learn.* If you're puzzled by these objective pronouns, figure out why they're objects, of what verb or preposition. In *Let's you and* me *learn this grammar, me* is objectively correct; *you and me* is another way of saying *us,* the object of the verb *let.*

Here are examples of the correct choice of the *subjective* case. *It is* I. *It is* he. *This is* she. In these sentences *I, he,* and *she* are another way of saying the subjects *it* and *this,* and that's why they're in the subjective case, too. Informally, everyone says *it's* me, *that's* him, *it* was *her, there were* us *and four others.* Formally, you should say *It is I, it was* she, *there were* we *and four others.* Answering the phone at home, you'd probably say *That's* me, but at the office you'd say *This is* she. Since this kind of switching about is so common, when people find themselves in Formal situations they try to change every objective pronoun they find to subjective, and are guilty of what is known as overcorrectness: *The boss wants* we *secretaries to call* him *Buddy. The editor would like* she *and* I *to revise the article.* English teachers have fits about overcorrectness, thinking it to be social climbing, but it's quite unconscious. Since compound subjects are more common than compound objects, people assume a pronoun that follows *and* has to be subjective. They say *He told Bob and* I, though they would never say *He told* I.

The following examples are also incorrect. Figure out why. *If it had been* her, *I would have smiled. We'll do it, you and* me. *Going there does not appeal to you or* I. *Toys are* us. *A number of* we *grammarians find this fun. It was hard for* them— she *and Bob.*

Whether you use the possessive or the objective case before a gerund (*she watched* his *dancing, she watched* him *dancing*) depends on what you're emphasizing—the action or the doer. *Bob approved of* them *going instead of him. Bob approved of their going instead of staying. He was sad to see* them *leaving. He was sad to see their leaving so soon.* You decide which meaning you want. In Informal, the possessive is never used with the gerund, even when there's ambiguity: *Your husband is against* me *smoking.*

Conjunctions are often interpreted as prepositions, which confuses the choice of the pronoun. *I'm taller than* (she, her). *He will do it, or* (they, them). *Everyone liked it but* (I, me). *She drives as fast as* (I, me). If you choose the subjective pronouns, that means you feel the presence of a silent verb or else you love subjective pronouns. The objective pronouns sound more modern and Informal. In the past, *than, as,* and *or* could not be interpreted as prepositions, and you had to use subjective pronouns with them. Some old clubhouse pros may try to bring this rule back into the Game, so watch out.

For Whom Are You Looking?

The choice between *who* and *whom* is confusing for several reasons. One reason was already mentioned: people have been told so often to use the subjective pronoun (*It is* I, *This is* she), that they lean toward *who*. Another reason is that whenever this pronoun is heavily stressed in speaking, the choice is *who*, and never *whom*. You want *who* to come? You gave it to *who?* In writing, this heavy stress can't be heard (unless the writer is brave enough to under-line), and *who* reverts to the calmer *whom*.

The main reason why *who* replaces *whom* is that it's interpreted as the subject of a silent clause, *who it is*. Instead of saying the cor-rect *Guess whom*, people say *Guess who*, meaning *Guess who (it is)*. Instead of saying *Whom do you want?* they say *Who do you want?* meaning *Who (is it) you want?* Instead of saying *Whom are you talking about?* they say *Who are you talking about?* meaning *Who (is it) you are talking about?* Instead of saying *I know whom we think we want*, they say *I know who we think we want*, meaning *I know who (it is) we think we want*.

You may want to scream at this point and say, "Why are you telling me how these mistakes arise? Just tell me what to do!" I'm telling you. Use *who* whenever you hear the silent verb after it. If you do this you're not making a mistake. You can't hear the silent verb where you really have to use *whom*. You say *With whom?* because you wouldn't say *With who (is it)?* You say *He loved whom?* be-cause you wouldn't say *He loved who (is it)?* You say *I am looking for whom, it was given to whom, it was liked by whom*, because you do not think of these whoms as beginning clauses. That's the solu-tion to *who* versus *whom*. It's the solution you've used uncon-sciously for a long time. The ear is now the test for correct *whoms*.

Educated people overuse *whom* just as uneducated people overuse *who*. They choose *whom* in error when it is followed by expressions like *I think, they know, we saw*. Errors: *He's one* whom *they say won't let you down. It was Bob* whom *she said started the fight. We'll ask* whomever *we find knows the way*. The case of the pro-noun depends on how it's used *in its own clause*.

Finally, try not to separate *whom* from its preposition. Say *from whom, of whom, about whom*, and don't say *Whom did you get it from? Whom are you asking the favor of? Whom are you talking about?* These sentences are awkward bcause they start with *whom* in the subject position and because the phrases are split. In-formally you say *Who are you sitting with?* Formally you say *With whom are you sitting? Whom are you sitting with?* is a poor third.

Fatherless Pronouns

Pronouns save us much time and effort. When we're doing a piece on Transylvanian vampire researchers we say *they* and *them* and save lots of time. Pronouns are so lovable they are used even when they shouldn't be, when it's unclear what they refer to. Faults in pronoun reference are common as Kleenex; editors need to check every pronoun. If the antecedent (the noun the pronoun stands for) is too far from the pronoun, if there's confusion about which noun the antecedent is, or if the pronoun doesn't match the noun—for example, a singular pronoun for a plural antecedent—the poor little pronoun is off on its own, and its parent must be found.

Faults in reference are common because the writer has a clear idea of the antecedent, but the reader doesn't, and can't get it from the pronoun. In speaking, faults in reference seldom occur, because we usually don't frame long sentences requiring lots of pronouns, and we can make antecedents clear by emphasis in our voice. We can say things like He told *him* what he owed to *his* mom, but in writing, the pronouns have to be sorted out.

Here are examples of lost pronouns.

> Each team member should decide whether they want to play.
> We should feed those who need it.
> There's a fly in your soup; do you want it?
> A hermit is happy, but it's hard to make a living at it.
> To Bob's way of thinking, he knows everything.
> To his way of thinking, Bob knows everything.

Faults in personal pronouns are not as annoying as faults in the use of *this, it, that, which,* and *such.* These are often used in a broad, vague way to refer to more than one antecedent. They can refer to a whole list of things, but not to two different things. The reader must never be forced to go back:

> He used to take the bus, but now it doesn't appeal to him.
> She told him she loved him, and gave him a flower, and this made him happy.
> I didn't wash my hair last week, which I never do.

This one may be OK:

> In the third quarter they fumbled twice, and in the last quarter they missed three field goals, and that's why they lost.

Faults in reference are akin to shifts: the writer forgets what she's said (prompting us to do the same). *If everyone doesn't pay their taxes, they'll get you. Everyone* and *no one*, by the way, are followed in Formal by singular pronouns *(he, his, him)* and in Informal by plural. Formal: *Everyone loves* his *mother.* Informal: *No one loves* their *mother all the time.* And while we're still on pronouns, remember in Formal to avoid saying *you* when you mean *one. One should never pour with his left hand.*

Conjunctions and Parallels

Coordinating conjunctions are the simple little words *and, but, or, nor, so, for,* and *yet* that join words, phrases, and clauses. What is on one side of a coordinating conjunction must balance what is on the other by having the same grammatical structure. When the sides are not balanced, the fault is called a *lack of parallelism.* Some nonparallel structures are easy to spot. *Betty loves swimming and to play tennis.* Some are hard to spot, because the sentence is complicated or there's a long list in it. Did you just spot mine? I should have said: *because the sentence is complicated or because there's a long list in it.*

The two things being coordinated by the conjunction don't have to be *like* each other; they only require the same structure. You can say: *Lying on the table are the oranges, bananas, and penguins.* You can't say *Lying on the table are the oranges, bananas and I can't tell what those funny birds are.* You can say *He is dark, handsome, and over thirty. Over thirty* is a phrase, not a single word, but it's an adjective like *dark* and *handsome.* In Formal you would change *He is dark, handsome, and snores* to *He is dark and handsome, and he snores.*

Informally, no one ever worries about parallelism. Informally anything can be joined to anything with the magic glue *and. She said that she wouldn't go, and if I wanted to and she knew I was going that would be OK.* In Formal that would be *She said that she wouldn't go and that if I wanted to go and if she knew that I was going that would be all right.* In Formal, words have to be added to show the parallelism. This helps in a courteous way to make everything perfectly clear, even at the risk of wordiness: *The artist lives in agony and ecstasy.* That becomes *The artist lives in agony and in ecstasy.*

To give you practice in drawing parallels here's a little drill.

> Life is a welcome burden and like a huge crumb of cake being carried by an ant.
> Life is a welcome burden like a huge crumb of cake . . . or
> Life is a welcome burden and is like a huge crumb . . . .
>
> She said she would not go but to pick her up anyway.
> She said she would not go but we should pick her up anyway.
>
> Tell the driver to drive fast and when you have to be there.
> Tell the driver to drive fast and tell him when you have to be there.
>
> I boiled the potatoes and macaroni for salad.
> I boiled the potatoes for potato salad and the macaroni for macaroni salad.

Do these yourself:

> Americans believe two things: that there is no free lunch but you can get 40,000 miles on a set of tires.
> By walking I save money as well as getting exercise.
> She is a woman of great beauty, and who has great wealth.
> I want to laugh and to sing and make love.

Some of these revisions may have struck you as fussy, but Formal is fussy. People love to fuss. If they didn't, we wouldn't always be saying, "Don't go to any fuss."

Comparing Adjectives

No big problems arise with adjectives, which is one reason people love them. Adjectives are the fourth most common part of speech, after nouns, pronouns, and verbs. Unlike nouns, pronouns, and verbs, adjectives are not inflected, except for a handful that change their forms in comparisons: *hot, hotter, hottest; good, better, best; bad, worse, worst.* The comparative form is usually a simple matter of inserting the word *more,* as in *more beautiful,* and the superlative form is a simple matter of inserting *most,* as in *most beautiful.*

Occasionally you'll wonder whether to try an *-er* or *-est* ending or fall back on the regular use of *more* and *most.* Should you say *redder, leafiest, blunter, slenderest, ruggedest?* In Formal, if you don't feel confident with an *-er* or *-est,* play safe with *more* or *most.* It's hard to err with these, but easy to make your audience think you're being cheeky if you say *cloudier, joyfullest, uncleaner, backwardest, hopefuller, stupidest.* With long or uncommon adjectives and with participles, don't use *-er* and *-est* (*tireder, laughingest*).

Another little problem arises with adjectives, and people get excited about this one since it has to do with logic. Certain adjectives are not supposed to be compared because they already have an absolute meaning: *infinite, complete, virginal, supreme, vital.* You've often heard about these absolutes, that you mustn't say *more exhausted, emptier, more full, almost pregnant.* But people say illogical things all the time, in order to speak forcefully. Jesus, for example, said: "He who has nothing will have taken away from him even the little he has."

Since Formal tries to be logical, show that you are trying, too, and do not say *very unique, increasingly comprehensive, less fatal.* On the other hand, don't be upset that these Informal exaggerations are constantly used. People just don't have the time to choose words with the most perfect precision. (Did you catch *most* perfect?) Adjectives ending in *-able* and *-less* should not be compared: *harmless, powerless, destructible, inflatable, unable.* In Formal, you can't use the Mad Ave comparative—better tasting, longer, smoother, milder—because no one knows what's being compared.

Of course, the main problem with adjectives is not misusing them grammatically, but overusing them stylistically. Adjectives are only words about words. But verbs, ah, verbs live.

Where to Put Adverbs

Since an adjective only modifies a noun, there's no trouble in putting it alongside its noun, but since an adverb modifies different kinds of words, and phrases, and whole sentences, it's often misplaced. It splits infinitives when it shouldn't and misses its cue in verbs. *He had been* always *helping* instead of *He had* always *been helping*.

One reason why adverbs are misplaced is that many of them are useless, and therefore no one knows or cares where they belong. Called on to intensify expression, they often make it weaker and vaguer. *I am* very *happy to meet you. I was* really *hurt not to be invited. He is* highly *praised for his omelets.* When you say you don't know *too much* about cars, how much is too much? As the adjective can be the enemy of the noun by distracting attention from it, so the adverb can be the enemy of what it modifies. Some adverbs are *infinitely* annoying and *literally* drive me up the wall.

The position of adverbs is no problem in speech, for they can be stressed or left unstressed wherever they are, but in writing care must be taken in placing them. Some adverbs seem to look in two directions: *He will hopefully plant tomatoes. He watched her carefully light the cigar.* Certain adverbs modify two or three things at once or have a general effect on the whole sentence. In Informal, *just, only, even, ever,* and *never* move around rather freely in a sentence. But in Formal, they should be placed as precisely as possible. *I only shop at Woolworth's* should be *I shop only at Woolworth's. I just want a cigarette, I want just a cigarette. I never will learn, I will never learn. He not only made a living but a fortune, He made not only a living but a fortune.*

A special kind of adverb comes near the start of the sentence and modifies everything that follows: *luckily, happily, apparently, significantly.* Since this kind of adverb neatly tells the reader how he should respond to the sentence, it's overused by writers who lack confidence that their sentences speak for themselves. *Logically,* these adverbs dangle, since what they modify is unclear. *Interestingly, x plus 2y equal 3z over x square.* What's going on *interestingly? Hopefully, we can find the square root, though no one has ever seen a square root.* Who is hoping or who is hopeful? *Most importantly, she adores me.* Most important of what?

Adverbs can be emphasized by taking them away from their normal place in the sentence (*Loudly she snapped her gum*) or by letting them split closely related words. *I want* never *to see you again.* Here *never* splits the verb and its object. *Bob, during lunch, saw Carol.* Here the adverb phrase *during lunch* splits subject and verb. *This is a wild, skinny,* very *hungry cat. Very* splits the series of adjectives. *He had been* quietly *eating hot dogs.* Normally the order would be: *He had* quietly *been eating hot dogs.* An adverb will normally precede its verb or the *important part* of a compound verb: *He usually doesn't sing so much* is better than *He doesn't usually sing so much.*

If it's kosher to split phrases with adverbs for emphasis, why not split infinitives too? You *should,* when you want to emphasize the adverb. When you don't want to emphasize it, you shouldn't. Here are some infinitives that probably shouldn't have been split.

> The weather is to always be taken into account.
> She likes to quickly walk to work.
> My cat seems to never be hungry.
> You should try to, if you want to quickly get ahead, learn to not split infinitives.
> I hope I don't have to, because I split infinitives, lose my job with the bank.

The infinitive should be split when the adverb is important.

> I want you to entirely forget what I said.
> He used to constantly chew tobacco.
> You have to deeply water your mango.
> It is rather for us the living to be here dedicated.

If there weren't a rule against splitting infinitives, if they weren't awkward, you couldn't emphasize the adverb by splitting the infinitive. Let's hear it for the rule. Just as there's a reason for every mistake, there's a reason for every rule. Rules aren't so bad, if breaking them and observing them allow us to express ourselves.

Lying behind the objection to split infinitives is a well-founded dislike of adverbs. Adverbs, get lost! *To finally resolve* should be *to resolve. To quickly go* should be *to speed, to run, to hasten. To flatly forbid, to completely drain, to thoroughly baffle.* Every adverb you don't use means one less you have to worry about placing.

Adjectives versus Adverbs

Another problem with the adverb, one that brings anguish to the nervous and amusement to the confident, is the choice between adjective and adverb *forms.* Before getting deep into the question, let's have a snap quiz. Pick the correct form.

feel bad,	badly
land soft,	softly
made wrong,	wrongly
weigh heavy,	heavily
fit loose,	loosely
sing different,	differently
go gentle,	gently

Which did you prefer—the -*ly* forms or the ones that seem to be adjectives? I recommend you use the first versions and avoid the timid -*ly* forms. Here highbrow usage is the same as lowbrow; only middlebrows say things like *The dress looks well on you, Slice it thickly, The engine ran smoothly.* Middlebrows avoid what seems vulgar, and vulgar usage ignores adverbs: *I paid him good, She talked excited, He hit it perfect, That was real nice.* But the vulgar avoidance of adverbs doesn't mean they're good for the educated.

In the quiz, the first versions—*bad, soft,* and the like—should be interpreted as adjective-adverb mixtures. In *she made it wrong,* for example, *wrong* can be thought of as modifying the noun *it* or the verb *made.* These double-purpose words come in mighty handy (not mightily handily).

Remember, too, that adjectives, not adverbs, follow the special linking verbs mentioned earlier—*feel, sound, look, turn, become.* Thus, *feel bad, look bad.* Some borderline linking verbs are *dress, treat, behave, act. Dress cool. You treat me unfair. You behave mean to me now but you used to act sweet.* In Formal, play it safe and keep away from the border.

The notion that adverbs are elegant has led to some incredible coinages: *doubtlessly, thusly, overly, muchly, importantly, lastly, firstly, diametrically, icily, uglily.* Climb all over anyone who uses these words.

Not many adverbs appear in speech, but writing is heavy with them. In speech we say *I'm TIRED* and get the message across, but when we write *I'm very tired* no one knows how tired we are. We can therefore omit nine out of ten *very*s, *too*s, *greatly*s, *really*s, *actually*s, *extremely*s, *quite*s, *rather*s, *slightly*s, *fairly*s, and *somewhat*s. If you're using lots of these, your writing needs more than these vitamin pills, it needs life itself, the sound of your real voice. Good adverbs are those that modify verbs *(Old folks walk about, not to and from).* Bad ones modify adjectives, or everything, or nothing.

Adverbs are essentially vague, like *essentially:* said *happily, immensely* rich, *endlessly* entertaining, *sometimes, later.* They'll trip you up when you write *rather appalled, very necessary, actually dead, badly suffocated, almost overwhelmed.* They'll sap your strength and you'll go around muttering *more or less, by and large, in general, on the whole, to a certain extent, to all intents and purposes,* until you're off to the hospital.

Pep Talk on Grammar

Grammar is a wide subject overlapping usage on one side and style on the other. Style is taken care of in our final chapter. I've put off till then some questions that could be treated as questions of grammar, such as the use of the subjunctive *(If I were),* absolutes *(The game over),* the reference of the pronoun *we,* and choices between *which* and *that, of which* and *whose,* etc. Faults in logic are sometimes considered grammar faults, but resist classification and are hard to talk about. They include *non sequiturs,* that is, ideas that do not follow *(It was raining and I lost my virginity),* and impossibilities or contradictions: *Look at the rat between the three garbage cans, Take your hands out of your pocket, There's lots of square space here, Crime on the subways is improving, Climb down, I'm the best of anybody, Empty the water.*

Problems in grammar are like problems in diction: you have to choose between *perhaps* and *maybe* in diction, and choose between *It was they* and *It was them* in grammar. Some people deny that such freedom exists where grammar is concerned, but it does. Some would argue that *perhaps* and *It was they* were fussy; some would argue that *maybe* and *It was them* were too Informal. Having prejudices in these choices can hurt your chances of persuading your audience.

It's a pity that people get so caught up in questions of grammar and usage when they should be concerned about what is being said. A grammar or usage mistake is not so bad as a poor sentence, and a poor sentence is not so bad as a foolish or false one. Why search for grammar faults in a pile of manure? Because what's manure to us may be someone's fertilizer. To attack someone's language is to attack him. We may have to do it indirectly, by referring to his misunderstanding of certain words, his lack of parallelism, his dangling verbals.

When others go after your grammar, it may not be the grammar they're after, it may be what you said or it may be you. That's why your grammar must be invulnerable. And you can always distract attention from it by having something to say. With something to say that you have faith in you'll say it confidently, and you'll say it passably. Faults of expression arise from having nothing to say. In the following chapters, we'll concentrate on finding things to say.

Before moving on to Good Sentences, let's look at some puzzles to test your mastery of grammar. Which is correct? *There are no nails and hammer, There is no hammer and nails, There is no hammer and nails, There is no hammer or nails, There are no nails and no hammer, There is no hammer and there are no nails.* I'll give you the answer in a minute. Here's a tougher one. *She lay sobbing. I sat smoking. Drop dead.* In each sentence, what part of speech is *sobbing, smoking,* and *dead*—verb, adverb, or adjective? The answer is that no one knows. You see why some professors get fed up with the traditional parts of speech and invent new systems for analyzing sentences. But this does no harm and keeps them off the streets.

Here's your last puzzle. Which is correct? *Bob and Carol blew their nose, their noses, his nose, his and her nose, his and her noses, his nose and her nose, his nose or her nose, his nose and hers, his/her nose, his and/or her nose, his and/or her nose or noses, his and her nose respectively.* There are dozens of ways of expressing this idea. Maybe there is no Right Way. Sometimes you find yourself in a no-win situation. When this happens, don't panic—try to enjoy the predicament. If you can't figure out what to do, whatever you decide won't make much difference. If you're anxious—let's say you're taking the bar exam—and won't commit yourself to anything less than perfect, cast the sentence a new way. The obvious solution to Bob and Carol's nose problems (or Bob's and Carol's noses' problem) is to recast the sentence: *Bob blew his nose and Carol blew her nose.* But no one would have been puzzled if you had used the original version—*Bob and Carol blew their nose.*

Many grammar puzzles are illusions. They're like those knots you pull and the knot disappears. If one-fourth of the people say *For whom are you looking?* and three-fourths say *Who are you looking for?* whichever you say, you'll be in good company. When usage is divided and there's no compelling argument in favor of one usage (what is traditional is not compelling), then choose what you like and stick by it. Do *you* like *There are no nails and hammer?*

Chapter Five

Good Sentences and Paragraphs

The Heart of the Sentence

You'll be pleased to know I'm not going to try to define a sentence beyond what was needed to explain punctuation and grammar. The reason is that a sentence can't be exactly defined. Every handbook has a slightly different version, and none of the definitions covers all cases. Anything spoken can be a sentence, depending on what's said before or after, and depending on whether the listener hears some kind of complete or satisfactory message. A single word like *banana* can be a sentence, if what's being said about the banana is understood, such as *I want the banana* or *Here is a banana*. But because Formal is based more on written than on spoken language, it's important for you to be able to recognize a sentence when you write one and correct it if it's not a sentence by Formal rules—whenever you're writing Formal. Otherwise, just figure a sentence is a word or group of words that somehow makes sense, and leave it at that.

Handbooks spend time trying to define the sentence because they have to warn people not to make the mistake known as a sentence *fragment*. It's easier to say what a fragment is than what a sentence is. A sentence makes sense, but just how it does that is a mystery. A fragment is not mysterious—it's the mistaken use of a period where no one wants a period sound. Which are the fragments here? *She's his neighbor. Who sings too loud. Grandma snores. Because she's stopped up.* If you know what a period is, you won't be guilty of this fault.

A different construction, the sentence lacking a subject or predicate, is incorrectly referred to as a sentence fragment. Such sentences are common in speech. They're not common in writing, since writing, which lacks the resources of the voice, has to spell out the meaning slowly and carefully. Here are examples of sentences lacking subjects or predicates: *Never in a million years. Which is true. A ballplayer who can do everything. Gone fishing. Two million dollars. A hundred years later.* These expressions make sense, and should be distinguished from real fragments caused by misused periods. Can these expressions, called clipped sentences, be used in Formal? Not in *very* Formal. Clipped sentences appear more frequently in writing today, giving it a fast pace and intimate tone. They're quite effective, but like any device, if overused they'll seem phony.

Sentences used to be called *periods.* The word *period,* meaning a *cycle,* reminds us of what the sentence should be. A sentence moves, and stops. A subject is announced, the listener assumes that something will be said about it, something is said, the predicate is completed, the voice falls. A sentence has one job to do: one big subject and one big thing to say about it. The subject can be a compound and the verb can be a compound and the sentence can have a number of main clauses, but no matter how much is said, all must add up: the sentence must have unity. In Formal, you can't say *George Washington was our first President and had a set of false teeth made of ivory.* The words express two ideas; they require two sentences. A sentence is not a bag into which words and ideas are thrown, not a clothesline on which items are hung. It's an act. During its moment of life, it can only do so much, and the more it tries to do the less it gets done. A very good sentence is like a slap in the face. The reason that writing transitions between sentences is so hard is that each sentence is a completion and each new sentence is a new start.

A sentence is a proposition that others will accept or refuse. To offer a sentence is to stick your neck out. You're saying, "Here's my subject and here's what I'm telling you about it." The sentence arches up over the magical moment when you link the predicate to the subject. There's often a heavy pause before the verb, because this is the moment everyone waits for. Sentences are created. Creation itself began when a subject met a verb: *Let* there *be* light. If a speaker lets her audience down, by offering them a dud predicate, she has no feeling for a sentence. Here are some fizzlers. *The hydrogen bomb is very dangerous. The Pope is in favor of the Church. Othello got mad at his wife. Two billion dollars was made by Octopus.* The subjects are *the hydrogen bomb, the Pope, Othello,* and *two billion dollars,* yet the sentences are awful. What's said about the subject is what's important, not the subject. This applies to the most common subject of them all, the perpendicular pronoun *I.*

Interest in a sentence does not depend on the verb either, though verbs are more important than subjects. Vigorous verbs are always welcome, but a sentence is more than its verb, or even the sum of its parts. A sentence depends on how the subject is treated in the predicate. In poor sentences the link between subject and predicate is lost. The subject becomes the focus, and may be buried under a heap of modifiers, or the predicate becomes the focus, and may be sapped of its strength by modifiers and afterthoughts. If a sentence has a job to do, it should be stripped for action. Words devoted only to the subject or predicate, rather than to the treatment of the subject by the predicate, drag the sentence down. Any word not helping predication should be cut; any detail not serving the point of the sentence should be cut.

Here is a sentence from *The New York Times* in which predication has been buried:

> If that time is used aggressively to overhaul drastically the grossly mismanaged Hospitals Corporation, it may be possible to save some jobs that otherwise would be lost.

That should be:

> If the mismanaged Hospitals Corporation is overhauled quickly, some jobs might be saved.

Whoever wrote that original sentence for the *Times* did not know how to write, or was being paid by the word.

Here is a sentence from a letter to the *Times* explaining why city buses arrive in groups:

> Having become . . . heavily loaded, they must stop more frequently to let off passengers, so there is both a first and second derivative positive feedback to the progressive clustering of independent vehicles.

That should be:

> Buses bunch up because the ones in front lose time in picking up
> more passengers and in letting them off.

Instead of thinking about building a good sentence, the writer of
the bad sentence was thinking about the jargon he was dying to
use. But a thousand socko words do not have the punch of a good
sentence.

Here's another example of writing done with words rather than
sentences. It's a brief review of the movie *Grease* from *The New
Yorker.*

> The grease is the Elvis Presley sort of hair grease, the society is
> proudly sexist and ritualistic, the film's commercial calculation is
> obviously shrewd. The movie runs on pure ozone, good times, and
> an easy homesickness for a past decade that the people who lived
> through it will not find particularly missable.

A fault in American prose as compared to English is that Americans are colorists rather than draftsmen. They get excited about
the words and forget the structure. This fault has been aggravated
by advertising, which uses words, phrases, and suggestions rather than sentences to get its effects. But the best ads have been sentences: *Pepsi Cola hits the spot, Wouldn't you really rather have a
Buick, Duz does everything, Winston tastes good.*

What Should Be Put in a Sentence

I've warned against overloading a sentence, but obviously we can
squeeze extra details in without wrecking predication. Details do
not always have to be relevant, but they should not be distracting.
In deciding what details to use, the writer takes tone into account.
In serious writing, with powerful predication, you want stripped
sentences. In unserious writing, you can toss in extra details. If
you were writing about a ballgame, could you write like this?

> Curly-headed Bob Firecracker from Chillicothe, Missouri, knocked
> the white horsehide pellet into the newly-painted bleachers in the
> bottom of the ninth to put the rampaging Cardinals over the .500
> mark, even though he broke his bat when he did it.

You could write that, but you would write better if you left out the distracting details. They should go somewhere else, even if the only place for them to go is the wastecan. This is better:

> In the bottom of the ninth, Bob Firecracker put the winning Cardinals over the .500 mark when he knocked the ball into the bleachers—with a broken bat!

The following sentences lack unity, though they offer fascinating information:

> My boyfriend lives two floors above me and he's a Sagittarian.

> After eating a big dinner of tacos, tamales, and refried beans, Bob asked Carol to marry him.

> Last Tuesday it was raining and I caught a cold and I was late to work.

> The explosion flattened the fireworks plant, which was built in 1960 by the Sperber Construction Company, a firm which has been in business here in Fernwood since 1880.

These sentences were silly, their lack of unity was so obvious. But it's surprising how many sentences, if examined for unity, are found lacking. Many sentences have no main idea, or have several ideas. Sentences lacking point flourish under pressure of deadlines. Copy expands to fill the available space.

The impulse to tell everything, a welcome, generous impulse when we're with friends who dote on our every word, or seem to, leads us to use extra modifiers—*There was this big huge truck*—and to bring in irrelevant details even when they interrupt. *Then I went to the butcher's—Jim, you know Jim, he's the redheaded one—I've always like redheads—well, this roast we needed—he asked how big it should be, and I said for ten, but I didn't really know if three of the people would be able to make it—Bob and Carol and Mary.* This flood of thoughts must be dammed in Formal writing. There we show we are energetic and friendly by saying as little as possible. Speech pours out; writing comes drop by drop. Speech should be slowed down and writing speeded up, so that they're more like each other and less like parodies of themselves.

We sometimes feel it's economical to make a number of points in one sentence and stuff the sentence good and tight. This doesn't work. The more points a sentence tries to make, the less significant they become. Sometimes when the writer makes a number of points in one sentence, she has a notion of how they're related, but her mind and the reader's work differently. The relationship of the ideas may have to be spelled out for him. If the writer has a reason for saying in one sentence that George Washington was our first President and had false teeth made of ivory, she better tell her reason right away. It's not enough to clear up confusion in the next sentence or two. The next sentence is too late, the damage has been done, the reader has raised an eyebrow.

Young writers come up with *amputated* sentences. *Hamlet had certain problems. She's a Terpsichorean. The devil is an angel. Bob looked for his glasses. Carol never ate hot dogs.* When a sentence raises a question, the writer should at least begin to answer the question in the same sentence. Sometimes a sentence omits the explanation of how the ideas are related. *Bob is a Leo and Carol is a Scorpio, but they get along well.* Revised: *Even though Bob's a strong-willed Leo and Carol's a strong-willed Scorpio, they get along well.* Another: *I grew up in St. Louis and I can't stand hot weather.* Revised: *I grew up in St. Louis, which is so hot, I can no longer stand hot weather.* Another: *He talked to the committee and they adjourned.* Revised: *He persuaded the committee to adjourn.* The connection between ideas or events should be explained—it only takes a word or two—if the connection is not obvious to *everyone.* Frequently, intelligent people do not write well because their minds are quick and skip over the connections between ideas that need to be laid out for the average reader. The good writer thinks like her readers. This gift of sympathy and imagination is more valuable to her than intelligence.

Awareness of other minds, sensing the likes and dislikes, the limits and talents of a reader over one's shoulder, is not something that can be taught to a writer. Sometimes it can be acquired through deep reading and the unconscious incorporation of good models. But any writer can learn how readers react by submitting her work to teachers and friends for criticism. Don't write in a vacuum. It's often said that a real writer writes only for herself. Don't believe it. The best way to remind yourself of *the others out there* is to read your stuff aloud as if someone was telling it to you.

Kinds of Sentences

If a sentence has one main clause, that is, one subject with its verb, it's a *simple* sentence. *Carol sneezed.* If a sentence has two or more main clauses, it's a *compound* sentence. *Carol sneezed and Bob said Bless you.* If a sentence has a main clause and a subordinate clause it's a *complex* sentence. *Bob said Bless you when Carol sneezed. Carol sneezed because she was allergic.*

Which kind of sentence is best depends on what you're saying. For stories, simple sentences are best, giving a fast tempo. For creating an aura of importance, compound sentences are best, the ideas frequently linked with no explanation as to why they're linked. Compound sentences are poetic and suggestive: the Bible is loaded with them. Complex sentences are best for discussion. In them ideas are related to each other and the relationship is named—*because* so and so, *when, which, after, although, unless.*

See how the effect of the sentence is changed by the kind of sentence it is.

Simple:	I went to her place. I found him.
Compound:	I went to her place, and I found him.
Complex:	I went to her place, where I found him.
	Many are called. Few are chosen.
	Many are called but few are chosen.
	Although many are called, few are chosen.
	She walked home. Her feet hurt.
	She walked home, and her feet hurt.
	Since she walked home, her feet hurt.

In simple sentences each idea is separate and important. In a compound sentence the ideas combine to form one idea that's more important than the separate ideas. In a complex sentence one idea is stressed at the expense of the other idea, which is subordinated.

Beginning writers use simple sentences because they feel that every idea they have is important. Too many simple sentences is kindergarten style, where nothing is sorted out and everything is equally emphatic. Compound sentences may be overused when the writer is trying to keep a narrative going or is aiming at a cumulative effect. *I got on my bike and I rode down the street and I reached the corner and I saw the fallen tree in the road.* Too many *complex* sentences gives an impression of timidity; the ideas all seem to require help.

Thus, the three kinds of sentences have advantages and disadvantages. Notice what kind you're writing because the use of one kind for too long gets tiresome, and its effectiveness is lost. In revising, you shouldn't just patch mistakes and change words, but change a number of sentences to a different kind. Choppy simple sentences suggest a simple-minded attitude, stringy compound sentences suggest haste or fatigue, and puffy complex sentences suggest the writer is a mouse. Proust expressed how feeble he felt and how complicated everything was by writing such long sentences that one, as Joyce reported, could fill an entire magazine.

Of the three kinds of sentences I praise the complex, since it is the most useful and should be the most frequent in Formal writing. Complex sentences are not awfully common in speech, and writers aren't using so many of them today as they used to. In the past, excessive subordination of ideas produced overloaded and over-refined sentences. Today, we do not find as much subordination as would be useful.

The more Formal the writing, the more ordering and relating of the ideas is required. In Formal, the writer sweats to make everything perfectly clear. She changes many simple and compound sentences, that would be natural in Informal, to complex.

Compound: He's an ex-drunk and he's our mayor.
Complex: Though he used to be a drunk, he's now our mayor.
My first boyfriend was Bob and he was a freshman.
My first boyfriend was Bob, when he was a freshman.
Try this on Carol. She needs practice.
Try this on Carol, who needs practice.

Do this one yourself: *Consider the ant, thou sluggard, and be wise.*

Complex sentences, despite their name, are clearer. If teachers nagged you to write longer sentences, they meant clearer ones.

Ordering the Ideas

To write a complex sentence you must subordinate one of the ideas. *I went to the movies, where I saw* King Kong. *When I went to the movies I saw* King Kong. If you can't tell which idea is more important, going to the movies or seeing *King Kong*, then coordinate by saying *I went to the movies* and *I saw* King Kong. But usually when there is more than one idea in a sentence, one of them is the main idea, and the others should be put in their place, or they will be insubordinate.

It's more important to be able to use subordination than coordination. We could do without most *ands* and *buts* between main clauses. In revising your work, you'll find yourself taking out unnecessary *ands* and *buts*. The *and* between main clauses is never really needed, and *but* relationships are often understood without your having to use *but*. Subordinating conjunctions, on the other hand, are much more instructive than coordinating conjunctions. Coordinators make sentences smoother and faster, subordinators make them smoother and *clearer*.

No subordination: *The used-car salesman approached us. He was very smooth and he told us he would give us a deal on a 1985 Mouse. It had good tires and low mileage, and he was only asking ten thousand.* With subordination: *The used-car salesman, who was very smooth, approached and offered us a deal—a 1985 Mouse with good tires and low mileage for only ten thousand dollars.*

Another example: *Last night I was driving my car and I missed the evening news, but I did see the morning news.* With subordination: *While driving last night I missed the evening news, but I saw the morning news.*

Another: *I graduated and I went into the Army, and then I worked in a store, and so I saved enough to get married.* With subordination: *By going in the Army after graduation and then working in a store, I saved enough money to get married.*

Change main clauses to subordinate clauses, change clauses to phrases, and combine sentences. You may be surprised at how much of this revision is possible and how it improves what you've written. A lot can be done, because in what you've written—just as in what you say and what you think—the ideas are connected somehow. Subordination clarifies the connections.

We'll now review the ways of making subordinate clauses.

Start them off with the relative pronouns, *that, which,* and *who.* Instead of saying *Tightening my prose is a problem. It's bothered me all my life* say *Tightening my prose is a problem that's bothered me all my life.*

When you're stumped in thinking of a way to follow up an idea, be inspired by the following list of conjunctions (or the list of connectives on page 135). Connect the ideas in terms of

Time:	Use the conjunctions *after, since, before, when, while, as,* and *until.*
Place:	Use *where, wherever.*
Purpose:	Use *so that, in order that.*
Comparison:	Use *than, as, as if, as though.*
Condition:	that is, one event depends on another. Use *if* or *unless.*
Concession:	Use *although, though, even though.* Some people sense differences in these, but I think you can use any of the three depending on the sentence rhythm.
Cause:	*Because* is a little more emphatic than *since. For* and *as* also express cause relationships, but they are weaker and can be ambiguous, especially *as. As he looked at her she looked at him.*

Other conjunctions can get you into trouble. *While* can be ambiguous. *While he looked at her, she looked at him. So* can also be ambiguous. *He looked at her, so she looked at him.* At least five other conjunctions besides *like* are now taboo—*being as, being that, plus, only,* and *let alone.* If you use these your goose is cooked. *Being that Bob is a Satanist, plus Carol is a Baptist, they argue like hell, let alone they don't speak to each other.*

Arranging the Sentence

Most people have never heard that position in the sentence is important, but it is. Should a main clause go before or after a subordinate clause? It depends. Usually the speaker or writer automatically puts the subordinate clause in the right place, but often she doesn't. Sometimes there's no choice; for example, you say *Don't stand up until the judge stands up;* you do not say *Until the judge stands up, don't stand up.* But generally, in Formal, try to put the subordinate clause *before* the main clause.

After he missed the shot, he threw his racquet.
Because he paid no tax, they called him in.
As the tornado struck, he thought of his insurance.
When you're out of Schlitz, you're out of beer.

These sentences would be weaker if the subordinate clauses were put after the main clause: *You're out of beer when you're out of Schlitz. He thought of his insurance as the tornado struck.*

When the subordinate clause comes after the main clause it can sound like an afterthought.

> You must have the car inspected, when the time comes.
> I have a widget, which is why he asked to borrow it.
> I detest hot dogs, though right now I'm very hungry.

Sometimes, though, you will want a falling or cadenced sentence for a funny or sad effect.

> I never watch the soaps, although my canary enjoys them while drying off.
> We never go to that place in the country any more at this time of the year.

You may have heard of the rule that you should try to put what is important in the sentence at the end of the sentence, because the end of the sentence is the position of greatest emphasis. This rule should be explained. The position of greatest emphasis has to be the predicate, and whatever is important in the sentence should be in the predicate of the main clause. The reason is obvious. Whatever comes after the predicate is an anticlimax. You can write sentences in which you say the important thing first, and then add a lot of extra stuff, but you should not write many sentences like that. Sentences that end when the predicate ends are strong. (Like that one.) Putting as much of the sentence as you can *before* the predicate strengthens the sentence. (Like that one.) Anything put in the sentence *after* the predicate is weakened, and will in turn weaken the sentence, for no sentence is stronger than its weakest part.

These instructions run contrary to your general experience, in which you're always being told to be brief, say what you have to say, get to the point. But a sentence is supposed to build up, not fall off a cliff, as these do.

> Someone at this table is a werewolf, he said as he sat down and arranged his napkin in his lap.

> The world is coming to an end, according to Reverend Swain, pastor of the First United Church at the corner of Locust and Vine.
>
> The suspect turned out to be a man, which was disclosed by the matron who ran from the room where the suspect was being searched after being arrested for possession of a suspicious-looking cigarette.

Arranging a sentence for emphasis is the master trick that separates the pros from the amateurs. In speaking, we all tend to say the important thing first and tack on extra stuff. In writing, do try to put the subordination and the modifiers at the front of the sentence. You will not lose spoken tone by doing this and you will avoid the monotony that may result from beginning every blessed sentence with the subject.

Do not open a sentence with a bang. If you have a bang in a paragraph, save it for the end of the paragraph. If you have a big bang to set off somewhere in the composition, save it for the finale. All writing should have some bangs, or it drones on like a textbook.

Sentences that do not build to a climax are called loose or accumulated sentences. In speech, loose sentences are fairly short, and no one minds them. In writing, loose sentences can go on and on and become very tedious. Loose, shapeless sentences are a disease of modern prose. In Latin and in German, where the verb is often put at the end of the sentence, the sentence can build to that climax. In any language, though, emphasis is achieved by doing things in an abnormal way, and that is why you *should* write sentences that build. *If it looks like a duck, walks like a duck, and quacks like a duck, it must be a—duck. With proper care a cold lasts for seven days, but otherwise it takes a whole week.*

Clauses that trail along after the predicate are bad enough, but trailing *phrases*, participial and prepositional, are even worse. Here are trailing participles:

> The teams played an evenly matched game, resulting in a scoreless tie.
>
> She couldn't resist ordering a widget for herself, thus overextending her credit.
>
> He had the good sense to take a cab, enabling him to be there for the appointment.

Here are trailing *with* phrases:

> The stock market soared, with the result that he celebrated more than he should have.
> Carol enjoyed smoking the huge cigar, with Bob watching her closely.
> Bob likes all the flavors, with blueberry ripple his favorite.
> That resort is so romantic, with the cabins by the beach.

Maybe you don't find anything wrong with those sentences. If you didn't, it's because they reflected our normal way of talking. But the normal way is not the best. It's bad enough to have normal ideas, but to say them normally is worse. What's the point?

Cute Tricks

Writers seldom think about arranging their sentences because the words usually come to them in the right order. *Carol kissed Bob good-bye when he left for work.* That loose sentence need not be changed to a climactic sentence: *When Bob left for work Carol kissed him good-bye.* The normal word order is *usually* right. But striking effects are achieved by breaking the normal pattern of the sentence, inverting the natural word order, throwing in interruptions or questions, and falling back on the passive voice. Here are striking inversions.

You'll always have the poor.	The poor you shall always have with you.
She wore a pants suit to the wedding.	To the wedding she wore a pants suit.
We don't have real evidence.	Real evidence we don't have.
I have devoted my life to Yale, to country, and to God.	I have devoted my life to God, to country, and to Yale.
To begin with, Marley was dead.	Marley was dead, to begin with.

Interruptions can also be clever.

> The movie was, if you must know the truth, a disaster.
> This criticism, the more you say it, strikes me as unfair.
> Her he chose, from all his girls, to do his shirts.
> Out of the water we fished, dripping sinisterly, a book on—what was it on?—grammar.

One of the easiest tricks of lively writing—witness the popularity of dashes and parentheses—is to break the flow—within the sentence, within and between the paragraphs. Interruptions are particularly welcome when you don't have any flow. Interruptions should be brief, as in this example from *Lolita: My very photogenic mother died in a freak accident (picnic, lightning) when I was three.*

When you're writing about something doing something to something remember that you have a choice between the active and passive voices.

Carol punched Bob.	Bob was punched by Carol.
The bride wore a white satin dress.	A white satin dress was worn by the bride.
The Army discharged me when the war was over.	I was discharged by the Army when the war was over.

In the switch to the passive, the object of the verb is thought to be more important than the subject, and takes its place. The subject does nothing then and is passive. The passive voice is used when what is being done is more important than who is doing it. *The car was stolen. We were gypped. He's tanned. Trash was thrown. The war was ended.* What about *I'm asleep*—active or passive?

All too frequently, though, the passive is used to cover up a mystery about who is doing what is being done. *It is thought.* By whom? *Data has been gathered, trespassers will be shot, he is considered, it has been suggested, it was decided, they are known.* When the verb is vigorous, putting it into the passive voice can sound ridiculous. *My nose was punched by you. Hot dogs are hated by her. The tree was struck by the car.* In short, the passive voice may be used (I just used it) when the verb is unexciting and the agent unimportant or unknown. In good writing these conditions don't often occur, and that's why the passive voice is seldom used. (I did it again.)

Seven Tips on Sentences

Let's go over the requirements for an acceptable written sentence. It has unity, or a single main point. No point, no sentence. Everything needed to make the point is in, everything not needed is out. Whatever is unclear or distracting is out. The ideas that are left have been weighed, consciously or unconsciously, and have been coordinated or subordinated. The sentence is built around the main point.

A sentence is like a juggling act: all goes up and comes down at the right time in the right place. The inexpert juggler sends stuff up, like a subject, forgets about it, then grabs anything that's handy and sends it up, too. Sentence juggling is not easy, but gets easier after years of practice. The expert juggler has the sentences arranged in her mind before letting them fly.

A good written sentence has stricter requirements than an acceptable spoken sentence. It's hard to compose a decent sentence and harder to compose a forceful one. But if it was easy, it wouldn't be worth doing or be so well rewarded. Good sentences can get you into the White House or even Westminster Abbey. The essential talent for a writer is not intelligence, wit, knowledge, or personality, but a feeling for sentences.

Here are seven tips to help you build them.

Keep sentences brief. In any art, energy and force derive from economy of means, and not because the artist has different ends and different means. Shakespeare tried to entertain, Mozart wanted to write good tunes and score musical comedy hits. They achieved their effects more swiftly and easily, and thus more powerfully, than their rivals. You should write the shortest possible sentences using the shortest possible words, in the shortest possible paragraphs, not because people are dimwits or because they're busy—they're not that dim or that busy—but because force comes from the elimination of the inessential. T.S. Eliot said, "Artistic creation proceeds by a series of destructions." In the next chapter I'll encourage you to destroy what you've written. A brief sentence does not mean a baby sentence, but a stripped sentence. A hundred-word sentence that's clear and worth saying can seem short, but a dull four- or five-word sentence can seem interminable. Nixon: *Death is always inevitable.*

Vary your sentence patterns. Try to write climactic sentences, even though they sound a bit unnatural. Here's a pointed sentence by Dr. Johnson: *No man but a blockhead ever wrote, except for money.* Today that sentence would be edited: *Everyone writes for money except blockheads.* Another kind of sentence to try is the balanced sentence. *I seem to see blankety blank, I seem to see higgledy piggledy, I seem to see dickery dockery. Men think, women know. Men do, women are. Men are men, but man is a woman.* Balanced sentences are for Sundays and holidays.

Mix up short, normal, and long sentences. Short sentences are a dozen words or less. Long sentences are, say, thirty or more words. The average written sentence is fifteen to twenty words. Most of your sentences should be around the average. Anyone can write shorter sentences by turning clauses into separate sentences or write longer sentences by tacking sentences together with coordinating conjunctions and by adding clauses with subordinating conjunctions. Ho hum. But the reader expects sentences of normal length just as he expects normal words. If he didn't expect them you couldn't surprise him with a long or short one.

Wake the reader up, if you want him to be awake. Use questions, exclamations, asides, commands, interruptions, and inversions. Unless you're doing pure reporting, all of these devices are available to you. You can address the reader. It's silly to always pretend you and he don't exist. But guard against saying *you, you, you.* He may not want to get involved, or think he's listening to his mother. If you address him directly, use a touch of restraint. *Holy smoke! Does that knock your socks off, kid?* You can be natural without being hyper.

Be brave and strong. As St. Paul says, "If the bugle does not sound a clear call, who will prepare for battle?" Don't overqualify what you're saying. Speak what you feel, not what you ought to say. When writing is dull, it's because the writer is timid. Don't stall, don't be nice. Avoid the passive voice. Throw out the adjectives and adverbs. Make the nouns precise, the verbs forceful. Remove the copulatives: don't say *He is distrustful,* say *He distrusts,* don't say *She's a good writer,* say *She writes well,* don't say *I am hungry,* say *I hunger.* Look at each negative statement, and try to recast it as a positive statement. *He did not agree, He disagreed. She did not accept it, She rejected it. She did not take her purse with her, She left without her purse.* The word *not* is strong in speech, where it can be stressed, but weak in writing.

Combine sentences. This tip seems to contradict *Keep sentences brief,* but both tips are intended to smooth the reader's way. Combining sentences may or may not save words, but often makes the reading easier. Young writers, erring on the side of short sentences, should try to combine them. When two or three sentences in a row have the same subject, combination is possible. *The factory is at 1500 Ohio Street. It is an old, red brick building. Repairs are badly needed.* Combined: *The factory, an old, red brick building at 1500 Ohio Street, badly needs repairs.* When a pronoun keeps reappearing, combinations are possible. *He used to lose a lot. Now he's given up playing poker. This has made his wife hap-*

py. Combined: *Since he lost so much at poker, he's given it up, which has made his wife happy.* Sentences that follow each other are related by time, purpose, comparison, etc., so combine them using the appropriate subordinators.

Don't distract attention. If you're writing seriously, avoid devices and expressions that call attention to themselves or to you. Sometimes the right hand should pretend not to know what the left is doing. Prose may be at its very best when it's a window and not a painting.

Don't like what you wrote. Admiring what you have down beclouds your judgment. The sentences you're fond of, you may have to get rid of. A writer is ruthless: she cuts down and hauls away great armfuls of brush and weeds, and sometimes flowers go with them. If you're having trouble with a sentence or a paragraph skip it and move on. You'll probably discover later that you didn't need it, and that's why it gave you trouble.

What's a Paragraph?

The word *paragraph* originally meant *outside mark.* It was a mark—a star, hand, leaf, dagger, or the special paragraph mark (¶)—that a writer or printer put in the margin of the page to show that a new subject was being introduced and to help the reader mark his place. Today these little marks aren't used. Instead, writers and typographers indicate a new paragraph with white space—by indenting a new paragraph or, in modern block style, by skipping a line or two.

Some publishers love white space so much they insist on short paragraphs, and divide the writing up not according to the ideas but according to the desired paragraph length. But a paragraph should not simply be a convenience for the eye; it should be an aid to the understanding. Paragraphs should help the reader follow the argument by offering the ideas in groups.

How long should a paragraph be? One-sentence or one-word paragraphs are possible. In dialogue, each speech by each speaker usually gets a paragraph to itself. But in other kinds of writing the paragraphs should not be too short, for this gives a choppy, hard-breathing effect, just as short sentences do. A paragraph should normally be from three to ten sentences long. Readers now expect paragraphs no longer than two or three inches.

In the past, much longer paragraphs were common. Long paragraphs were and are a sign of Formality. But remember that the paragraph is a device of writing, not of speech. Since less reading is done nowadays and since writing is becoming more like speech, the taste for long paragraphs is disappearing along with the ability to read them. It's a good idea to break up a four or five hundred-word paragraph into three shorter paragraphs and allow the modern reader to rest his weary eyes. Paragraphs are getting shorter, but if they get too short they'll slow the reader. When you paragraph, keep in mind the expectations of the audience and the natural divisions of the discussion. Sometimes you must negotiate between the two demands.

I won't spend much time talking about the paragraph. Since paragraphing is only a device for the eye, it's of minor importance. When handbooks talk about developing a paragraph, they're really discussing the big problem in composition—joining sentences. All of the sentences in a paragraph should be related to each other—that's true. But that's not saying much, because we know that all the sentences in a composition should be related to each other. How we divide the sentences into groups is often arbitrary.

Paragraphing can be done two ways: the sentences can be grouped after the whole composition is written, or the paragraphs can be written one by one according to a plan as little compositions in themselves. The writing comes easy with a good outline that lists subtopics of the right size for each paragraph. But good outlines are hard to get, and most writing is done without them, as we know. It's not enough to be a master of diction and a master of the sentence. Another skill is needed: the ability to develop an idea through a paragraph and through the whole composition. The choice of words and the shaping of sentences require thought, but paragraphs require planning. The ability to work with the larger structures, with the design, is a special skill and the one most often neglected. Many writers choose words well and write strong sentences, but get lost in the paragraph. They're like tennis players who master several strokes but have no serve. In a paragraph the sentences must follow, and in a composition the paragraphs must follow. Nothing follows anything unless there are controlling ideas for paragraphs and the composition. Composition means putting things together, and you can only put things together that go. Where do they go? Where are you going?

Pursuing an Idea

The hardest part of writing is writing consecutive sentences. In writing poetry this is no problem because the poet has a license to flit around. In writing narrative or description, this is no problem because the writing simply follows time order or space order. In writing discussions and arguments, this is *the* problem—making the thoughts follow. The mind does not come up with consecutive thoughts unless it has been disciplined to do so; there's a great difference between the way the mind naturally works and the way sentences have to follow each other like elephants holding tails. Since this is the main problem in composition, I'll talk about it here and pursue it thoroughly in the next chapter.

There are two ways of proceeding: the way of the painter and the way of the composer. The painter begins with a design and fills in the details. The musician begins with a phrase and then elaborates it into a grand design. Some compositions call for the way of the painter and some for the way of the musician. Few people are good at both. Young writers should use the painter's method and work from a design. But because they lack experience it's hard for them to come up with good designs. The reason they don't plan their compositions is they don't know how. Planning is in the next chapter. Here we'll look at the musician's way of building. Speech and music have much in common, since both proceed in a linear way through time. Rhythm and tempo are just as important in writing as in music.

Most people have had little practice in pursuing ideas. They have an idea, and then they have a different one. Here, for example, is a writer working on an essay about hot dogs. She starts with an ordinary idea: *Hot dogs are pretty good sometimes.* (The first idea doesn't matter, any idea gets you started.) Next idea: *I had a good hot dog the last time I was at the stadium.* Next: *That was some game.* Next: *I wish I was there right now.* Next: *That cheerleader was cute.* You see what has happened. Instead of moving in on the first idea, the mind has moved on. What was the first idea? *Hot dogs are pretty good sometimes.* Let's stay with that. Why pretty good? Are they good or aren't they? Why sometimes? On what occasions are they good? What makes them good? What makes them bad? By pursuing these few questions one could easily develop enough material for the essay. Though people think about themselves, they're not in the habit of questioning themselves. That's what pursuing ideas is, questioning oneself about the topic.

Maybe the writer has to do an essay on cats, and starts thinking: *Cats are not as demanding as dogs.* Next idea: *I only see my cat Reggie about once a week.* Next: *Reggie is a good old boy, a real tom. A ginger cat.* Next: *He has a big piece out of his ear.* Next: *I wonder how that happened?* Once again, the mind of a writer is not supposed to move *on*, in a natural browsing way, but move *in*, in a relentless, gnawing way. *Cats are not as demanding as dogs.* Why not? Should they be? Are dogs too demanding? Are cats not demanding enough? What is being demanded? How does a cat demand? How does a dog demand? What is better? Why? You see, this is the way to pursue an idea and develop a paragraph—not by putting down thoughts as they come but by asking questions about each statement you'd like to make. The procedure seems slow, destructive rather than creative, going backwards instead of forwards. But that's what thinking is—driving into the subject, not bouncing off and moving on.

Don't think of a paragraph as a collection of ideas on a subject, whether it's hot dogs or cats. Think of it as something to build, piece by piece, on the first idea. You could have a million thoughts about hot dogs, but you can't write a six-sentence paragraph with a million thoughts. You've got too many thoughts. In fact, your mind is like a beehive. What you have to do is to stay with the thought you started with, then stay with that thought and the next, then with those two and the next, and so on. It's hard, but gets easier with practice.

Do *not* proceed this way: *Reggie is my cat. He's a ginger cat. Some people call them marmalade cats. One called Morris used to be on TV. Reggie is a tom who really gets around. He has a piece out of his ear. His right ear.* Instead, proceed this way: *Why did I name my cat Reggie? I suppose I thought the name sounded elegant and debonair. Reggie lived up to his name and still lives up to it. He doesn't look so elegant and debonair as he did ten years ago, when he was young, and not missing so many pieces of himself—such as his right ear. But now he is even more elegant and debonair in his manner. He enters a room as if he were Louis XIV, the Sun King of France. But Reggie is only Moon King of Nyack. Every night he holds court,* etc.

Each sentence picks up an idea from the previous one and works with it. The mind stays focused by asking questions about the previous sentence. If what you've put down gets you nowhere, scratch it and try something else. The reason writing takes so much time is that a train of thought can stop after you've been following it a while, and then you have to start another and follow it to see where it's going. You don't have to go far; you only need five or six sentences for a paragraph, and once you've gotten them you'll have a number of ideas to pursue in the next paragraph. You'll make countless false starts. Writing is like panning for gold—lots of time and effort, but the gold is left when you're done.

If pursuing ideas is hard for you, get practice this way. Have someone give you a sentence, then force yourself to write three or four sentences about it. Doing this will convince you you're wrong ever to say you have nothing to say. When you get a sentence down, it automatically begins to suggest a critique of itself. Whatever is said has to be incomplete. A statement cries for help, needs to be explained or improved, either by adding an idea or taking a bit away. The sentence is a thesis. The next, if it follows the first, is an *and* or a *but* sentence. You add to or subtract from what you've said. There's nothing unnatural in this; it's the way thought proceeds. Thesis, antithesis, synthesis. Yes, but, and. Some thinkers have said that that's how history proceeds. Whenever you put a sentence down, somewhere in the wings is the next sentence talking back. It's there all right—just call it forth. Its cue is *but,* the most wonderful word of all. *I will give it to you but. . .I love my wife but. . .* Use this priceless word often. It was Ibsen's dying word. Get your sentence down, say *but,* and see what happens.

Paragraph Form

Young writers are told that a paragraph should have a beginning, a middle, and an end. They are told that a paragraph should have a topic sentence near the beginning, and maybe a thesis or concluding sentence at the end. They're told that a paragraph should start with a transitional expression to link it to the previous one.

This advice is not helpful, and I wish I hadn't mentioned it. Paragraphs are not written according to a model. Good writers don't think about paragraphs, they just write. As they write, of course, they keep their topic in mind, but they don't worry about topic sentences or the arrangement of the paragraph. A paragraph doesn't have to build to a climax, or open, or close. If you look at books in which you've underlined important sentences, you'll see that these sentences come anywhere—at the beginning, middle, or end of paragraphs. If you can skim a book by reading the first or last sentence of the paragraphs, there's something wrong with the writing. In good writing, each sentence is important, and you can't pick out the ones to underline. You don't need a topic sentence in a paragraph, but you'd better have a topic. If you have a clear idea of your topic, you'll have a hard time not coming up with a handful of topic sentences.

It would be nice to write paragraphs full of tricks, little compositions in themselves, with beginnings, middles, and ends. But thinking about *form* while writing only distracts you. Questions of form may be considered once you've done a draft. Then you can divide what you've written into paragraphs of the right size, rearrange sentences, and maybe add little touches to show that you're opening and closing paragraphs.

Only advanced and fluent writers come up with whole paragraphs that have not been previously planned for. Others need a clear or controlling idea for each paragraph in order to keep from straying. A plan has many benefits and no risks. No one needs to follow a plan exactly, and any plan can be left behind when the writer gets hot. Sad to say, most young writers have neither fluency nor plan; they use neither the musician's method nor the painter's. They need to learn both, learn to draw up a design and to follow where the ideas lead. Writing calls for alternating the methods, allowing the thoughts to flow, while checking them according to the design. One can have a good design, but the writing can be dead, lack fluency. And one can write fluently but wander off the topic. Writing is an art like the others—a balancing of conscious form and unconscious inspiration. Too much form means dullness; too little form, the work is shapeless, pointless.

Paragraph beginnings are no problem. Did you notice that I just started a new paragraph? Probably not. Which shows that one can start a new paragraph without preparing for it in the previous paragraph and without sticking in a transitional idea or expression. Paragraphs *should* open with sentences that sound like beginnings. Questions or definitions get the paragraph off to a good start, as in these examples: *There are three basic types of hot dog. The cat is man's best friend. What is a hot dog? The cat is a domestic feline; that says it all. The hot dog is a frankfurter or wiener sausage on a soft roll.* When you're revising, check whether your paragraph beginnings sound like beginnings. You needn't pay special attention to the closing sentences of paragraphs. Paragraphs are not long, and don't have to be brought around. They can stop abruptly, without closing chords.

Joining sentences is harder than joining paragraphs, which are expected to introduce new topics. New topics within reason, that is—you can't talk about cats in the first paragraph and hot dogs in the second without explaining how you got from one to the other. (When you have to explain what you're doing, something's fishy.) You move easily from one paragraph to the next if the paragraphs are subtopics under the main topic of the composition. Connecting the paragraphs does not depend on clever transitions but on having a design for the composition which includes these paragraphs.

Some bold writers—John McPhee, Tom Wolfe—make a virtue of abrupt transitions, moving from one time to another, one scene to another, one speaker to another. Sharp breaks should not be too frequent, and are more acceptable when put into a pattern.

Making Transitions

If the paragraphs are related to each other through planning and if the sentences follow each other by staying on the topic, the writing goes merrily along. The problem of transitions is the whole problem in writing. Writing is joining things. It's not like the song of a bird, it's like engineering, bookkeeping, or bricklaying. It can be taught *or* it can be learned: it can be done.

When the writer has her material and her building plan, she won't have trouble with transitions. But sometimes a little work has to be done on some of the pieces to fit them in, and that's where tricks come in handy. One trick in making the writing appear to have more coherence is to repeat a word used in the previous sentence. The repetition of just one word makes a connection between sentences that are about quite different things. Pronouns link sentences. Another trick is to stick with the same subject through the sentences. *He does not believe in democracy. He has not cut his hair in two years. He eats alfalfa. He never wears shoes.*

The easiest trick in linking sentences is to use transitional expressions like *meanwhile, furthermore, on the other hand, similarly, as a matter of fact, in other words.* The English language has a great store of these expressions called *connectives* or *conjunctive adverbs.* They are used all the time in writing and are signs of written and Formal style. If you use too many of these glue words, you run the risk of making the writing sound artificial and lacking the tone of speech. Beginning writers usually do not use enough of these words; academics use far too many. Professional writers avoid them.

Some of them are so stuffy, they are nearly unusable: *accordingly, rather, nevertheless, moreover, indeed, to be sure, thereupon,* and *in sum.* Don't use these smug words unless you want to sound like a professor. *However* is particularly overworked, and I never touch it myself. Use *but* or *though* instead. Give your reader credit for being able to see connections between ideas, and don't steer him by opening every paragraph and every other sentence with a connective. No one wants to be lectured to with a lot of *thuses, thens, therefores,* and *howevers.*

A *few* well-chosen connectives do add grace notes to your writing. (See how I managed to start that sentence without *however?*) I'll now tick off the connectives that are still useful.

If you're *adding* another thought, use *besides, also, then too, what's more, and then,* and *furthermore.* If you're *listing* thoughts, use *first, second, third, in the first place, in the second place, next, finally, last.*

If *comparing,* use *similarly, in the same way, likewise, equally important, equally so and so. By the same token* is pretty tired.

If *contrasting,* use *yet, and yet, still, however, in contrast, on the contrary, on the other hand, to be fair, otherwise, still, or else, alternatively.*

If showing a connection in *time,* use *earlier, afterwards, later, before, at that time, then, since then, meanwhile, in the meantime, subsequently.*

If *summing up,* use *in brief, in short, to repeat, as I have said, once again, in other words, as has been said.*

If offering *examples,* use *for example, for instance, as follows, that is.* Be careful with the Latin abbreviations *e.g. (for example)* and *i.e. (that is).* In Formal you don't use abbreviations. And if you don't say *e.g.* and *i.e.,* that's a reason not to write them.

If you want to point out a *cause* relationship, use *so, and so, hence, thus, then, as a result, consequently.*

If you want to intensify the next idea, use *in fact, after all, of course, surely, certainly, in any case, at any rate, to tell the truth, to be sure, whatever the reason.* But these don't help much.

These connectives, like the conjunctions listed on page 121, remind you of ways to develop ideas. Connectives are similar to conjunctions, but conjunctions (usually) follow commas, and connectives follow periods or semicolons. *Carol has her problems; for ex-*

ample, Bob loves hot dogs. But she still cooks them. After all, she's his wife.

The glue in these glue words is weak. The ideas have to match up. Success in making transitions depends on the ideas. You can say *The Germans love music and eat sausages.* You can't say *The Germans love music and began the war.*

A writer's skill is shown in the smoothness of her transitions. You can tell a good writer just by the way she uses *and* and *but* and by the way she leaves them out. *But* is a great word for writers. The only problem with *but* is that the reader occasionally does not understand your reason for using it. Casey Stengel: *They say you can't do it, but sometimes it doesn't always work.*

And is a troublesome word, causing no end of logical problems. *The world is a closer place* and *Stud deodorant is a part of it. She's a Scorpio* and *all three of her sons married Scorpios. I am an American,* and *I am proud of it.* You can begin a sentence with *and,* of course, but you'll have a sneaky feeling that the new thought should have been worked into the sentence before. *He still likes girls. And he's ninety-six years old.* In Formal that should be *Even at ninety-six, he likes girls.*

Putting in the conjunction or leaving it out is important. Take the saying *Love me little, love me long.* If this idea were not put so well it wouldn't have become a proverb. It might have been put as *Love me little, and you will love me long* or *If you love me little, then you will (or I hope you will) love me long.* This last way, the clearest way, would be right for Formal. But sometimes the clearest way is a little dull.

If you can dispense with a conjunction or connective (or anything) without a serious loss in smoothness or clarity, do it. Writing that's crawling with *ands, buts,* other conjunctions, and connectives is condescending to the reader or fishy. These words cannot paper over cracks in the thought. How to think without cracks, without stopping, involves our next two chapters.

══════Chapter Six══════

Writing: Before, During, After

The Need to Plan

There are three steps in writing: planning, actually writing, and revising. Young writers must put a lot of effort into what they do before and after writing. As they gain experience they can spend less effort on planning and revising. These are the steps in writing that need to be taught, and these are the only steps that can be taught. First, the plan.

Your parents probably told you there were at least two ways of doing a job—the easy way and the hard way. The easy way is planned. Writing is a job like any other; it just differs in requiring a shocking amount of effort. Even great writers squawk about having to write. Dr. Johnson said, "I wonder that so many people have written who might have let it alone." In view of the strenuous work, it's surprising that so many people do not plan their compositions, to save themselves effort while writing. They'll draw up a neat plan for a birdhouse, but won't plan a paper or report that could affect their careers.

The main reason they don't plan is that planning is even harder than writing. It requires prolonged and concentrated thought, and that's hard for everybody. Also, they may feel that a plan will inhibit them as they write and halt the flow of ideas. This notion is silly, because the plan assures a steady flow of ideas and saves the writer from drowning in them.

Some people have to start scribbling right away. They need to get something down. Engineers say they need paper to talk with—talking paper, they call it. A certain woman who loved to write everything down once said, "How do I know what I mean until I see what I say?" The critic Harold Clurman was asked what he was going to say about a play he had just seen, and answered: "I don't know yet, I haven't talked to my pencil." It's true that right things to say, lovely things, come once you begin to write. But if you have many things to say, you need a plan to sort them out.

The hard way to write is to begin scribbling away. You may get fifty or a hundred good sentences down, but when you try to fit them together—they're like pieces from different puzzles. If you know the tricks of making transitions you can fit almost anything together—as you can make clothing fit by opening seams and taking in and letting out material. But that's work. Instead, make things to size. The easy way is to refrain from writing as long as possible, and spend your effort in thinking and planning. That way you don't commit yourself to sentences and paragraphs you have to fiddle with or throw out later on, or that you keep, even though you shouldn't, just because you've sweated over them.

Most people write the way a musician composes, by making a start and going on from there to the finish. I tout the painter's method, making a design and then filling in the details. I may have contributed to the notion that writers go from small to large, work up instead of down, because that's the way I've gone in this book—from word to sentence to paragraph, and now to the whole. Maybe I should have started with what the writer should start with, the plan. The writer, of course, chooses the words and sets them down one by one, but without some notion of where she's going, the words don't come. The words, the details of writing, make it succeed, as details make every art succeed, but they do so only by contributing to the overall design. When you find yourself blocked, skipping from subject to subject, fumbling for words, wrestling with sentences, that means the plan needs work.

In planning, you have to start at the finish and work backwards. Thinking sometimes feels that way, that you're moving backwards or sinking. Hard thought can make you dizzy. This feeling of going backwards is common among writers, because they, unlike other thinkers, start with the conclusion—an attitude, a belief, a thesis, a story they want to persuade others to accept. The writer has to go back in her own mind to find support for what she is presenting to the audience. She has to keep an eye on three things at once—

herself, the subject, and the audience. She handles the subject, questions herself, and deals with others. Scientific problems are straightforward in comparison.

Many writers have trouble beginning because the beginning is farthest from the end, which they already know. The plan has to be worked out backwards and written forwards. The real work of writing—everyone knows it—is getting ready. The severe discipline lies in what must be done before the sentences appear. Once the typewriter keys or the pen starts moving, the battle is over; the writer breathes easier.

Thinking and Writing

Thinking is like certain other words—*art, poetry, grammar*—in that it stands for a category of activity and also for the ideal type of that activity. We may wonder what our cat is thinking, but whatever it is, it's not what IBM wants us to do when it gives us signs saying *THINK*. Thinking covers all kinds of mental events— jumbled up sensations, perceptions, images, concepts. Some of these can be steered in the right direction and some cannot. In the general sense of the word, thinking is equated with consciousness. In the ideal sense, it refers to the ability to control thoughts, follow them up, and communicate them.

When the mind is working well, directing thought, it works in an impersonal way duplicable in other minds. When mathematicians see an equation, their minds analyze it in the same way. They're thinking. When musicians read a score and follow the music in their heads, they're thinking. When you express yourself clearly in sentences, you're thinking, and when your audience reads or listens to what you say, they're thinking. As a sharable and impersonal activity, thought seems opposed to *creativity* and *originality*. Thought is strictly controlled by form; its forms are called *languages*. Our ability to use our primary language, the language of words, is usually considered the best indicator of our ability to think.

Like it or not, we're judged in this world according to our intelligence, which is judged by how we use our tongues. The word *dumb* means not only silent but stupid. Beautiful but dumb blondes do not marry millionaires, they marry other dumb blondes. One may wonder why intelligence is so highly prized, if it doesn't make people happier. That it doesn't pay to be too smart is proverbial. Psychoanalysts are smart, and commit suicide at ten times the normal rate. Apparently happiness is not so much our goal as is success. Intelligence brings success.

When people buy books on English, they're not just seeking to avoid mistakes but to become more intelligent. They know that the powers of the mind and the powers of expression are functions of each other, and grow or decline together. This view is not an error, though it is an error to suppose that one can get smart fast, or that if he uses the new, magic words he'll take over the company.

I've talked about thinking for this reason: if you're going to write, you should admit what writing is, and what it is—let's have no secrets—is thinking. If you can't think you can't write. Learning to write is learning to think. Everyone knows this, but pretends it isn't so, for though they want to write, they feel they can't improve their thinking. Of course they can. If writing were not thinking, not such a serious matter, then people wouldn't be so afraid of it. They know that by writing they expose their minds to others. It's pride that silences the would-be writer. The reason writing is not taught in schools is not that writing can't be taught, it's to spare feelings. Don't worry about hurt feelings. Get the stuff down, no matter how bad it is. So it's not *Hamlet,* at least it's yours. A jabbering monkey is more fun than a silent genius. And every genius used to jabber.

Many words can flash in our mind while the trained part of the mind selects the right word. Many sentences can be framed and rejected while the chosen one is being spoken or written. Mental events are electrical, but sentences are built slowly. People speak and read only about a dozen sentences or a few hundred words a minute. Going faster than that becomes a meaningless trick.

The mind spends much more time composing written sentences than spoken. Written style can be elaborated into something very slow and artificial. That's often what's wrong with writing, and that may be why most people don't like to read, however much they love to talk and listen. Written words, put together like cars in a freight train, are far removed from the flashing thoughts of the mind.

The writer should try to speed up her writing, making it less slow and unnatural and more like talking. Though writing is read a little faster than speech is spoken, it seems slower and duller, and it is. The writer should try to write as if she were dictating. This is the best way to write, and it's a way of getting you to write. You're used to talking. Writing should flow, and slow down, and race like speech. Put the stuff down fast. You can always tidy up later.

Inside the mind it's like a silent movie—images, words, phrases are flashed; all is dim, jerky, chaotic. The writer has two jobs: to control this circus through articulate speech, and to get the little black marks on the paper to speak. With experience she has more and more thoughts that are *sentences*, and she stops writing down *things* she would never say.

Concentrating

What happens when people think who aren't much used to it? They let anything pop into their heads. Their minds, instead of working like a machine, stand there like a blackboard on which anything can be written by an invisible hand. The student reading a discussion of the causes of the Civil War keeps turning her thoughts to her boyfriend, or worries about the soap opera that's on television while she's reading. A businessman at a sales conference keeps thinking how much the ties cost that the other men are wearing. A voter listening to a politician is not really listening—only a few key words get through—because he's thinking of how the politician looks and whether he can win. No one's mind is always under control. A human being is not a brain kept in a glass jar. Our needs and emotions are fierce and keep breaking in on us, stopping the train of thought before it goes anywhere.

Concentration, the ability to keep the mind from being interrupted, is not a hard skill like playing the violin, but an easy one, like meditating, relaxing, or swinging a golf club. The first thing to do in getting the knack of concentration is to eliminate distractions. Internal distractions of the mind—worries and desires—are bad enough without having to cope with external ones. Turn off the radio and TV. Shut out noise. Don't answer the phone. Stay away from members of the opposite sex. Stay away from members of your own sex.

If you worry, you can't concentrate. But look at it the other way—if you concentrate, you can't worry. Sit down and concentrate, and don't get up until something is accomplished—a chapter read, an outline planned, two pages written. If the mind starts to wander, catch it before it goes very far. Referring to a plan reminds you what to focus on. Your concentration will break from time to time, but don't be anxious when this happens. Don't start thinking about yourself—*I* can't think, *I* can't think— but get back to the subject. An English wit, Sydney Smith, said that he never could find any man who could think for two minutes together. But a lot can be done in under two minutes if one is thinking well.

Once you're off the track, getting back takes effort. You feel frustrated, feel you've been wasting time. That's why it's better to stray as little as possible, by following a map—your plan. We seldom notice just when our minds begin to wander, since everything happens so quickly in the mind. Wrapped up in what it's doing, it forgets where it's going. It's most liable to wander at the moment the thinking gets tough. But that's the crucial moment; that's what you watch for. Real thought only begins when the mind meets an obstacle. Most people give up or try a detour around the obstacle, and the detour takes them away instead of over. The obstacle should be faced: Why can't I think this thought? What don't I know? Maybe the obstacle can't be climbed, but if you try at least you'll know how far you can get. For the climb the will has to help and provide the power of concentration. All advice on writing is useless if one cannot learn to concentrate, and stay with a question the way a dog stays with a bone.

Everyone concentrates from time to time, and does it unconsciously when the work is interesting. So try to get interested in what you're doing. Convince yourself you want to do what you have to do. Some minds are stubborn, though, and need to be subdued, as some dogs need to go to obedience school. The mind has to learn NO. When it wants to wander off, yank it back. This sounds easy, but it's hard, as people are not in the habit of watching what their minds are doing. Here, then, is the trick of concentrating: dividing the mind into one part that works and another that watches.

The best way to divide the mind is to start a dialogue between the parts. Let the will question the intelligence and boss it around: What do you mean by that? What's this word? How can you say that? Back to the subject, please. Look at the problem a different way, you boob; you're getting nowhere. Break the problem into parts. Let's do a diagram to get the picture. What are other ways to look at it? What would a scientist say? a historian? a child? the devil? a conservative? Why are you stuck? What are you stuck on? Are we barking up the wrong tree? What's up there? Do we have a case or not? What are the facts? Stop moving off the topic. Do you know what you're talking about? You want a break? Want to eat a donut? Smoke? I'll let you if you state the problem clearly.

The will disciplines the mind by firing many such questions and orders at it. The will can coax and tease the mind or, if necessary, badger and cross-examine it. Writing is the result of this dialogue. People who go around talking to themselves aloud are considered odd, but people who sit around talking to themselves, whether silently or aloud, are thinkers. They are the ones who become articulate and win the Game of English. Athletes and performers are always muttering and giving little lectures to themselves. Why shouldn't a writer do the same, especially if writing is the most difficult game? Writers tend to view what they've done as a collaboration, maybe between their inspired self and their critical self, or maybe with their Muse or an imaginary reader over their shoulder. Maybe that's why they're so fond of saying *we* and *us*, when no one knows who *we* is. Writing only looks and sounds like a monologue; it's really a condensed dialogue.

Let's say you want to write an attack on privilege, on the tax benefits of being wealthy. How do you write it? Do you just tell what the tax law is and what privileges it provides? Do you just offer a series of facts? What you're expected to write is what *you* want to say, and you have to think about the subject in relation to yourself. You have to concentrate on you and the subject. You are part of the subject. The thinking that writers do must include thinking about themselves.

That's why you should get used to questioning yourself as if you were two people. This does not mean that when you write, you're expected to write about yourself. But you have to think about you, you have to think about what you're thinking. Here you are, working on your piece on the income tax. To start, you could ask: What result do I want? Why am I talking about the rich? Do I envy them, admire them? What should I think about them? What do they do with their money? Do they deserve it? Do I deserve *my* money? What does *deserve* mean? How did they get rich? Can I get rich, too? Should I? Why? Why not?

Here are enough questons for a lifetime. You may only have time to work on a few of them and maybe you'll find them unanswerable. But you have to work on hard questions like these. Though they may strike you as leading away from the topic of the tax laws, they are really leading you into the topic. How can you talk about *inequities* and *privileges* unless you examine what *you* mean by these words? Any subject that involves right and wrong involves personal judgments and thus involves you.

If you can't find answers to your questions, then what do you write about? You write about how far you got into the questions, how they might be answered, whether they can even be answered at all. You'll have plenty to write without having plenty to say. Thinking proceeds by asking good questions, and a good question is one whose answer is unknown. Thinking is done with questions, not with answers.

Very little writing is straight reporting, and personal judgments are involved in deciding what should be reported. Writing cannot be totally impersonal, although most Formal writing tries to sound impersonal. How it sounds is one thing, but how the writer thinks is another. It's impossible for her to stay completely out of the picture. If she has to think, and not just remember, she has to think about herself, and question herself in regard to the topic. It's hard to do this. When people question themselves, they come up with answers they don't like. If they don't like them, who will?

Every subject can be as hard or as easy as you want to make it. There's no end to the thinking to be done on any subject. You can't run out of questions. The supply of *why* questions alone is inexhaustible. *You* are an especially handy inexhaustible subject. Let's say you're doing a piece on the sex life of the praying mantis. Why? Start with *you*, before going on to *it* and *them*.

Gathering Ideas

Gathering ideas, strange as it may seem, is fun. As a matter of fact, some people pay others to listen to them do it. Analysts are paid to listen to their clients free-associate, and that's what gathering ideas is. When members of a group gather ideas they *brainstorm* to get a torrent. Planning or arranging ideas is work, but gathering ideas is fun, like picking a bouquet.

In gathering ideas you want a big sheet of paper for jotting down whatever comes into your mind on the topic. Jot down words, abbreviations, phrases, slang, anything. Don't write sentences, because that slows you down. You wouldn't use these sentences in the composition anyway. In gathering ideas, the aim is to get a big bunch without worrying how good they are. Do not list the ideas. Scatter them all over the page. Put them in groups if you like. If you list the ideas, that may suggest a plan for using them, and you don't want a plan yet.

Ready with the sheet of paper? Our topic is hot dogs. Pretend you have to write an essay on hot dogs. Take five minutes now to gather ideas about hot dogs, and I'll do the same. Start.

Here's what I jotted down: are they hot where dogs hush puppies hotfoot dogfish dogwood dog days dogpatch color: pink red brown gray juicy dry wrinkled short 3 to 12 inches bun size flat buns soggy buns toasted buns buns too short too long fall apart buns vs. rolls where from who invented why how popular other countries where eaten ballparks picnics kids what's in 'em yuck don't ask cereal fat beef pork chicken spices flavoring chemicals what parts of animals best to know best not to know why want to know rely on taste who likes 'em I don't why kids like 'em don't taste like meat kids not like meat easy to eat hold in hand reason for bun shape whole thing what else mustard yellow brown kinds of mustard how much mustard sauerkraut Coney Island with chili ketchup pigs in blanket hot dog on stick deep fried frankfurter or wiener skin casing artificial casing snappy chewy skin past present future of hot dog big future meat substitute

I can sort these ideas; I see that they fall into groups that would make good topics for the four or five paragraphs or sections I want to write. First paragraph: What's a hot dog and what good is it? Second paragraph: Where, when, how eaten. Third: Reasons for hot dog success. Fourth: Past, present, future of hot dog. Fifth: The Ideal Hot Dog. With a plan such as this, writing a good essay shouldn't take anyone more than half an hour. You could write a whole essay on why hot dogs are called hot dogs, without having the foggiest idea of the answer.

Let's try another topic. Ready? This one is not cats, it's earthworms. Dig the earthworm for five minutes. Back already? Here's what I jotted: fishing putting worm on hook all fish love irresistible what a way to die worms don't seem to mind or do they handling worms can of worms dirt in can where dig rotting vegetation best eat worms I'm gonna eat some worms why do kids eat 'em must look good I used to don't now why not used to play with 'em appearance disgusting, movement disgusting? people don't like or pretend not to where's head where's tail worms crawl in worms crawl out do worms crawl do snakes crawl night crawlers snakes and worms worst worms like snakes snappy muscular worms cost of worms raising worms big money usefulness of aeration of soil leveling of lawn how many worms

how many species   sex life of worm   top speed length of worm
robins vs. worms how robin catches worms   looks listens
other birds   early bird catches   why   worms in city   worms on
sidewalks

Here are a number of ideas to work with without my having to read
any articles about worms, but there's no law against reading an article or two before gathering ideas. With these ideas, five or more
paragraphs could easily be written. First paragraph: Worms and
fishing. Second: Finding and keeping worms. Third: Appearance
and activities of worms. Fourth: Bad things about worms. Fifth:
Good things. If I knew a lot about worms and fishing I'd write the
whole essay on that. This gathering of ideas is awfully easy once
you're used to it.

This technique of snatching any idea from anywhere should be
used for even the most rarefied topics. The writer is expected to
think deeply through concentrating and questioning, but is also
expected to think widely and inclusively, to make sure that what's
interesting or important will not be ignored. This technique of
ranging through a field like a hunting dog may seem at first rather
wasteful, but saves time in the long run, and brings a lot that you
can work with within reach. You needn't worry about finding
enough ideas. Questions provide an infinite supply of them. Every
subject can be seen and handled from different points of view.
Every subject is related to others which you can bring in. Really,
couldn't you talk about any subject? If you were asked to write on
vodka, couldn't you move on to drinking? If you were asked to
write on differential calculus, couldn't you talk about why you never got that far in math? No one is required to be an expert on everything. You can sneak off the topic to topics nearby. Knowledge
is supposed to be a seamless web, or one big subject. An old definition of an educated person is one who can talk indefinitely on any
subject. She can do this, not because she knows more than the uneducated person, but because she can articulate or join what she
knows. Being educated means being skilled in listening, talking,
reading, and writing.

Focusing Your Topic

Choosing a topic is probably the most fun there is in writing, but it
may take work—candidates for the doctorate can spend years
looking for a topic—and it may take luck—white sharks and god-
fathers pop up from nowhere. But you shouldn't agonize over the

choice of topic. Any topic can be handled interestingly. The poet Cowper wrote an epic about a sofa. Hemingway wrote well on boring, silly topics—shooting big game, killing bulls, war.

You're part of the subject, and that's how you make it exciting. If you're bored, you'll be boring. If you've been assigned a topic, at least you're not responsible for choosing it. And there's no need to fret at having to write on a disagreeable topic; it's good discipline. Greek and Roman students were trained to write on both sides of a question: to praise baldness, suicide, and obedience to tyrants.

You might consider shying away from topics you have strong feelings about. Your feelings will show, and no one cares about them, except your mom, sometimes, and you're not writing for her. As a judge withdraws from a case in which he has an interest, writers should perhaps do the same. It's hard to write about AstroTurf and the designated hitter when you're foaming at the mouth.

Pick those topics you have your own ideas about, for nothing is more stimulating to the writer than the belief she's saying something for the first time, and nothing more discouraging than the feeling that all she can offer is a rehash. Writers plagiarize when their topics are too ambitious. Check whether you have the knowledge or experience to handle the topic. You wouldn't write about life on a commune without having been to one.

The narrower, more limited the topic, the easier the writing will be. To inexperienced writers this seems like nonsense, for they assume that the bigger the topic the easier the writing. But the work of writing does not lie in accumulating a certain heap of words or in thinking easy thoughts on big topics; the work lies in thinking of things for you to say, and whether you say anything depends on whether you can narrow a focus and put outside the focus the infinite number of things that might be said. *Everything* is a topic on which nothing can be said.

Inexperienced writers should not tackle grand, abstract topics like patriotism, education, punishment, equality, justice, freedom. It may be that these are the only subjects worth talking about, but you run risks in talking about what you don't know about. Big topics are the worst. General ideas—*loyalty, capitalism, God*—these are either boring or inflammatory.

For a five-hundred word article you'd work on a topic like Dinner at Chicago's Best Restaurant, for a thousand word article, a topic like Chicago's French Restaurants, and for a book, a topic like A Guide to Chicago's Restaurants. But focusing is not so easy when the topics loom. Asked to write on inflation or the French Revolution, you might very well feel threatened.

To narrow your focus on a topic, work right away on the question of tone, weighing what you can and would like to say with what the audience wants you to say. Do not think about a title. Wait until the writing is finished; titles are too important to be chosen quickly, and they must be accurate. (Since the audience wants to get the tone from the title or the first sentence or two, snappy titles and openings are not always appropriate.)

Your focus on the topic will remain unclear if you are thinking of the writing primarily as self-expression or as a study of the subject, and neglect what the audience wants. It's always tempting—and always a mistake—to forget about Them, who make the writing *work*. Thinking about any of the three separately—you, it, and them—wastes your time. In thinking about hot dogs, mull over what you can say about them and what the audience is willing to hear. You *could* go on for hours about hot dog facts and put everyone to sleep. You *could* deliver a jeremiad against hot dogs and infuriate all the hot dog lovers.

If you solve the problem of tone, you don't have to worry about the other nagging questions that writers are supposed to ask themselves, such as: What's my point? What's the big idea? Why am I telling them all this? Forget these questions. When you write, you don't have to have a single purpose or main idea or thesis. Ideas are for inventors, messages are for Western Union. Writing is discourse, or talking about a topic. If you want to talk, you just talk. You don't have to defend yourself, or say "I am now writing about the widget because people are not sufficiently aware. . . ." or "In this paper I intend to prove. . . ."

If the audience doesn't have to know the writer's purpose, the writer doesn't either. Did Shakespeare understand his purpose when he wrote *Hamlet?* The writer's purpose in discussing the topic need be nothing more than to discuss the topic. She doesn't have to *say* anything, but needs to hit the right tone. If she has something to say, she's in luck, because her job will probably be easier. It would be harder only if the audience doesn't want to hear what she wants to say—which happens. If the writer winds up saying nothing, but saying it with the right tone, she will be doing exactly what most writers have always done. You can write a wonderful piece on hot dogs without deciding what they are, what they should be, whether they taste good, whether people should eat them, whether you like them, etc.

The message in writing is often overvalued, because its presence is what distinguishes writing from the related arts of painting and music. But writing is primarily a formal art like the others, and a good writer is one who has done her lessons and learned the form. Audiences looking for *instruction* are hard to find. If your audience ever starts asking, "What's your point? Why are you telling me this?" they're doing so not because you have nothing to say, but because you don't know how to say nothing. You have no tone.

Thinking How to Do It

In any composition, the larger the part (word, sentence, paragraph, chapter, the whole) the more important it is, and the more important it is, the more attention it should get. When the unskilled writer hears the command *Write!* she immediately starts thinking of words and sentences and gives no thought to the paragraphs and the whole. Writing is done with words and sentences but it's not about them. It's about you, it, and the audience. What can you tell them about it? What do you want to tell them? What do they want to hear?

Sometimes the topic determines the tone. If you're speaking over a coffin or writing a dissertation you can't clown around much. Or the audience determines the tone. When the audience is all important and the topic is of no importance, the writing is called *academic*. When the writer's personality determines the tone the writing is *stylish*. Tone can be anything—ironic, deferential, lascivious. There's even the solemn tone of no tone, which for some reason is thought to be ideal for reporting the news.

As you decide on the tone, think about the *basic mode* of the piece. Is it going to be telling, describing, explaining, or arguing? Telling and describing are usually associated with fiction, explaining and arguing with nonfiction.

Telling can be narrative or dialogue, a report of what happened or what was said. Telling is the easiest kind of writing, for there's no problem in arranging the material; it's arranged according to time. But since telling is the easiest and commonest mode, it's the hardest to excel in. Most great literature is telling.

Describing is another easy kind of writing, a listing of impressions that does not attempt to go below the surface. The material is arranged from the large to the small, from the whole to the part, or from the general to the particular. Describing is thus a narrowing of focus, and is often anticlimactic in its effect. Straightforward description gets tedious quickly, and a writer usually tries to inject it with some dramatic interest or create a little excitement in moving from one part to another. Readers skip description, so writers can do it, too. Mark Twain once inserted into a description the words *a solitary esophagus winging its way into the sunset* and apparently no one noticed his little joke.

The danger in description is overwriting, trying to pump in excitement with modifiers and mere verbal emphasis. The poor writer turns to this because description focuses on the subject and prevents *her* from saying anything. The safe way to do description is calmly and briefly. A picture is worth a thousand words—of description—but no picture can tell a story, only an author can; telling is an event.

Explaining is more complicated. Explaining is presenting information, and interesting questions arise as to how the information can best be presented. It's usually arranged in one of the logical ways I'll get to in a minute.

Arguing is a special kind of explaining. Explaining and arguing often overlap; behind every exposition is an argument, in the sense of a point that the writer is trying to make. The word *argument* is used in two senses: as the design or purpose of a piece of writing, and as the attempt to persuade. The word is ordinarily used in this second sense and has bad connotations. *Don't argue with me. No arguments during dinner.* Because argument is disliked, the cleverest kind doesn't look or sound like argument.

The four modes of writing seldom appear in their pure form. Exposition pops up everywhere, in narrative, description, and argument. Narratives and descriptions can conceal hidden yet powerful arguments. If the modes are always getting mixed, why bother thinking about them? Because the less you mix up the modes, the better your chances of maintaining the tone. In going from mode to mode you confuse the reader. What are you up to? Are you describing, or are you telling a story? Are you explaining what happened, or saying it should never have happened? It's a poor tactic to interrupt a hot argument for a cold explanation, or slow down a narrative with description. Modes in writing, like modes in music, set up the proper responses in the audience and get results merely by being sustained. So when you tell, tell dramatically. When you describe, describe vividly. When you explain, explain carefully. When you argue, argue convincingly.

Do not decide too quickly on the *tone;* your stance towards your material may change as you work on it. A surprising benefit in writing is the way it forces us to change our minds; it's unlikely that we bring our full faculties to bear on any subject until we write about it.

As the nonfiction writer works towards finding the tone, so does the fiction writer grapple with the *point of view.* Should it be first person, third, or mixed? Should she be omniscient? Use a persona? Use a narrator? Have the same view as the protagonist's? Complicated questions of this kind arise, questions beyond the scope of this book, but solvable through experience.

Planning

There's a lot to do before you get to write—gathering ideas and pursuing them, focusing the topic, deciding on the tone, finding the facts, drawing up the plan. These are not separate steps and do not have to be done in order. The mind doesn't work that way. It spends time on one job, switches to another, then back again. I've talked about what has to be done as if there were separate steps in order to impress on you all the work that needs to be done before you go onstage to perform. Since ancient times, writers have complained that *invention,* or finding something to say, is the most difficult and the most important part of writing. But even when one has lots to say, a good way to say it is never easily arrived at. Organizing the material and drawing up the plan is the hardest part of writing and thus the part most often skipped.

Planning is hard enough without having to put the plan in the form of an outline. Most students have been asked to submit outlines that follow a form: a topic outline or a sentence outline. The sentence outline is the sillier, for how can you write sentences without knowing what's before or after them? Formal outlines have Roman and Arabic numerals, capital and small letters, and there has to be at least two of everything. It's hard enough to think in advance of what you're going to write without having to fool with alphabet-soup outlines. An outline belongs to you. Do it the way you want. See it as a friendly timesaver, not as something to turn in to the teacher for your punishment.

Those who complain they can't write don't have an outline. They don't lack things to say, but try to say everything at once. The point of an outline is to let you do all the things you want to do one by one in good order. You take an outline or shopping list to the store; if you're used to the store, you put the items on the list in a certain order.

There are different ways of ordering the items in an outline. The obvious way of proceeding when writing about events is to use *time* order. *Goldilocks fell asleep on the bed, and then* . . . .

The second obvious way of proceeding is to use *space* order. Things are described according to where they are in relation to other things. *In the first row sat the sleek professors. In the next row were the twitching instructors.*

Ordering the items logically is more complicated, usually carried out in one of four basic ways. You can use *examples. Women are naturally superior to men: they bear children, live longer, and do not lose their hair.* In giving examples—facts, figures, illustrations—you can assert something and then give examples of it, or use the more unusual and effective way of giving the examples first and then saying what they are examples of. Whatever you say that's disputable should be backed by examples.

Another logical way is to explain *cause and effect* relationships. You can talk of causes first and induce the effects, or talk about effects first and deduce the causes. The deductive way is preferred. People talk of causes first when they don't know the effects. *Bad people go to hell. If Vietnam goes, all of Southeast Asia will go.*

Another logical way is to *analyze,* or break the subject into its parts. *There are five kinds of ape: gorilla, chimpanzee, orangutang, gibbon, and man.* You can go from the whole to the parts or from the parts to the whole, as this book does.

The last way of proceeding is by *comparison.* Comparisons are risky, since no two things are exactly alike, so far as we know. They're only alike in certain respects. A remote comparison is an *analogy,* a close comparison is a *definition.* Comparisons are more prevalent in writing than is generally supposed, since definitions are comparisons. Overt and extended comparisons are tedious. Definitions are tedious. Implicit comparisons are better, and are unavoidable, if every common word, standing as it does for a class, involves comparisons. *Roy Cohn is a lawyer.* Here Cohn is being compared to other men called lawyers. Contrasts are easier to do than comparisons, but are even less interesting, since it goes without saying that things are different. This accounts for the weakness of negative statements: *Blank blank is not blink blink.* So?

Don't make your plan too elaborate or detailed. It should have a topic for each paragraph you're going to write. Paragraphs vary in size, remember: you can have an item in your plan that you may be able to handle in one sentence, or one that you'll want to extend through two or three paragraphs. The most helpful kind of plan is one that includes *ideas*, as jotted propositions or questions, rather than just *names* of topics. This gives you a clearer idea of how to develop the paragraph.

Here's a good sketch (all sketches, all notes, all outlines are good) for a quick piece on beer cans: billions of cans   colors   collectors   aluminum   pop-up rings   snap tops   litter   back to bottles   keeps colder. Here's a better sketch: see cans everywhere   billions   U.S. big garbage pit   some cans beautiful worth collecting   should be more collectors to pick them up   aluminum cans returnable   may be the answer but price for returns too low   pop-up rings dangerous   may swallow   snaptops spray you and break fingernails   are they improvement over rings?   Today's Beer Can!

In drawing up a plan try to use climactic order. People read what keeps them in suspense. Don't announce your purpose (readers might not like it). Keep your cards close to your vest or whatever. Don't think about opening or closing your work. These are easily added afterwards, if needed. Short compositions needn't open or close. In long compositions you may want some little formalities in getting underway and in concluding. Conclude only if there's something to conclude. Don't merely explain what you've done; don't apologize, don't sum up, don't repeat if you have no new ideas or insights to add. First impressions count, last impressions last.

Finding the Facts

By now you should feel confident you can handle any topic. You can discuss any topic merely by reflecting on it. But sometimes mere reflections will not satisfy your audience or you. You'll want to hunt down some facts, not because knowledge is an end in itself, as they say, but because you don't want to get caught making a mistake in a question of fact. A mistake in grammar is a misdemeanor, but for a mistake in fact you can be brought up on a felony charge.

You can't keep from making some mistakes. No one has a monopoly on truth, no one can check out everything that's supposed to be a fact. But you can steer away from embarrassing mistakes by offering as few facts as possible. (Facts by themselves, remember, quickly become boring.) And you shouldn't present as fact what you dimly remember or what you think really ought to be a fact. At least ninety-nine percent of the opinions in the world are thought to be facts, and that's a fact. Few writers are bold enough to invent their facts; they let their subconscious minds do it for them. Facts are so esteemed by the public that they are often imitated. The media are filled with pseudo-facts, which tip off their own falseness by sounding a little too precise. Consider these facts culled from the headlines: *Shakespeare had 190 IQ, study shows homos happier than heteros, cave has six and a half million bats, cat urine increases gas mileage, orgasm machine shows masturbation more satisfying than intercourse.* What sage was it who said there were no facts?

If you present something as a fact, that means you can back it up, that you have someone to blame the fact on if it turns out to be wrong. You don't have to check every fact. The facts you assert as your own experience are not going to be questioned. Facts that are commonly known are not going to be questioned. Facts that are not commonly known have to be checked. You can say that hot dogs are delicious or that they vary in size, color, and taste. But you can't say that Americans ate two billion hot dogs in 1986 unless you have someone to blame this statement on. You can say George Washington was the greatest American or that he was married to Martha. But you can't say he had a lot of girlfriends or that he was the richest man in the country, unless you can offer an authority to back you up. Whether you actually cite the authority depends on the tone of the piece.

Writing is superior to speaking in one important respect. It allows the writer time to check the facts. This makes for work, and the writer may have to find many more facts than she will actually use, as she explores the terrain around her subject. She wouldn't want to write that bees die after they sting, if bumblebees don't, or write that black slaves were materially better off than poor white farmers, if they weren't. Of course, she could go ahead and say these things. It's a free country. She can blow herself up skipping and hopping through a minefield of facts.

One way of making sure you have the facts is to apply the standard questions that reporters tack to their desks for reminders: Who, What, When, Where, How, and Why. Kipling wrote: "I keep six honest serving men, They taught me all I knew; Their names are What and Why and When and How and Where and Who." (It's interesting to see that in Kipling's day *Who* comes last, and in our day— the day of the Owl—*Who* comes first.) These six questions protect you from sins of omission and help you to grasp the scope of your topic. Which one will you emphasize—the Who, the What, the How?

Though you're now convinced of the preciousness of facts, you still may not know where they are. Chase them down in their hiding places through legwork in a library, and fingerwork on a telephone dial. Professional writers and researchers stay away from the library as much as they can and do their research over the phone. They know that those they call are surprisingly eager to offer information—everyone likes to be asked. So never be shy about phoning or asking. If you're writing about Japanese beetles, talk to the county agricultural agency—about marijuana, talk to your local police, about gun control, talk to the National Rifle Association, about women priests, talk to a local clergyman.

Of course not all research can be done over the phone; you may have to go to the library. Libraries have many dead ends and detours, so don't dash in and dash around. If your topic is narrow, technical, or of recent origin you had better check with the reference librarian to see where the materials can be found and whether your library has them. There are now a surprising number of guides to reference materials *according to subject*. Whether you ask the librarian for help should not depend on whether you're an extrovert, but on the nature of your topic.

Some people go straight to the card catalog. But since this catalog lists books, it's not much help. For almost any assignment, facts you require are to be found in reference works or periodicals, or they are hidden deep within books. Don't think of calling for a pile of books; get the *right* book or two and read just the right parts.

Orient yourself to your topic by reading about it in a general or special encyclopedia. Articles in the encyclopedia include bibliographies, or lists of relevant books and articles. The smaller the bibliography, the more useful it is. Encyclopedias are lovable since the information is compressed and since many articles are written by experts. What the encyclopedia knows, you don't have to.

In taking notes on what you read, keep these tips in mind. 1. Do no serious or deep research until you have a plan for the writing. Your plan may change as research proceeds, but if you don't start with a plan you'll waste time. 2. Write your notes on small cards. Make sure that each card somehow indicates the name of the book or the article you're using and the page you're on. By putting single ideas and single facts on separate cards you'll be able to move the cards around later on to help arrange your own argument. 3. Jot down facts, and put arguments in your own words. Paraphrase only good arguments you might use. 4. *Copy* only those statements that are *quotable*. A statement is quotable when it is extraordinary or wrong, when it comes from an authority, or when it expresses an idea so well you could not say it better.

Copy very little. You're taking notes: a note is only a note. When you run across something useful, decide right off whether to compress it into a few words or copy it out exactly and fully. Do paraphrases any way you want, and use lots of abbreviations. *Copying* has to be perfect, because if you ever quote what you've copied, fairness requires that the quote be full and exact. Don't forget to mark what you copy as being copied, since you don't want to plagiarize, accidentally or on purpose, for that's a choice between being a boob or a crook.

Writing

It's easy to talk about the steps that lead to writing, but the writing itself, that's a mystery. You just do it. When you learned to talk, you had to learn it all by yourself, and you must do the same with writing. In learning to talk you prepared for it by listening to others for a year or two before you could do it, and in learning to write you have to prepare for it by many years of reading. If you haven't read much, or haven't read closely, you will find writing a torture—not because you have nothing to say, but because you're not used to the mere mechanics of writing. All the composition courses, drillbooks, and cute teachers in the world cannot turn nonreaders into writers. If you can't write without frequent mistakes, you have to catch up on reading.

After that, learn writing by doing. Write anything—tirades, nonsense, letters, reviews, harangues, prayers, abuse, stories, poems, bawdy pieces—anything that comes easy. The hand has to get used to writing, has to take over the mechanics—spelling, punctuating, paragraphing. Anyone can make sounds on a piano and anyone who can talk can write something, but with practice anyone can make agreeable sounds on a piano or learn to write agreeably. To make beautiful music or write beautiful prose, of course, requires a gift. Some writers lack the necessary feeling for sentences, and are said to have a tin ear, like unmusical people.

But many unmusical people learn to listen better, and many poor writers learn to listen to what they write.

Like a pianist, a writer will lose her place from time to time. When this happens to you, talk to yourself, focus on what you've just put down, try to make the idea clearer by saying what it is. That you have a subject means you felt a predicate nearby. If no respectable predicate steps forward, move on and work on something else in the meantime. If an idea refuses to come clear, it may very well turn out to be an unclear idea.

Famous writers are always being asked how they write, and they can only say such things as: I crank myself up at dawn, I write on a portable down in the basement, I scribble on cards and then on pads, I turn purple. Obviously, they don't quite know what goes on. Their hands seem to know what to do. There's no best time or best way or even good way to write. Dr. Johnson said: "A man may write at any time, if he will set himself doggedly to it." You may have to do that. If you sit there long enough glaring at your notes or outline, you'll get bored and then start to write. Glare at the outline then, and start to fill in what's missing. Writing is only a matter of turning scratch notes and outline into a hasty draft. In this draft use abbreviations and initials to maintain speed. Don't expect the draft to be good. And don't write with a pencil; the smell of cedar is intoxicating.

If you can't think how to begin, for goodness sake, don't begin at the beginning. The importance of the beginning is overrated. Some teachers of writing make students throw away their first paragraph or first page or first chapter. In writing it's the middle that counts. Begin to write the part most interesting to you, for that will be the easiest. Just as the choice of the title is the final touch, the writing of the beginning and the ending should be the next to final touches. Besides, you have to know what's in the middle before you can do a proper beginning and ending. A redeeming feature of writing is that you can do any part of it at any time (before your deadline). As Dr. Johnson said: "Sir, it is no matter what you teach them first any more than what leg you shall put into your breeches first. Sir, you may stand disputing which is best to put in first, but in the meantime your breech is bare."

The fact that writing can be done anytime is not always a blessing. If the writer postpones the work, she'll feel guilty. Or she may work too long and hard, striving for the unattainable goals of accuracy and eloquence. In either case she'll learn to hate to write. The best way to write is to do it, get it over with, turn it in. Many people write better under time pressure in class or at work than when they are at home.

The idea is to write urgently but not frantically. Writing that comes fast is never as good as it seems and needs a lot of revising. Writing that comes slow lacks natural flow and spoken tone. If the writing doesn't come, stay where you are and keep struggling with it. Something will get done. It won't be easier tomorrow. You needn't be in a receptive mood to write, though you have to be in a receptive or creative mood to find new ideas or make breakthroughs in problems. The writing is not so much a matter of finding ideas as of revealing ideas already found. A writer's mind is like an udder: it fills up and is then milked. Milking is a relief. It only hurts on a dry udder.

Blocks are a big problem for those who write for a living, but amateur writers seldom have trouble with production. Their problem is finding readers. If they are dedicated, they will keep at their art, just like actors, painters, and musicians. Practice has its own rewards. And practice is the way to get to Random House as well as Carnegie Hall. Not to mention having a gift and being lucky.

Creative Writing

Whatever kind of writing you do—letters, reports, briefs, memos, or sonnets—the *basic* problems of expressing yourself are the same—finding the point of view and the tone, planning the whole, choosing the right language, hammering out decent sentences. With the basics mastered, you're ready to write anything.

Those who turn to creative writing (narrative, dialogue, and verse) suffer from a vivid imagination and a strong need to make something of their own. Everyone has some imagination and the desire to create. Everyone wants to talk, everyone wants to write. The writer is one who keeps on writing until people listen. You can tell you're a writer if you like to write though you know how hard it is (Thomas Mann said the writer is one who finds writing more difficult than others), if you get excited when you read certain passages and think them beautiful, and if you find yourself frequently composing—framing consecutive sentences and hearing people talk inside your head. While ordinary people hear notes and words, musicians listen to music, and writers, to sentences.

Though *writers* are born and not made, there's no problem in teaching anyone who knows the rudiments of writing how to be competent in a particular kind of writing. Nearly all that is written is done within a strict form—the short story, the three-act play, the textbook, the editorial. The requirements of form can be taught by a master and learned by an apprentice. Tuition is needed, not intuition. If creative means original, creative writing has to be the hardest kind. When there are no models to follow, writing is excruciating. But there are models for whatever you want to write, and you should read aloud and copy these models.

You shouldn't think that because you are creative you have to avoid the established forms. When a form is strict, it's because the product is in demand. Chase after the Great American Novel and you may never be heard from again. Instead of writing verse that no one wants because it's free, keep your job at the bank and write me some good letters for a change. Some traditional markets are languishing—stories, verse, drama—but the market for books and screenplays is booming. Of course, when a writer is really good, she can be overwhelmingly good, creating new forms. Works of art are judged—at least by the wiser judges—according to their merits rather than their formal shortcomings.

Revising

The word *revision* originally meant *taking a second look*. Now it means *changing* or *improving*. Evidently there's no difference between taking another look and wanting to fix up what you see. What if you like what you see? You may like parts, but no writer ever likes the whole thing. All writers revise, and are constantly being drawn back to the scene of their crimes. A few lucky writers are experienced enough to make revisions as they go along, as each sentence is being put down. Since inexperienced writers have to make numerous and painful revisions they should lay their hands on word processors. Professionals use them too, and are sometimes embarrassed to admit how infatuated they are with them.

All writing is rewriting. Revision only extends the criticism brought to bear during the writing into the period after the writing. Each sentence as it is put down represents a triumph over its competition. The triumph is always temporary, the number of competitors is infinite, and a bigger, faster, meaner sentence can come along at any time.

That figure of speech was intended to remind you that revision is a nasty business. You are not supposed to like what you see; you're supposed to attack it. If you create on Monday, on Tuesday you're still fond of your accomplishments. If you look at the stuff next Monday, you'll see it more clearly. The longer the time between first and second draft, the better the second draft will be. This draft, with polishing, you may be able to tolerate. If the second draft fails to come clear or provide satisfaction, there's something wrong with the plan: you'll have to devise a new plan and rewrite the whole piece. Though you will always feel that more revision is needed, if you revise too much you get far away from the original flow. Certain writers, like Conrad, revised too much, and made their prose stiff and careful.

Revision time is subtraction time. You probably have said far too much already. Trying to amplify now is like starting all over again. Confucius says, "If one word does not succeed, ten thousand are of no avail." Force, drama, excitement come from the Idea, the Story, and not from touching up the sentences. If you habitually add and add at revision time, that means you should spend more time on planning.

If you add, you may jam up the flow. If you paint and polish, you'll get a surface that's too shiny. Let's say you've written: *I always like to say that golf is a good way to ruin a good walk.* In revising you cut lazy modifiers, so you cut *good* from *good walk.* You're not writing for Mom, so you cut *I always like to say* and just say: *Golf is a good way to ruin a walk.* You hope to jazz this up, so you write *Golf is a great way,* and then change that to *Golf is the best way to ruin a walk.* Maybe you want to drop a name and attribute the saying to a wit, so you write: *Golf, as Schlomo Pinkus says, is the best way to ruin a walk.* Where does all this get you? You seldom improve writing by adding and polishing. You improve it by stripping. *Golf is a good way to ruin a walk.* That's the way to say it. In revising, Kipling used a brush to block out words, and never touched a pen.

You can pick away at your writing like a slave in a jute mill, but the idea is to get it down quickly and leave it pretty much alone. The temptation to add and polish leads to overwriting. In overwriting the writer is obviously struggling. All beginning writers of any promise overwrite, since they do try hard, they know they are writers, they have something to say, they press their argument, they enliven their diction. But they must cool off. The secret of commercial success is very often *under*writing—bland, smooth, a comforting drone that doesn't even try to say anything. If you're providing two hundred pages of copy every day for the *Times (Los Angeles* or *New York)*, you had better master underwriting.

When you revise, you apply what you know about good diction and good sentences and paragraphs. In final proofreading you work on little details; in revising you look at the parts in relation to the whole. Big revisions are made first, since that can relieve many smaller problems. If you feel that parts are not in the best place, drop your pencil and pick up the scissors. Cut the composition into paragraphs or sentence groups and shuffle these around until you come up with a better arrangement. Or draw arrows showing what goes better where. If you don't need the scissors, keep working with the pencil, repairing mistakes, crossing out and changing words, recasting bad constructions. Anything that causes a lot of trouble has to go, has to be completely redone, or has to go away and stay away. The writer's best friend is the wastebasket.

Sometimes you'll run across a bit you can't bear to let go. When that happens ask yourself why you're defending it. The more you fight, the more suspicious it is. You want to keep it because it's unusual, it's personal, it's you. But that's probably why the audience won't like it. We seek praise for what we're *not* good at. "Murder your darlings," a Cambridge professor told his students. The runts in the litter have to go. I could have written several books with the adorable sentences I couldn't fit into this one.

When you revise, ask yourself these questions. Was the main idea clear, or does it need more emphasis here and there? (Often the main idea is not just clear, but belabored.) Have I used enough examples and illustrations to be persuasive? Have I given the audience too much credit or too little? Have I gone too fast or too slow? Is this paragraph necessary? Is this sentence necessary? And ask the most telling question of all: How would I like somebody to tell me what I just said?

Be sure to look for your kind of fault. Everyone has faults in personal style, since no one—hardly anyone—is a perfect person. Timid writers are wordy, write unemphatic sentences, resort to the passive voice. Those for whom things are simple write too simply, without qualifying and without persuading. Four-flushers send up clouds of smoke. Professors spend a lot of time clearing their throats. Whatever faults are in you will be discovered in your writing (which is a good reason to write).

Writers should face, but often ignore, the question of seeking and heeding editorial assistance. They are a proud lot and don't like to be helped. A writer should seek whatever help she can get. She's not required to accept it, but she'd be foolish not to listen. Collaboration and editing often result in improvements. Shakespeare probably accepted assistance with his plays, since plays are subjected to a lot of revision. Writing done by committees is supposed to be terrible, but committees have produced the Bible, the King James translation, the Constitution of the United States, and the Communist Manifesto. Homer's work is the final version of the efforts of many poets.

To be interesting, writing must be personal. Revising and editing, oddly enough, usually make writing less personal yet better. The good editor helps the writer to express herself. Elbert Hubbard described an editor as someone who separates the wheat from the chaff and publishes the chaff. Only a writer could say something so nasty, so untrue, so enjoyable.

Condensing

Condensing or tightening writing is only cosmetic surgery, but can make the difference between beauty and ugliness. Let's have more of it. Writers don't cut enough because they love the words they worked so hard to find. If they cut too much, they have to make up the losses. But cutting is so easy it makes editorial work more fun than writing: growing things takes sweat and patience, cutting things down is a kick.

When you condense you may be shocked at how much you can get rid of. Paragraphs can be reduced to sentences, sentences to clauses, clauses to phrases, phrases to words, and words can be thrown away. What's left? Only what's alive. Prose should be lean and muscular, though not be so compact it's unnatural, so muscle bound it can't move. Boiling writing down can be carried too far, and what's left can lose its flavor like the prose in condensed books. But doing too much cutting is seldom a danger. Skinny sentences are hardly so common as fat.

Sentences should breathe, have a certain ardency or glow. Occasionally a writer wants a fat, sleepy sentence to make a weak statement. Here's a hippo of a sentence from the Republican Party Platform of 1976: *The Republican Party favors a continuance of the public dialogue on abortion and supports the efforts of those who seek enactment of a constitutional amendment to restore protection of the right to life for unborn children.* This sentence might have been expressed: *The party favors the discussion of abortion and supports the efforts of those who support an amendment to restore protection of the right to life for unborn children.* The original sentence is unclearly vague, the revised sentence is clearly vague. The trick in being vague is to be vaguely vague, that is, don't get caught. Being obscure and evasive is more frequently called for in writing than teachers like to think. An awful lot of writers constitutionally take the fifth. But if you write this way, don't do it inadvertently, because you might start to believe in it. Too often, flabby, sniveling sentences are not written intentionally but because the words poured out too fast. Pascal once wrote to a friend that he would have written a shorter letter but didn't have time. Serious revision takes lots of time. Condensing takes little time, and becomes second nature with a bit of practice. Let's practice.

Combining sentences may spare a few words and always spares the reader the period pauses. It's easy to combine sentences that have the same subject. *Carol is strong. She can throw the ball as hard as a man. She's the best pitcher in the league.* Revised: *Carol throws the ball as hard as a man and is the best pitcher in the league.* Another: *First the car was serviced. Then it was washed and waxed.* Revised: *The car was serviced, washed, and waxed.* You can put several verbs into a sentence. You can turn sentences into clauses. *We hope that you will come on the sixth. It's Bob's birthday. He will be twenty-three years old.* Revised: *We hope you'll come on the sixth, which is Bob's twenty-third birthday.*

After hearing me praise the subordinate clause, you may be surprised to hear me recommend that you change many subordinate clauses to phrases. Change the ones in which the verb isn't forceful. Most clauses that start *who is, which is,* and *that is* should be changed to phrases.

Bob, who is presently a salesman, dreams of being a rock star.

Bob, a salesman, dreams of being a rock star.

Napoleon, who had just become Emperor, married Josephine.

On becoming Emperor, Napoleon married Josephine.

He told me a story that was scarcely believable.

He told me a scarcely believable story.

When the subordinate clause has the same subject as the main clause, it can be shortened.

> After Bob bathed the dog, he got ready for the guests.
> After bathing the dog, Bob got ready for the guests.
>
> When I was a young girl, I did countless foolish things.
> When young I did countless foolish things.
>
> Carol took the train because she wanted to be there early.
> Carol took the train to be there early.

Many clauses and phrases can be reduced to single words.

> Because the tires were overinflated, the ride was bumpy.
> Overinflated tires made the ride bumpy.
>
> We sat out under a sky that was filled with stars.
> We sat out under the star-filled sky.
>
> In order to write better you will have to write more.
> To write better, write more.
>
> The dress was too hot for her to wear in the summertime.
> The dress was too hot for summer.

Certain words should ring alarms in your mind, alerting you to flab. Slow, roundabout phrases (*there is, that is, it is, it's a fact that, for your information*) should be reduced or left out. *It is easy to lose, Losing is easy. There is a bright future for us, Our future is bright.* Try not to use *thing*. It's often accompanied by some description of what the thing is. *You silly thing, You're silly.* Sentences with the phrase *and that's why* or *the reason is that* should be turned around. *He loves her and that's why he gave up hot dogs, He gave up hot dogs because he loves her.*

The alarm words *kind of* and *sort of* can usually be omitted. *This kind of perfume smells good, This perfume smells good.* You don't need to say *in the world* because that's where things are. *This is the best lesson in the world, This is the best lesson.* You seldom need to say *today*—just use the present tense. *Some* and *any* should always sound alarms. *There are some risks involved, Risks are involved. Yes, we don't have any bananas, Yes, we have no bananas. It was done without any fuss, It was done without fuss.*

The articles *the, a* and *an* can often be omitted. *The segregation of the men and the women, Segregation of men and women. The waiting time has been cut, Waiting time has been cut. Bring a lunch, Bring lunch.* If you say *one of,* readers wonder about the others. *Nietzsche was one of those crackpots. . . .* And the others?

Check for unnecessary negative statements. Lionel Trilling: *Freud has no desire to encroach on the artist's autonomy.* Whoever said that he did? The double-negative device called *litotes* is limp: *He treated me not unkindly, He treated me well. This page is not without humor, This page sparkles.* Avoid the *negative-if* clause so beloved by academics: *If it does not blah blah, then it does blah blah.*

Take out lazy adjectives and adverbs. *True facts:* strike *true. Serious problem:* strike *serious. Deeply moved:* strike *deeply.* You'll recall from the diction chapter how common wordiness is, and how much the writing is improved when it's cut. Quaint redundancies can help set an Informal tone, but in Formal a single redundancy can sink you: *In terms of sheer size, Canada is the second largest country in the whole wide world.*

Now you have your turn. I know you're dying to; it's fun to be mean. Hack away at this sentence. *On the table there were a great number of dolls that had been made by hand.* Did you cut that to *On the table were many handmade dolls?* Another. *The farmers here grow the apples which are used mainly for the juice.* Did you get rid of the farmers and say *Apples are grown here mainly for juice?* Do the rest of these yourself.

> I like the kind of a cat that has curly whiskers.
>
> He spoke to his audience in a boring manner and went on without any conscious awareness as to how his audience was responding.
>
> Even though there is a lack of water, I'll water my grass which is dry anyway.
>
> It is the most serious drought in twenty years that is affecting farming in Iowa.
>
> Perhaps the main cause to be deduced for the rebellion was that the people were beginning to not get enough to eat.

When you write a sentence like this last one—it happens—don't tinker with it. Scrap it and try to express the idea simply. If you don't like the idea when it's expressed simply, scrap it. Somewhere, somehow, there's much more to say. If the words fall short of the number you have to produce, go back, get more ideas by thinking widely or deeply, and plenty of words will come.

Proofreading

Sooner or later you will have to submit your work. Proofreading is the last desperate scrutiny of your manuscript before you hand it over for your reward or punishment. The circumstances of proofreading are scary, the work to be done is minute and at times upsetting. No wonder it's done poorly. Few people proofread their letters, and few students proofread their exams. But proofreading catches mistakes, and nothing should leave your hands with even one mistake. Reading maketh the full man, conference the ready man, and writing the *exact* man.

The majority of mistakes—these are in diction, spelling, grammar, and punctuation—result from carelessness and not ignorance. This carelessness is redoubled when the mistakes are not caught by proofreading. So what is worse—being ignorant of the correct form or forgetting on *two* occasions to use it? Those who are offended by mistakes don't care whether the mistakes result from stupidity or from laziness. In either case, you lose, and they win.

Once you're used to proofreading it's not so scary, but routine and maybe even enjoyable. A copy editor or composition teacher catches mistakes the way an anteater catches ants. Here's how to find the ants in your writing.

First, check the form. Do you have the right margins and spacing? Then check the title and opening. Do they set the tone? Is the title accurate?

Now comes the trick of proofreading, a trick requiring you to do two things at once, like rubbing your belly and patting your head. You have to coordinate looking and listening. Novices listen too much and look too little, tired proofreaders look too much and listen too little. Unless you have been proofreading all your life, you must do it out loud. Reading aloud catches ugly constructions and faulty spelling and punctuation. Reading *aloud slowly* is the only fast way to check spelling and the word division at the end of lines. You can't look up all the words in the dictionary. You can't analyze the grammar in every sentence to check the punctuation. Misplaced words can only be caught by reading aloud, since the ear is the test for these.

This is how to proofread. Read the manuscript twice, aloud and with feeling. If you're some place where you can't read aloud, read softly while moving your tongue and lips. Pause at the end of each sentence to listen to what you heard. If everything sounds OK, move to the next sentence. Stumbling while reading shows where repairs are needed.

After rereading the manuscript, reflect on it and decide whether to do it over. You've already revised once or twice, but maybe you've thought of improvements that justify rewriting the whole piece. In deciding, recall that the planning, rather than the actual writing, was the hard part. Writing goes fast. Planning and proofreading go slow.

Finally, hand the paper in, send the memo, sign the letter, sigh with relief. Maybe pray for mercy. People will be merciful if you haven't made mistakes. Generally, writing just has to look right. Lying, misleading, and plagiarizing may pass; mistakes don't.

No one much likes to submit writing. They feel it does not do them justice, or it does. In either case they must step to the bar. Whoever heard of a proud writer? Writers seem to miss the satisfactions that other artists enjoy. Shakespeare never published. If he was disappointed imagine how I feel. Don't expect too much.

Chapter Seven

Persuading

Writing Is Persuasive

We speak for the same reasons a baby cries: I am! I want! It's surprising, in view of the basic purpose of language, that we so often use it without having the foggiest notion of what we're after, and so often lapse into talking to ourselves—badly. Chances of getting what we want must improve when we know what it is. The writer should know what she's after. If it's money, attention, respect, or mastery of a certain form, then that should be her aim. Instead of thinking What can I say? she should first think What do I *want?* Whom do I wish to persuade of what?

The *general aim* of expression is the general aim of life: to be praised. Casanova wrote: "I expect the friendship, the esteem, and the gratitude of my readers." All writers long for such praise, and the fear of not getting it makes them clam up. Even when they're misleading or manipulating an audience they're still looking for praise in some form for doing a bad job well. Writing can have any number of *special aims:* to inform, analyze, amuse, enrage, flatter, brag, unite, warn, sell, deceive, seduce, convert. The writer does not have to let anyone know what she's aiming at, but to do a good job she ought to know herself. Writing has a moral benefit for the writer if it prompts her to think about her motives.

The art of doing a praiseworthy job and getting what you want is the art of persuasion, called rhetoric. Expression always includes this element of persuasion. When you calm a child, you're persuading her to stop crying. When newspaper editors arrange the front page, they're persuading others that this is the important news and that it can be arranged in order of importance. When you send a letter without erasures you're persuading others of your efficiency. To do business is to persuade.

Whether the persuasive aim is overt or hidden, standard devices of persuasion are used. These devices work because they please, enabling you to get what you want from the audience by giving them what they want. Persuasion involves a contract with the audience; something is expected from each party. Writers do not become good persuaders if they resent having to adjust themselves to the audience. The writer needn't try to please everyone like a whore, but should try to please someone besides herself. Grabbing the mike is not enough: if you don't coo or yell or drone the way you're supposed to, the audience may not listen.

The audience expects to be persuaded. They know the writer wants something, and thus they resent being confused about her intentions. They want her to show she needs them. Her job is to know what she needs and go after it. She doesn't announce her purpose, but indicates it through tone.

She needs something to argue. This may seem odd, because when people are at home they don't like an argument—*You should take an umbrella, You should have another piece of pie.* But they accept it from strangers, for they know that the persuasion will be well mannered and can be ignored. They don't just want exposition, don't just want to be told, they want to be asked. No matter how much straightforward exposition a writer has to present, it will be presented better if it has an argumentative edge. An encyclopedia article on, say, horseshoe crabs will be more readable if the writer conveys her impression that these creatures are extraordinary. In Formal, the writer is usually expected to pull a disappearing act, so the audience can concentrate on the subject, but this disappearance should only be an illusion.

Publishers are often mistaken in thinking that audiences want news and facts and other forms of pap. By not offering ideas, issues, and values they lose readers, as Hollywood lost its adult audience in the forties. A personal attitude toward the subject gets the audience to listen. Turn to the editorial page of your newspaper and compare the editorials with the letters to the editor. The letters are readable because they are written by real people with axes to grind. So when you express yourself, sound like a person who wants to say what she's saying.

Readers may look at stuff, but if it has no voice they won't listen to it. No voice, no style, no reader, just print, and lots of trees cut down for nothing. Writing for the masses loses its voice as it's homogenized, deodorized, and flavorized by a gang of market experts, and the product is like a salty, sugary, imitation barbecue-flavored, imitation potato chip. Never think you're feeding your audience; assume you're talking to them and they can talk back. Don't tell them anything you wouldn't like to hear. Holden Caulfield always knew a book was good when it made him want to call the writer up.

What's Wrong with Rhetoric?

Persuasion is used for bad ends as well as good. Lawyers lie and win cases, politicians lie and win elections, advertisers lie and make bags of money, parents lie to children, the sexes lie to one another. Many thinkers have observed that we have language in order to protect ourselves from the truth and to permit us to lie. Faulkner liked to say that writers were too busy to know whether they were lying or stealing.

Then what can be said about the role of truth in persuasion? Is a good speech, a good ad, or a good argument the one that succeeds, or the one that tells the truth? Should those who teach rhetoric tell their students not to lie, or tell them the truth about lying? That's a good question, because I don't know. One may get to heaven by honoring the truth but fall short of Madison Avenue or Capitol Hill. It seems to me that much can be said in favor of lying and a little can be said against it. But I won't go into the arguments for and against. Who am I to encourage people to lie? Nowadays no one seems to need lessons. If they receive, as it is said they do, a thousand advertising messages a day, they soon learn for themselves how to hit others where they live.

In these pages I've praised rhetoric of the better sort—language that is simple and direct—so I can't contradict myself now and start praising the other kinds. But my kind of language is not always rewarded, not even in the schools, much less in society. The language that persuades and is rewarded is often unclear, pretentious, or deceptive. There is so much fraud that the term *rhetoric*, like *propaganda* before it, has become a term of abuse. But one should not distrust rhetoric, one should master it, since it's not about to go away. To say that a certain speech is only *a lot of rhetoric* is itself the use of an unsubtle rhetorical device, name calling.

Rhetorical devices are plentiful, and they're all good, as devices, if they work. As the Chinese say, "Black cat, white cat, catch mice, good cat." From one point of view, *equivocation,* or twisting the meanings of words, is diabolical, and from another point of view, comical: *Kentucky—where the corn is full of kernels and the colonels are full of corn.*

Rhetoric at the highest moral level, where the speaker respects herself, the audience, and the truth, is far above rhetoric at the lowest level, where audiences are pandered to and manipulated through their fears and desires. But whatever the level, rhetoric is always rhetoric, always impure, never completely truthful. There cannot be a perfect speaker or perfect audience. Any speaker who claims she's leveling with you is one to distrust. Any statement making a special claim to be true has to be dubious. No one says *Truly, two and two are four,* they say *Truly, women are far more interesting than men.* One of the most effective and time-honored devices of rhetoric is a lie: saying what you're not going to do and then going on to do it. *I come to bury Caesar, not to praise him.*

Despite its shortcomings, rhetoric should be treated with respect and should be learned because the alternative to it is force. Those who refuse to persuade or to listen to persuasion fall back on power, and power, as we know, comes out of the end of a gun. Rhetoric takes the place of guns among the weak and gentle, and that includes a lot of people.

Another reason rhetoric is good to have around is that having to persuade others helps to make persuaders less self centered and more aware of other minds. Expression always requires some subjecting of one's own personality to what is common and impersonal. Though persuasion may have selfish ends, it cannot be done in a selfish way. In ancient times it was claimed that only a good person could be good at rhetoric, because she would have to forget about herself both in speaking for the audience and in swaying them through reasoning.

Mastering the tricks and strategies of rhetoric is not necessarily corrupting, and it's usually beneficial. You don't need to know much about rhetoric to sell mouthwash or militarism. Subtle rhetoricians are hardly so dangerous a threat as the ignorant and the innocent. To become skilled in rhetoric one must learn to think like others, and this takes sympathy and imagination. From time to time persuasion calls for both speaker and audience to forget personal interest and pursue an argument wherever it may lead. An audience is a blessing in that it prevents the speaker from being herself. One's thoughts are free, of course, which means they are worth nothing. Only an audience gives them value. Dr. Johnson said, "No sir, a man has not a right to think as he pleases; he should inform himself and think justly." The only way to find out if you're thinking justly is to see how others respond to what you say.

What Is Arguable

In presenting a topic, the writer begins her argument that the topic is worth discussing. The experienced writer knows that the audience really wants an argument. She also knows that they do not want controversy or contention, and suppresses whatever urge she may have to sock it to them. Arguments have to be slipped across. The audience thinks they already have the arguments. They have so many they can give you some.

For practice in preparing arguments I'll now offer you some propositions you might want to work with. Decide whether to argue for or against, and see if you can find at least three or four points to support your views. (In thinking of arguments, gather wild and free thoughts, ask the reporter's questions, and cross-examine yourself.) Try a few of these easy propositions.

> Dogs are better than cats.
> If one is old enough to fight, he's old enough to drink and vote.
> No one should make more than two hundred thousand dollars a year.
> If everyone is equal, everyone should be allowed to have a machine gun.
> The hand that rocks the cradle rules the world.
> Every girl should have a pony.

That exercise was hard to do in your head, and I wonder if you were clever enough to jot your ideas down and try to sort them out. Ideas come and go fast, and you want to catch them on paper. But the point of the exercise was not to remind you to make notes. The point was to think about which side of the proposition you chose to support. You probably chose to argue that dogs are better than cats if you have a dog. If you make a lot of money or intend to, you probably chose to argue that high incomes can be justified. I suspect you did not argue any proposition you did not *immediately* like. Our minds are quick: when they are not already made up on a question, we quickly make them up. We can always change our minds, of course.

Resume the exercise. This time try to find arguments on the other, or unsympathetic, side of the case. Once you've done this, ask yourself which had the better arguments—the side you favored or the other side. You probably still came up with better arguments for your side. Did you have trouble finding arguments on the other side?

Now consider whether knowing some arguments on the other side will not help you argue your own case better. In thinking of arguments against your case you'll be prompted to find answers to them. An argument is effective only insofar as it answers a counterargument. What goes without saying does not have to be said. Good arguments only appear when the counterarguments are strong. Only a dubious proposition is arguable.

For thousands of years writers have been trained in persuasion by having to argue both sides of a case. and this is still the best training. In the Middle Ages, philosophers had to draw up thorough arguments in *Sic et non* (yes and no) form. Debaters today do not always know what side of a case they will have to present. When a lawyer prepares a case, he prepares not only his but his opponent's as well, for he can't risk being surprised by a good argument from the other side.

This willingness to grapple with both sides of a question strikes many who aren't used to it as artificial and hypocritical. They see it as unprincipled sophistry, as ignoring right and wrong. They fear that the habit of weighing both sides leads to liberalism and skepticism, undermining value, doctrine, and authority. They're right. That's what happens when people habitually consider both sides of a question. The open mind is messy, mixed up, and quite often useless. In an open mind, so many ideas are welcomed that pretty soon the place resembles the Marx Brothers' famous stateroom.

What happens when you draw up arguments for the other side and find them convincing? Should you change your mind? You don't have to. Anyone can persist in thinking and acting the way she wants even when she knows she's wrong. You can make two hundred thousand a year and think it's wrong, cheat on your spouse and think it's wrong, take the Hippocratic oath and perform radical cashectomies. But doing this may hurt your self respect, which may hurt your confidence. Good arguments haunt you.

Fortunately, no one can always tell good arguments from bad. Many more questions are arguable than we like to think. Most propositions, and *all* propositions involving the idea *should*, are reasonable enough to argue, however unreasonable they may be under the All-Seeing Eye. How about these common assertions? *Capital punishment is necessary. Marriage is finished. The German people are guilty. God is dead. Intermarriage is the only answer.* Those who can instantaneously tell a reasonable proposition from an unreasonable one outnumber those who can't, but they're probably overconfident.

Preparing an Argument

The struggle between ideas can be so fierce it makes people shut their eyes and ears. But to argue well you must look and listen. One is either afraid of the struggle or not. The First Amendment protects us from those who are afraid to watch ideas mix it up.

When writing, you talk to yourself and cross-examine yourself, and when preparing an argument you do the same, but more fiercely. A good way is to pretend you are your opponent—it takes two to tango. Let's say you strongly believe the following is correct, but someone is going to make you argue it: *Since rich women can afford abortions, the government should provide abortions for poor women.* What you want to do is get a piece of paper and sketch a dialogue, such as this.

Con: Well, rich women afford many things poor women can't afford.

Pro: Well yourself. Abortions are special. They're not like other purchases. They're health care, which is provided for the poor.

Con: They're special all right. They're murder.

Pro: We're not arguing about abortion, we're arguing about whether poor women can get them.

Con: Let them save for it like me. I save money.

Pro: They can't. They can't save twenty dollars, much less two hundred.

Con: How do *you* know?

Pro: I guess I don't. I imagine a few of them might be able to save enough, but not many. But why should rich women get abortions and only a few of the poor?

Con: Life is unfair. Why should government pay for abortions?

Pro: Who else?

Con: Get the private sector to pay.

Pro: How?

Con: Persuade them.

Pro: If they don't?

Con: Ask local government.

Pro: They won't; they're afraid of the voters.

Con: Then ask the federal government to do it. They have ways of bypassing the voters. But you won't get Congress to vote to pay for abortions.

Pro: We women will make it hot for them.

Con: You good at making things hot?

Pro: They say women are. I'm learning.

Once you get a dialogue of this sort going, you'll soon collect enough material to work into an argument. Dialogues like this are easier than you think and require little imagination. People do not think them out and they argue badly because they prefer to simply state what they believe, repeat it, yell it, try to force it down someone's throat. Argument is much more often self-assertive and self-defeating than a genuine attempt to reach agreement.

In preparing an argument, remember that there may be many views of an issue, not just yours and your opponent's. During the Cuban missile crisis, John Kennedy asked his brother Bobby to play devil's advocate and present the argument against bombing Cuba. His argument won: it would not look right for the big U.S. to surprise bomb little Cuba. In the deliberations no one pointed out that the Cubans might not like being bombed; no one presented the Cuban point of view. So remember in arguments to include the simpleton's point of view as well as God's and the devil's.

In preparing an argument, try to think of as many ideas and points as are relevant, even though only a few will appear in the argument itself. And it's good strategy to make several points, even when only one of them is crucial. A repetitious argument is suspected to be weak. If an argument, like a chain, is no stronger than its weakest part, no point you make should be weak. One fat generalization can ruin an argument: *All animals are sad after sex.* Several unsupported assertions in a row turn an audience off. Protesting too much is common: *And thus I have proved that my client does not own a dog, that if she did own a dog it did not bite Mrs. Jones, and lastly, that Mrs. Jones was never bitten by a dog.*

In selecting your arguments, pretend that your clever and cruel opponent will put everything you say under a microscope. You must find the flaws before he does. In logic, as in grammar, *pinpoint* the mistakes even if you don't know what to call them. *Exactly* where do the following arguments go wrong?

> My parents believed in Quetzalcoatl, which is why I do.
>
> If people believe that it's possible for a person to be right, then there is such a thing as being right.
>
> Stale potato chips are better than nothing. Nothing is better than ice cream. Therefore, stale potato chips are a lot better than ice cream.
>
> The wish is psychologically equivalent to the act.
>
> Abortion is a form of killing engaged in to evade the consequences of sex.
>
> The decision to go into Nicaragua was morally right but prudentially wrong.
>
> The point of sexual reproduction is to replace yourself with a superior creature. Religion tells us that all individuals are equally valuable. Therefore, sex is pointless.

How to Win an Argument

Anything a persuader says or writes that turns out to be untrue wrecks her case. Let's say you're ready to buy an old desk at a garage sale. The seller claims it's maple, but you see that it's cheap pine. You refuse to buy from someone who's even under suspicion of lying. Audiences are like that; they get huffy when offered terminological inexactitudes subsequently proven inoperative. For her own protection the persuader should be honest with herself and try to discover if she's telling the truth, not because the truth is sacred—maybe it is—but because it has a way of coming through in the bottom of the ninth.

Though the audience deep down inside wants the truth, it never wants to be hit over the head with it. The persuader should be modest about revealing a naked truth, and if it's not pretty, dress it up. A naked truth: *Scientific studies show that Americans are thieves.* Half-dressed: *Some studies indicate that most Americans will steal.* Dressed: *A few studies by psychologists suggest that most Americans, given the right circumstances, are prepared to steal something small.* Another example: *Workers do more work in a four-day than in a five-day week.* More acceptable: *Certain test cases have shown that workers can do more work in a four-day than in a five-day week.* Another example: *Blacks do not make good swimmers.* More acceptable: *So far, blacks have not had real success in winning championships in swimming.* Even better: *Black athletes have not yet shown much interest in swimming titles.* You see in these examples what you already know: you can get away with saying anything, even the truth, by saying it diplomatically. A diplomat is one who says *Unless I'm mistaken, your soil here in the Sahara is rather thin,* or *I didn't succeed in gaining victory in the first set, and in the second set my more experienced opponent prevailed, while in the third set I proposed a draw and regrettably it was declined.* Diplomacy may not always work in international politics, but in the real world it works fine. Gentle, diplomatic statements have a way of sounding more accurate than forceful statements probably because they are. Of course, being too careful makes the writing dull. Decide what your audience will be willing to hear.

Facts do not have to be blown up. One way you can tell you probably have a fact is that you feel no need to garnish it. Trying to improve it, without real proof, may ruin it. Fact: *Some people maintain that the world is flat.* Nonfact: *Scientists recently proved that the world is flat and if you go too far, you'll fall off.* Fact: *A two-ounce hot dog generally has a gram or two more protein than a four-ounce slice of pizza.* Nonfact: *Hot dogs are more nutritious than pizza.* (More protein isn't necessarily more nutrition.) When you have a fact, just say it accurately, don't inflate it: that way it won't burst.

Now let's have a little practice in putting the truth forward in a proper light. Here are ten assertions; assume they are true, and try to express them in such a way that an audience will accept them. (Don't tone them down so much they're wishy-washy.)

Taking the train to Florida is better than flying.

No woman should wear a girdle.

Not eating eggs prevents you from having strokes.

Kansas City boys are the cutest in the country.

When a Democrat is president we have a war, and when a Republican is president we have a recession.

Your grass needs fertilizer.

Using Blizzard toothpaste prevents cavities.

The Church interferes in politics.

That pizza last night made me sick.

Women are much more sensitive and complex than men.

In working with these sentences you probably noticed that some were worse than others; some were matters of personal opinion, some dealt with facts, and some were disgusting mixtures of fact and opinion. These are the three different kinds of statement, and each kind has to be handled in a different way to be persuasive. *Kansas City boys are the cutest* and *No woman should wear a girdle* are clearly statements of opinion. The writer shows she's offering an opinion by obvious exaggeration. What is clearly opinion need not be qualified. You don't have to say *I feel, I think, I believe,* because no one wants to listen to a mouse. An audience rejects opinions offered timidly. Don't say *I believe Diet Rite is better than Tab* or *Croquet may be the finest sport,* just say *Diet Rite is better,* and *Croquet is the finest.*

Certain sentences were presented as matters of fact: *Blizzard toothpaste prevents cavities, Not eating eggs prevents strokes.* These are the dangerous statements. Facts can be verified. If the supposed fact is not so, the writer has insulted the audience. That's why she should not present opinions as facts. All of us confuse facts and opinions, and pretend to have many more facts than we have. No one goes around asking herself every time she wants to say something: Is this fact or opinion? But a writer should try to be careful. Facts are rare, elusive; courtroom trials are laborious attempts to find the simple facts. But despite the scarcity of facts and the dullness of most of them, they are often worth looking for, and last longer than diamonds.

Two more of the assertions pretended to be facts since they brought up the business of cause and effect: *When a Democrat is president we have a war,* etc., and *That pizza last night made me sick.* The first assertion was acceptable as it is in Informal where exaggeration is permitted for the sake of a forceful or funny statement. In Formal the assertion would have to be weakened (or abandoned): *In this century wars have tended to begin when a Democrat was president and recessions when a Republican was president.* The assertion *That pizza last night made me sick* would have to be explained in Formal: *That pizza last night made me sick because I get sick every time I eat a whole pizza.*

Now we come to the awful mixtures of fact and opinion: *Taking the train to Florida is better than flying. Your grass needs fertilizer.*

The Church interferes in politics. Most of our assertions are like these: they sound a little plausible, but can't be verified like facts or dismissed like opinions. These assertions need to be defended, qualified, or explained. *Taking the train to Florida is better than flying because it's not too slow, it's cheaper, and stays on the ground. Your grass probably needs fertilizer since it's not a deep green like mine. The Church interferes in politics in areas that have nothing to do with doctrine.*

Just as you should have some sense, while writing, of when you start foaming at the mouth or falling asleep, you should have some sense while arguing of what kind of assertions you're making. If you're offering opinions, offer them forcefully, because audiences admire force and may thus come to share the opinions. (Of course, if you don't want your opinions shared, that's a different story. Then why offer them?) When you have a fact, present it modestly and accurately.

Whether your assertions are accepted depends on how they're presented. A badly presented truth ceases to be true, a well-presented untruth becomes true. Language is an imprecise medium for the truth, since words mean so many things and suggest so many things. The categories of true and false seldom apply to assertions, despite the popularity of those True-False tests one finds in magazines and social sciences. So if an assertion of yours is in any way doubtful, soften it or add to it some defense, explanation, or example. The more unusual or doubtful the assertion the more help it needs. How would you handle that last sentence—*Women are much more sensitive and complex than men?*

How to Lose an Argument

The best way to lose an argument is to believe there is no argument, that the other side knows you're right and is just acting ornery. Overconfidence and self-righteousness prevent anyone from seeing the arguments on the other side and guarding against them. An arguer should really be grateful to her opponents, for without them she would have no argument to present. They should be treated respectfully for reasons of strategy as well as courtesy. Part of the audience may share their views. Also, vicious attacks are generally disliked. Do just enough to win. Refuting others can be harsh and combative, so it must be done politely. Sarcasm, ridicule, and mockery are out of style today, except in the home.

The arguer should guard against showing her feelings, especially anger. This may be hard to do, since our familiar route to articulateness is outrage: a newborn is symbolically whacked to begin his career in self-expression. We all complain so much that we confuse complaints and arguments. An argument taken personally becomes a complaint. But heated words are only hot air. Effective writers, like effective lawyers, try to accentuate the positive and avoid whining.

There are certain rhetorical devices to be used gingerly because they backfire. You should not impute motives to others or in any way caricature the opposition or their arguments. If you have to talk about the opposing view as you answer it, try to be fair. The cleverest ploy is to act kind and understanding to your opponents. With so much folly in the world there's no need to set up straw men to knock down. Real men do fine, and can be knocked down with a breath—with one good question.

A tempting device is the *reductio,* or pushing the opposing argument to the point where it becomes silly. *If guns are outlawed only outlaws will have guns. If pornography is censored, that will lead to censorship of other writing. Washington will soon be telling us businessmen how to blow our nose. A million here, a million there—pretty soon you're talking about real money.* The *reductio* is usually a clumsy, undignified blurring of distinctions. If you want to be annoying, try using it; it's a good tool for that.

Rhetorical questions, or questions whose answer is supposed to be understood, can be effective, used sparingly, but are a bit old-fashioned, and if you try them on smart alecks you will get a smart answer instead of the right one. *You want me to risk having a baby? What about the Joint Chiefs—you think all of them are crazy? What if every woman had an abortion? What has violence ever accomplished? Is it a sin to pay $180 for a man's cologne?*

How to Destroy an Argument

First, the bad news. Almost everything you assert can be subjected to destructive questioning. Now the good news. Almost everything that anyone asserts can be subjected to destructive questioning. Assertions are so vulnerable that people have a silent understanding to do little questioning of each other. "Questioning is not the mode of conversation among gentlemen," as Dr. Johnson says. It is the mode among arguers. Just a little practice in analyzing statements for their logical defects gives you very sharp teeth.

The first thing to do in analyzing an argument is to find its premises. Arguments are often based on faulty evidence. *People on welfare should not be given so much money; they're lazy.* Is it true they're lazy? *Criminals are sick people and require medical attention, not punishment.* Are there no differences between criminals and sick people? Are the crimes of no significance? Instead of attacking the conclusion, find the shaky premise of the argument. An unacceptable conclusion is seldom caused by an error in reasoning, but almost always by an unacceptable premise.

Since the general method used in argument is to show that some general principle applies to your proposition, the way to break up the argument is to destroy this link—by pointing out distinctions, by insisting that different things are really different. Simply by asking for clarifications of the ideas, you destroy the argument, as in the following examples.

Argument:	Pornography is wicked because it arouses lust.
Analysis:	What is lust and why is it wicked?
Argument:	She's against abortion because the Church has indoctrinated her.
Analysis:	What does it mean to be against abortion? Is a view wrong because it's held by the wrong people—in this case, the Church? What does indoctrinated mean?
Argument:	Property is theft. America was stolen from the Indians. I get to steal, too.
Analysis:	Isn't there any property to which people are entitled? Do you have any? When the white man stole America, he had the army. Do you have an army?
Argument:	Italians act like children.
Analysis:	Do other people act like children? What do Italians do that others don't?
Argument:	The universe is good because God is good, and the universe is proof of his goodness.
Analysis:	Is the universe good? Does good outweigh evil? How do you know?
Argument:	Death can't be so bad, because people who have been resuscitated no longer fear dying.
Analysis:	Do they fear death less now than before? Did they actually die?

These examples give you the idea. Don't refute or contradict an argument. Don't answer with your own arguments; if you don't propose an argument, you can't lose it. All you need do is ask one or two polite questions. Why deny an argument when you can question it? The arguer is obligated to deal with questions about what she's proposed. The most effective way to attack any argument is also the easiest—by asking to have the ideas made a little clearer. For asking deadly questions like these, Socrates' fellow citizens executed him. Maybe you don't want to become that good at it, but you want to be good at it, if only to examine your own arguments and be ready in case someone tries it on you. It's humiliating to have an argument sink under you. We need to take our ideas and beliefs seriously, and will even die for them. Losing an argument is not like losing a Ping-Pong game.

When you think about it, it's amazing that so little of this simple questioning is done. When a person says *We Germans are a nation of poets and philosophers*, the answer is heard: *We Italians are just as good as you Germans.* The proper response should be a question: *What, you mean most Germans are not slobs like everyone else?* When one says *There's too much competition in school*, another answers *Life is competitive* instead of asking *How much competition is too much?* People fight unclear ideas with their own unclear ideas, rather than with clear questions. They get so used to dealing in unclear ideas they forget to ask others, as they forget to ask themselves, to make the ideas clear. Unclear or general ideas cause great mischief in the world. They do help people live active lives based on beliefs, but some action we could do without.

Don't shy away from questions because you think they don't really say anything or that they're impolite. One good question is worth several doubtful assertions. As a wit once said, "For your information I have a question." Insinuations *(He went to Moscow, I will go to Korea, You're soft on street crime, You have ring around the collar)* can only be countered by questions. When you are questioned, fight back. *Why does a Jew always answer a question with another question?* Answer: *What do you mean by why does a Jew always answer a question with another question? Does he? Do all of them do this? Shouldn't they?* and so on forever.

Since I had fun pricking arguments, maybe you'd like a turn. It's great fun, except when the arguments are your own. Here are some unclear propositions. See if you can't zero in on their vulnerable spot with a clear question.

Drunken drivers must not be allowed to drive.

Private organizations should be allowed to choose their own membership.

If a person doesn't work, he shouldn't eat.

Students should have a voice in hiring and firing teachers.

No state is worse than that in which the richest people are considered the best.

By remaining in a society you are promising to obey its laws.

Anyone who does not protest the war is an accomplice.

Those who have suffered from discrimination deserve special assistance to catch up to those who have had advantages.

Personal Appeal

In making a personal appeal the speaker or writer relies on the audience's liking or admiring her. She should therefore be likable or show she's trying to be. In speaking she will command the basic skills of a speaker. She will not be afraid, but will look her audience in the eye and speak loudly, slowly, and clearly. She will show she wants to be liked by being well groomed and well dressed. If she's writing, she can't rely upon appearance and voice, but has to please the audience with words alone. It's easier to charm with looks than with words.

If one's looks are known, it's even easier. A famous comedian can say anything and people laugh. A football star holds up a can of beer on television, and people buy the beer. A pretty girl in an expensive dress gets in and out of an automobile, and both men and women flock to buy it. Patriarchal males and girlish females have strong appeal. The ideal male is the president, the ideal female is Miss America, and it's hard to say which ideal is the more difficult to achieve.

Do these remarks imply that personal appeal is low and undignified? I can't say that, for I've been guilty of admiring the masculine and feminine. There's no question that personal appeal is a basic and powerful persuader, and one would be foolish not to exploit it. As our society comes to rely more and more on television, personal appeal becomes ever more important. Writers will feel increasing pressure to be friendly, assured, confiding, as if selling something in one's living room.

If you seek to increase your personal appeal, remember that whatever is an asset or a liability in your personality shows up as an asset or a liability when you express yourself. One usually knows if she's gushy, surly, timid, etc. It's easy enough to advise removing the liabilities, but that will take work. T.S. Eliot said: "At the moment one writes, one is what one is, and the damage of a lifetime. . .cannot be repaired at the moment of composition." If the writer has many moments of composition, though, some repairs can be made.

When you approach an audience you don't want to be guilty of the personality faults that suggest deficiencies—being apologetic, hesitant, confused, bashful, squeamish. These faults are disabling because the audience thinks you're not eager and ready to address them and that you're wasting their time. They're right. You shouldn't try to say anything unless you want to and are ready to. Timidity has to be conquered, whether in speaking or writing. It's conquered by getting experience. If you think you can't speak, you must, or if you think you can't write, you must. Just do it. Human beings get used to anything. Timidity is often cured by getting angry. Even the lowliest worm may turn and bite the foot that steps on it. Anger is a road to eloquence, though a rocky one. Be brave or get mad.

Excesses are not as bad as deficiencies. Famous writers dither and babble, and get away with it because their energy and boldness are loved as virtues in themselves. Speakers behave deliriously, like quiz show emcees, and the audience loves it. No spark of life— that's what audiences do not forgive. It's hardly possible to be too animated, though one can have the wrong kind of animation and be too chummy, cute, excited, or nasty. Audiences are disappointed by expression that's cold and rational, and assume that the speaker or writer is more interested in what she's saying than in them.

My advice to work at being charming may fall on some deaf ears, for some people aren't interested in pleasing and persuading. Because of their own troubles they would rather stay silent or would even rather antagonize others. I'd like to think that those who want to sulk or lash out are not among my readers.

That was flattery. Did you recognize it? People seldom do; that's why you needn't be shy about using it. Flattery is so common in ads it goes unnoticed elsewhere. President Carter was elected after asking for a government as good and as decent and as honest and as loving as the American people. *Cosmopolitan* shamelessly says, "We believe in marriage if *you* do." You really have to exaggerate before an audience discovers it's being flattered, and when they do they'll forgive you.

The question sometimes arises whether the speaker or writer should be sincere. The answer is no. Being sincere suggests an uncritical attitude toward one's material. Acting sincere runs the risk of appearing sanctimonious. Forget about sincerity. Sincerity is a virtue only because its opposite, hypocrisy, is a vice. The young overrate sincerity because it's one of their virtues. Hitler was sincere. Be honest rather than sincere. Sincerity is respect for what's going on in one's own mind, honesty is respect for what goes on in the minds of others.

These remarks lead back to the old question of whether the speaker or writer should lie. From the moral point of view, liars should be encouraged so they will be discovered sooner. From the nonmoral point of view they should be discouraged because lying is too hard to do well. The poor liar is not allowed to say what he wants but is always satisfying some demand. Thinking that people are victims of liars is like thinking that johns are victims of prostitutes. And lies are much too hard to remember. "The pleasure in telling the truth," as Mark Twain observed, "is that you don't have to remember what you said."

Emotional Appeals

Effective writing appeals to the emotions and not just to the reason. If you want something from people, you must move them. The emotions are not dirty—only about half of them are—and appealing to them is not dishonest. Rhetoricians have always admitted that a writer's success depends on three things: what is said, how it is said, and who says it. Of these, the least important is what is said; what is suggested is what counts. Many ads for cars, for example, do not even mention the size of the engine. Cardinal de Retz said, "Everyone is open to insinuation, but scarcely anyone is open to persuasion." Ads can move people without being witty, eloquent, or even pleasant.

Like everything else, emotional appeals have been named and classified. When they work they're called *emotional appeals* and when they don't they're called *logical fallacies*. The most common way of appealing to the emotions (emotions are basically *for* or *against)* is to call things by good or bad names. This is the favorite rhetorical device of children and adults. *Name calling* ranges from out-and-out denunciation and abuse to subtle and imperceptible slanting of the language. Some bad names being heard are *racist, sexist, populist, establishment, old boys' network, regulation, welfarism.* There are so many bad names one wonders whether humans are not more aggressive and nasty than kind and loving. Do you know?

Slanting of language is more subtle. Many words have favorable or unfavorable connotations—some have no denotation at all—and skillful use of the connotations brings about the desired effects in the audience. *Fight* is good, but *violence* is bad. Lyndon Johnson: *We will fight in Vietnam until the violence stops.* Do you think *cults* should be taxed but not *religions?* Are you *neutral* or *indifferent?* A good old man can be called *senior, elderly, dignified, silver-haired, experienced, vigorous, wise in years, fatherly;* a bad old man can be called *jowly, balding, rumpled, stooped.* Just as language can be slanted, so can evidence: favorable or unfavorable facts are emphasized or obscured, half-truths are offered, quotations edited and twisted, motives attributed to others, and straw men set up in order to be knocked down.

Another emotional appeal is the *bandwagon* appeal. The audience is called on to feel or act a certain way because their associates seem to be doing the same. All racial, ethnic, patriotic, and party appeals rely on this need to belong to a group, a need so deep and powerful that appealing to it is often the main thing a speaker does. Bandwagon appeals can be base or noble, depending on where the band is going. *Let us extend a helping hand*—a noble appeal. *Love it or leave it*—a base appeal. People don't seem to mind bad music from a band, just so it's loud.

Another type of appeal is the *appeal to authority. Doctors report, History shows, Pismeyer of Yale says.* In our time, respect for any authority that is not scientific has weakened, and the appeal to authority works better with older and more hypocritical audiences. In arguing logically, you can use authority only to support other points of argument.

Another appeal is the direct *attack on the person* holding the wrong views. The personal attack is a good one, though sometimes its appeal is to prejudices. *You're only saying that because you're a man. A draft dodger is a coward. This witness is a convicted criminal and cannot possibly be believed.* The personal attack is not illegitimate. Lawyers use it on hostile witnesses. If one is a criminal it may well be true he's a liar too, or a draft dodger may be a coward. A fault in our politics is that the personal attack on politicians is avoided even when appropriate. People should say *Don't vote for so and so: he took campaign money from the oil companies, he paid no income tax for three years, he's a millionaire, he has twelve children, he wears too much makeup.* Such information can not only be relevant but can win for you.

Another appeal is the *blush*, or appeal to shame. *Everybody on the block gave; won't you? This is the holiest day of the year.* Another appeal is to the *purse. Our tax dollars are being poured down the welfare rathole. This new million-dollar tank can be destroyed by a twenty-dollar shell.* Another appeal is known as the *stick*, or threat. *If you don't eat your spinach, you get no dessert. In a year or two, the Teamsters will have an atomic bomb.* Threats are forceful persuaders, but are seldom considered in discussions of rhetoric because their effectiveness lies in the threat rather than in how it's expressed. But threats are everywhere, and are the basis of social and political control.

In short, there is nothing wrong or undignified in using any type of emotional appeal. They are not offenses against truth or logic; they become offensive only when used clumsily, insulting the audience. But audiences are seldom insulted by appeals to their emotions, for that's where they live. They have real interests and needs that are in themselves a truth to be understood and respected by the writer. Success in persuasion depends less on devotion to the truth than on knowing what the audience wants to hear. So important is knowledge of the audience that trial lawyers exercise most of their cunning in the selection of a jury. Mencken said: "The average man does not get pleasure out of an idea because he thinks it is true; he thinks it is true because he gets pleasure out of it."

In most arguments no distinction can be made between logical and emotional appeals. If I say women should not administer the sacraments of the Church because they have never done so before, is that a logical appeal? If I say policemen and ministers who commit adultery should get the sack because we hold them to a higher standard of behavior that we do others—is that a logical appeal? Arguments emulsify logic and emotion. It's not easy to separate the two, especially when we feel the emotion and believe it to be true. Emotional appeals should not be thought of as logical errors, for respectable arguments are riddled with them. Is it an *error* to think that your spouse is beautiful or that heaven exists or that fast-food hamburgers are delicious?

Logical Proofs

Logic plays only a minor role in persuasion. What is logical need not be argued. The discipline of logical thinking helps to destroy arguments rather than find them. In Formal one is only expected to *act* as if she were being logical and not emotional. Appearing to be logical, acting calm, cool, fair, reasonable, that is more important than being logical. The more sophisticated the audience, the more reasonable the persuader should be in her manner.

In arguing logically, whatever is a matter of personal belief or opinion is supposed to be laid aside. Facts should be put forward and supported when necessary by evidence. The tone must be calm and reasonable, no matter how outrageous the facts. The tone is not only cool but impersonal. Try not to refer to yourself or what you *think* or what the audience *thinks*. Refer to yourself only if introducing evidence from personal experience.

Your basic method is to show that the particular subject you're talking about is a member of a larger class, and that general principles, which people agree on, can be applied to the particular case. If you're arguing that the power of police to search should be restricted, you would convince your audience that they would not like to be frisked. If you're arguing that police should be free to make searches, you point out how many sacrifices of privacy people already make in the interest of public safety. If you're arguing against having to wear a helmet when riding a motorcycle, you point out how this infringes on privacy, particularly on one's right to dress as he pleases. If you're arguing in favor of helmets, you point out that the rider is a member of society, and society has rights in protecting one of its members from hurting himself.

After the particular example is referred to the general class or principle, then supporting examples, facts, or illustrations should be added. Logical arguments are not hard to develop since they move from the particular to the general. They move outward, like ripples on a pond, and lead quickly into large issues. The easy development of an argument is one of the reasons people love to argue. Take the argument about wearing a helmet and see how it opens up. Society does restrain someone who's trying to hurt himself. Does society have this right? If society has this right, does it outweigh the individual's right to do what he wants? How can we tell which has the stronger right? What does society lose if it gives up its rights in this case? What does the individual lose? After working through the argument one might conclude that society has the right to restrain suicides, but interfering in suicides is not the same as interfering with a motorcyclist who loves to have his hair in the wind and sun. Or one could conclude the argument through *compromising*, deciding that society can make riders who are under twenty-one wear helmets.

Though it's easy to argue, by making this move from the particular to the general, one can take the argument only so far. Everything that is is a member of a class, but is also different from other things. Comparisons, analogies, and extensions of principles can only be pursued so far until they break down and no longer apply. Every comparison becomes at some point untrue, since everything is what it is and not another thing. Nothing in the world is exactly identical to something else. And nothing is entirely unique. Aquinas well described thinking as *combining* and *separating*.

All of us have been treated to many overextended comparisons, such as these: *If white ethnics can make it, so can black people. Handguns are no different from other lethal weapons like knives. Nations grow old and weak. A zygote is a human being.* Test yourself now on this argument by analogy, and figure out what's right and what's wrong with it: *The law should crack down on obscenity, though it can't be precisely defined, as it cracks down on cruelty to children, which also can't be precisely defined.*

In arguing you have to use comparisons, but guard against extending them to the point where their falseness becomes apparent. To argue well, keep comparisons brief and simple and use several comparisons instead of pushing a single one.

When one is arguing logically and referring to general truths and principles, she may neglect to examine the general truth or principle itself, and fall into the error of relying on a *generalization*. Generalizations have a bad name, even though our knowledge consists entirely of generalizations from experience. Two and two are four: a generalization. Tomorrow, or somewhere else, two and two may be one, five, or a temporary or new number. Night follows day. A generalization. The earth might stop rotating, like the moon. A good generalization is one that a particular audience will accept. A poor generalization is one they won't accept. If the audience believes that one swallow makes a summer, you may tell them that. But sometimes the audience just looks gullible. There's a smart person born every minute.

If the writer believes she may say only what is logical or truthful, she might as well hang up her gloves. She should waste little time thinking about whether her propositions are right or wrong, true or false. She should think about whether her audience will accept the propositions, and her defense of them, if there is any. Look at the following typical propositions and you will appreciate the folly of thinking in terms of true or false. *America's young people (will, will not) fight for their country. Cats (do, do not) like ham. Actors (are, are not) selfish. Students today (can, cannot) read or write. Love means (always, never) having to say you're sorry. Washington is (the enemy of, controlled by) private enterprise. He loves me, he loves me not.* In this puzzling world where very few assertions (some say *none*) can be verified, you have an easier time if you present and work with the ones that entertain your audience.

When you're arguing, you sometimes have to talk about cause and effect relationships. My advice is to talk about these as little as possible. They are difficult to discuss and often have no bearing on the argument. The purpose of your argument is a certain practical result that is to come. To talk about causes makes you talk about the past. Forward-looking people are admired. The analysis of cause is chancy, and most events are too complicated to be analyzed for their cause. Whatever occurs does so as the result of much that has happened before, not as the result of some cause or a few causes or an immediate cause. No person ever acted from a single, pure, unmixed motive, and groups of people do not do so either. Just as you should not go around assigning causes to events you should not say this or that was a person's motive. The imputing of motives is not only unfair but a waste of time. People do not know why they do what they do and they're not pleased when you tell them. So stay away from causes of events and motives of actions. What about these? *He beat his wife because he got drunk. I use drugs because my parents didn't love me. Lt. Calley was convicted because they needed a scapegoat.*

Sometimes the causal relationship is expressed indirectly, without using *because* or *since*. *I have strong oral needs and can't stop smoking. If you forgive others, God will forgive you. One-fourth of all highway accidents are caused by beer drinkers. She got diabetes from eating too much sugar. Tight underwear gives you migraines.* You get the picture. If want to appear to be logical—and who doesn't?—avoid assigning causes. If you talk about a number of causes and weigh them for their relative importance, you will be safer (and very likely less entertaining).

Reasoning

Reasoning means talking in a calm or reasonable manner, and it also means ideal reasoning, or thinking in a cold, logical, analytical way, unaffected by personal attitudes, prejudices, or beliefs. This second kind of reasoning, true reasoning rather than the show of it, is extremely difficult and rare. It seems impossible for any human being to be perfectly reasonable. When Martin Luther cried out, "Reason is the devil's whore," he was pointing out that the human mind cannot work correctly. But he was also blurring a real distinction between reasoning that is a show and reasoning that is close to the ideal.

To reason properly, one should lay aside beliefs. Whatever is thought to be right or wrong can only be a matter of belief. Few people will agree with that statement, since most people have fervent beliefs that certain things *are* right or wrong. They believe in an abstract or absolute right and wrong, and associate these with good and evil, or God and the devil. Particular rights and wrongs lead them to believe in a general good and evil, and belief in a general good and evil reinforces their belief that certain things are right or wrong. The mind interpreting reality, moving as it does from the particular to the general and back again, invents the categories of right and wrong (and applies these categories to nearly everything).

Though people may nod in agreement at Hamlet's truism, "There is nothing either good or bad but thinking makes it so," very few of them are willing to question their belief in good and bad. In reasoning, this belief must be put aside if one hopes to analyze what a certain thing is in itself. Maybe because our emotions are basically love and hate and because we have a right hand and a left hand, our minds are far too easily inclined to think in terms of pairs, opposites, dualities, as if there were only two great boxes to put everything into. When the mind goes blithely along sorting everything out as right or wrong, popping it into a box where it's hidden from view, the mind is hardly working at its best. Shark = bad. Fighter pilot = good. Weed = bad. Flower = good. Suicide = bad. Money = good. When the snake told Eve she would *know* good and evil, he told a whopper.

Let's look at some examples of how belief in the right and the good interferes with analytical reasoning. When the nation's leaders decided to go to war in Vietnam, they thought along these lines: We have to do it. Vietnam is our ally. Our credibility as defenders of freedom is at stake. It's right to draw the line here against communism, which is a wrong system.

Thoughts such as these shoved out of the picture other important questions: what happens if we fight *there,* what happens to *them,* what happens to *us,* what happens if we *win,* what happens if we *lose?* No one thought we could lose. How could we lose, if we were right? Instead of thinking in a practical way of consequences, the leaders thought overconfidently about the cause of the situation and emotionally about the rights and wrongs of it. The Confederacy knew they had a *right* to leave the Union, and look what happened to them. By voting for what is right rather than for what is possible, lawmakers bankrupt their governments. Thinking about the future must range widely, not plod along wearing right-and-wrong blinders.

When an issue causes serious disagreement, it generally has a crux, or single point over which the disagreement arises. When people argue, they avoid the crux because they want to keep on arguing or they dislike the solutions. But a reasonable arguer locates the crux right away and refuses to move off of it to talk about other things. The crux of the abortion question is not sexual behavior or male oppression, but whether one should be allowed to kill a fetus. The crux—killing—should be discussed. What can be killed—soldiers, animals, the feeble, the dying, no one?

Another emotional issue is capital punishment. People think along these lines: Is it right to kill? What made the criminals go wrong? Are they bad? Are we good? Once again, the thinking proceeds along lines of right and wrong instead of practicality. The reasoning should be: What happens if we execute criminals? What happens if we don't? These two questions would give us enough to work on without our having to indulge in emotions of hatred of or compassion for criminals. Is this being too rational? What could be a better subject for reason than killing people? Reason requires that no thought be embraced because it's pleasant, or avoided because it's unpleasant. Reason does not deny that emotions exist, it requires that they not be brought into play during the analysis of a question. One can be tenderhearted and still be tough minded. So when you reason, see that right and wrong are left outside the door, as prayers are left outside the classroom. People don't agree about praying and don't agree about right and wrong. It's upsetting that they don't, but if you want them to agree with you, you have to reason with them and never get mad.

Thinking freely, without reference to good and evil, is called free thinking, or rationalism. It's extremely rare, so rare that one wonders why people get so upset at the very idea of it. Free thought can be upsetting, since it undermines certain kinds of authority and punctures beliefs and dreams that help people get through the day. But what authority or belief is secure, if it can't stand inspection? In the Age of Reason, the eighteenth century, a number of famous rationalists believed that common people could not reason and should not try, that they should not be required to look into their beliefs. In our country today, this view will strike most people as condescending. Our democracy is based on the belief—unfortunately, it's only a belief—that people are reasonable and can be reasoned with.

If you want practice in reasoning, here are some propositions to analyze. See if you can work on them in a purely *practical* way.

> It's part of a teacher's job to make sure the Pledge of Allegiance is recited.
> A confessed homosexual minister or priest should not be given a parish.
> The one million illegal aliens in New York City should be deported.
> Equal pay for equal work.
> Starving peoples should not be fed, because they will continue to overbreed.
> Women should not be allowed to have more than a certain number of children.

I hope you could reason out these burning questions without getting smoke in your eyes. If you can't come up with a long argument on each of these questions, you're not used to reasoning. If you're confused by tough questions like these, that's good. You should be confused—you won't think unless you're confused. A teacher's job is to confuse students—no wonder there's no money in it—and a student's job is to be confused—no wonder they act so strange.

But don't give up in confusion. If you reason long and hard enough, you're bound to come up with a few arguments you can live with and a lot you can use. Remember that in the arena where ideas are the weapons, the fighter who keeps a cool head may win. Everyone loses sometimes. But don't quit. As Freud said: "The voice of the intellect is soft, but is not quiet until it has gained a hearing."

═══Chapter Eight═══

Pleasing

Personal Style

The means of pleasing an audience are usually discussed under the heading of *style*. An interesting word, *style*, for its contradictory meanings: it means distinctive or personal style—it once meant *handwriting*—and it also means stylishness, or fashionable style, which is not personal at all. You can succeed in writing by having a good personal style or by mastering any of the current fashions in writing. The one is like music and the other like Muzak. You can let it all hang out or you can wear dark glasses and a wig.

It may be hard to see that personal style is valuable, because when we learn to write there is so much Form to master. For twenty years people tried to teach me to write, and did it by telling me what not to do. Parents, teachers, and bosses peer over our shoulder, give us lots of erasers, and stand ready to wash out our mouths with soap or stab us with red or blue pencils. We get the idea we will never be allowed to express ourselves in any natural way. Each move we want to make seems to be against the Rules. Though teachers tell us, Just Be Yourself, when we try it we are told, You Can't Do That! We feel we're being jived, and don't realize that this feeling is a stage everyone must pass through in learning to write.

Like playing an instrument, writing must be tediously learned. One in a hundred takes to it easily. Once it's learned, then you can express yourself, then you can sing. It's not a torture intended to break your spirit, though it may feel that way. It's our only way of communicating with many people. In learning the piano we start in a faulty, wooden way, but once we can play, we're not supposed to sound like the teacher or like someone's recording.

Writing is thinking, thinking is talking to yourself, and only you can do that. If you're out to lunch, you'll have nothing to say and will have to mimic and plagiarize. Too many young writers fear that if they do not come on in the accepted way and sound slick or humble or whatever, their teachers won't let them into law school or medical school or advertising. They put down stuff they would never say, forgetting that the point of writing is to solo, not blend with the chorus.

Trying to sound like others is, of course, easier than trying to sound like yourself. Even easier than that is trying to sound like the place where you work. Since no one knows what an industry, company, or office sounds like, it's safe for awhile to sound like one, and make pompous, shifty, and inane noises. But sooner or later, if there's real work to be done, someone in the outfit will have to start sounding like a person. In the long run *business English* is the worst way to do business. A business cannot talk. Would you want to be a spokesman for an industry? Or a mouthpiece? When all the communications are coming from houses, offices, boards, chairs, and desks, the human voice cuts through loud and clear.

Here is a chair talking:

> Even now we are in the process of formulating new service concepts to deal with changing health care needs of subscriber groups. And, of course, we plan to adhere to GHI's longtime guiding principle of innovative service at controlled cost for families who participate in our programs in both private industry and government service.

Here is a person:

> We're doing our best to keep up with changing demands for services, while we try to keep costs down for our members.

Here is an airplane talking:

> If by chance your choice is not available due to previous passenger selection, please accept our apology.

Here is a person:

> I'm sorry but we're out of that.

Printed apologies and thank yous are only *litter*ature.

Here is a house talking:

> We have examined *Pinckert's Practical Grammar* and have con-cluded that there is no specific market for it. Unfortunately it does not fit into our (perhaps artificial) categories.

Here is a person:

> I and three other editors have read your book and we all liked it. But it's a little odd, and if we took a chance on it and it didn't sell, the oil company that owns us would give us the sack. Try those brave, rep-utable publishers, Writer's Digest Books.

Today many people feel they are not being addressed as persons by persons. To reach them you should talk to them, not talk down to them like an officer or expert and not suck up to them like an ad. When you're writing a business letter, pretend the addressee is sitting right across from you, and just tell him what you want to say. Some offices used to have a sign: *Say It Quick*. Is courtesy ev-er quick? A good letter is written to someone, not just about some-thing. Whether speaking to a crowd, writing a scientific paper, or scribbling a note for the milkman, sound like a person, and mem-bers of your species will hear your cry.

If you have no voice, no one listens, but if you fall in love with your voice and talk too much, no one listens very long. Beautiful voices only disguise for a time the lack of substance. It's better to say something—or try to—than just seem to. During the '79 fuel crisis President Carter was warned by his political expert, Patrick Cad-dell: "Too many good people have been beaten because they tried to substitute substance for style." Being good and not wanting to be beaten, Carter substituted style for substance, and was beaten anyway. Slamdunkers and skywalkers may make the All-Star Team but not the Hall of Fame.

To develop your personal style it's best to do a lot of writing on sim-ple enjoyable topics until your own voice gets strong enough to hear. Once you're more experienced, studying and imitating other styles helps make your own more flexible. As composers use certain formulas, so do writers come up with sentences that fall into patterns. The more patterns you master, the easier the writing goes, and that's where the exercise of imitating comes in handy. (Try imitating a number of writers you admire, not just one.) Writers used to train by imitating famous stylists; today this is seldom done for fear it will constrict one's originality. But it's still a good way to train the ear. You might have fun doing parodies—all good writers can be parodied, their voices are so clear and peculiar. And no matter how much you work on your style, your basic style will stay the same. If you're cheerful, decisive, or meticulous, that shows up in your writing as it shows up on a smaller scale in your handwriting. All valuable papers are signed.

Once you have found your style you will come to trust it and write with more ease. Less agony and more ecstasy. You won't spend all day searching for the ultimate way to say it: *She had a foxy look, She looked like a fox, She had a face like a fox, She had a foxlike face, She had a face such as one sees on a fox, She had a face such as one sees in a fox.* Oh, to hell with it! In any art little things mean a lot, but you must also spare yourself for the big things.

Readability

Readability is hard to analyze. It does not depend on short words, short sentences, and lots of names, though these help nowadays. It depends on who's talking to whom about what. Writing can be clear and simple, and be totally unreadable. If it's beautifully clear and simple, though, it's readable. Writing needs beauty of some kind, and there are many kinds. A professor can find a piece unreadable because it's *not* difficult, an editor can find it unreadable because it's not marketable, a sociologist, because it's not couched in the jargon that's his bread and butter. Audiences do not always look for easy reading even when they're just flipping through magazines at the hairdresser's. If the reader thinks the material important, he'll read despite the difficulty. The kind of reader—"Fit audience find though few"—is always to be considered, not just the demographics.

Simple writing gets boring. Complicated writing is wearing. Writers can succeed by writing simple stuff for simple audiences or special stuff for special audiences, but the most esteemed writers are those who address a wide audience without aiming at the lowest common denominator (also known as The Bottom Line). It may be right to say that the *best* writing addresses as many people as possible and tries to be simple and direct. But of course there are many styles of writing that pay, many uses of language besides declaring—suggesting, deceiving, puzzling, arousing, pontificating.

Writing for special audiences runs the risk of being impersonal, dull, and jargony. Writing for mass audiences runs the risk of being impersonal and dull. Much writing today is so dull it's embarrassing, and that's why publishers love fewer and shorter sentences, pictures, white space, and one-sentence paragraphs. *Reader's Digest* not only has ads but cartoons: the reader has finally been digested and is ready to be eliminated. Many people now believe that readability means something that needn't be read, that a nonbook is a book and a library is a media center. What happened to the readers? They're still out there, waiting for you to say something. Instead of thinking of writing as an industrial product with a shrinking market, remember what it used to be—a person talking.

Though readability is a relative virtue, we can still talk about what helps or hurts it among *most* audiences. Writing that lacks energy, writing where the sentences go nowhere and nothing is asserted—can anyone like that? No one likes wordiness or the piling up of qualifiers and modifiers. In writing, as in any art, whatever is excessive results from weakness in the concept or idea.

To get the reader underway, the tone of the piece should be sounded early and clear. The audience approves the tone, and it's not sounded too loud or long. It's not too breezy (cute), too pompous (solemn), too solemn (lugubrious), too funny (facetious), too technical (unintelligible), or too ironic (confusing). The writer can modulate the tone—writing without surprises is dull—but the surprises are in the material, not the point of view. The audience assumes the writer has settled on a point of view before lifting her pen—though this is often not the case.

Tricks of style are used—sound effects, questions, appeals, figures of speech—but used without drawing attention to themselves. The greater the variety of tricks, the less conspicuous a particular trick will be. The artistic principle of nothing too much applies especially to these flowers of rhetoric. One rhetorical question on a page—fine. Two questions—disaster. A writer can sneak two metaphors into a sentence, add a third, and collapse the whole sentence. Tricks of style are like high notes and trills for singers· they embellish the performance but may also jeopardize it.

Readable style avoids unnecessary synonyms: *sorrowful and tragic, clear and lucid, risky and unsure.* It shies away from lists, "laundry lists." They're boring. Terms are not defined, since they are being used the way the audience uses them. Readable style does not correct itself. *He was the handsomest lifeguard I ever saw, I suppose. The two parties will not agree; but maybe they will. Everyone is religious, or else they know someone who is.*

Readable style uses a variety of sentences. The anticlimactic or loose sentence, the characteristic sentence of modern style, is avoided as much as possible. This is the timid sentence that starts off all right, and then has a lot of items tacked onto it, like this sentence now, and it just goes on and on until it finally peters out, with a trailing "with" phrase or a trailing participle bringing up the rear, plus any other bits and pieces the writer has lying around.

Readable style does not mumble *more or less, part and parcel, by the by, as it were, by and large, what I would like to say is, in my view, in the final analysis, as such, it seems to be the case that,* etc. Certain expressions only prove that silence is golden.

The writer should choose words that are predicted or anticipated by the reader. If he's given too many unusual words, his anticipations have to be corrected, slowing him down. If he slows down too much he'll stop. Words should be normal just as pencils should be yellow. You can use some big words, but if they're all big, then none of them is. Idioms and natural turns of expression speed the reader along. Sometimes you'll even want to risk being trite to make the reading smooth as silk and easy as falling off a log.

You can get away with using lots of adjectives and adverbs in speech and in Informal writing, where there is generally a shortage of them. In Formal, fight off the temptation to overwrite. Occasionally you can hit a home run with a modifier, but steady singles with verbs are what you want. Don't say *upward, downward, pulsatingly, throbbingly, the giant piston moved.* Say *up and down the giant piston slid.* Instead of writing *This great statesman grew up in a tiny village,* and then sweating to fix up *great* and *tiny,* just write *This statesman grew up in a village.* Don't say *He has a small, black, nervous, curly-haired poodle dog.* Say *He has a small black poodle.* Have you met small poodles that weren't nervous and curly? Many adjectives tell us what we know—*warm sun, given subject, visible scar, bad cold, shining stars, personal friend.* There's nothing *wrong* with adjectives; it's because they're so handy and useful one grabs them rather than look for a better noun or a better sentence. *A mild form of madness* might be *a quirk, kink, obsession, or hangup. A very tall, skinny person* might be *a beanpole, stork, giraffe. She treated him like a loving parent, she mothered him. I'm very fond of, I adore. I do not have much experience, I lack experience. Use* adjectives—don't just throw them in or throw them out.

Long sentences sink if all they can deliver is a measly adjective: *This blah blah blah blah blah is unfortunate.* Sentences that end with an adjective have their focus on the subject rather than on subject and predicate. Writing doesn't just name, it asserts something about what it's naming; it doesn't just describe, it comments. Don't say *The rose is red, I am negative, This problem is difficult.* Say *The red rose blooms, I worry, This problem would make anyone pick his nose.*

Another fault in modern prose is the triumph of nouns over verbs. Some call this *noun plague, nounitis, nominalization, reification*—each term being an example of the problem. Emerson said, "Things are in the saddle and ride mankind." Things are also in the saddle in modern sentences. Don't lose a verb inside a noun.

Bad	Good
We had recreation.	We played.
Give me a welcome home.	Welcome me home.
It gives me pleasure.	I'm pleased.
It's an additive.	It's added.
The college expansion was rapid.	The college rapidly expanded.
There should be an outreach to these people.	We should reach out to these people.
There is a necessary choice between the punishment and forgiveness of criminals.	Criminals must be punished or forgiven.

Abstract nouns often end in *-tion,* so when you have a . . . *tion* see if you can't change it back into a verb. *We made an examination, We examined. An observation of mine, I observed. The separation of church and state is desirable, Church and state should be separated.* When an abstract noun is the subject, try to find an active verb to use with it. *Punishment is a problem, Punishment eludes, puzzles, worries. Clarity is desirable, Be clear.*

Don't try to make new verbs from nouns—to *critique, concertize, distance, waitress, structure.* Don't turn adjectives into nouns—*I'm a black, a pink, a crazy, a rapee, a retrenchee, the most.* Don't encourage nouns by using them as adjectives and stringing them together—*county tax assessment record keeper, State of Alabama law, anti-missile missile missile, Singer Sewing Machine Sales Representatives' Fourth of July Picnic Dance Contest Winner Award.* Nouns have weighted writing down so much, particularly those thousands of nouns that are mere concepts, it's no wonder people watch the Tube. If you're lucky, that can be a Family Strength Acknowledgment Experience.

Brevity

Everyone knows that brevity is the soul of wit—even Polonius, who said it, and who was so tedious Hamlet had to kill him. Brevity is a rare and thrilling quality in writing, and marks the distinguished mind. We admire those mental powers that see things clearly and express what they see simply and clearly. Mathematicians and scientists talk of elegant proofs and demonstrations; elegance is another way of talking about brevity. Here is brevity.

Dr. Johnson: Marriage has many pains, but celibacy has few pleasures.
Julia Child: When you are alone in the kitchen no one can see you.
Abraham Lincoln: As I would not be a slave, so I would not be a master.
Martin Luther King, Jr: A riot is the language of the unheard.
Garibaldi: Only a slave has a right to go to war, against a tyrant.

And here is the first sentence of Bertrand Russell's *Autobiography:*

> Three passions, simple but overwhelmingly strong, have governed my life: the longing for love, the search for knowledge, and unbearable pity for the suffering of mankind.

Only clear thinking finds such clear expression. In each quotation the diction is simple; the words do not have punch, the ideas have power. That kind of force, the force of the idea, is hard to achieve, but should be aimed at all the same. Wordiness tries to cover up weakness; brevity reveals strength.

Being brief is not to be confused with being quiet or taciturn. If someone is a man of few words, those words are probably poor ones. To talk well you must talk a lot, like Hamlet or Don Quixote. Today the style in speaking is to be cool and say little, while the style in writing is to be so verbose that many people who once read have turned to stamp collecting and raising houseplants for excitement. Here is a significant passage of modern prose from the science pages of the *Times*.

> Most people can prevent flatus for a time. But it can build up and cause pain and eventually must be released. Sometimes flatulence that is normally well controlled passes at embarrassing moments. This results from a relaxation of the rectal muscles.

Do we learn something new every day?

Both the modern speaking and modern writing styles are mistaken. In talking you should try to be loquacious and in writing you should try to be brief. If you succeed in either you will stand out.

You have to decide whether you want to stand out or sort of merge in. In a world where everyone shuffles papers you may not get paid to be brief. Journalists, bureaucrats, and professors get paid for words. Upsetting this applecart will not butter your parsnip. You may have to drivel and bloviate like your elders in the information industry, to report, review, refer, research, comment, confer, criticize, analyze, and plagiarize till kingdom come. As Jesus put it: "They think that they shall be heard for their much speaking." If you enter law, politics, or business you will discover that brevity and clarity can be disadvantageous, in addition to being hard work. But however Goethe felt about it, I'm glad he spent sixty years working on *Faust*. Of course, with a Wang word processor he could have done much, much more.

Using Force

Writing has to speak with a certain force if it is to command attention. Much of what is written today lacks force or has the mere show of it. People get so used to the false assertions of ads they begin to suspect all assertions. They think that writing must either be dishonest, hyped like advertising, or honest, with the poor writer chirping away like a cricket and nobody listening.

Here's a typically modern, overassertive sentence from *The Whole Earth Catalog:* [This is] *not only the best how-to book on drawing, it is the best how-to book we've seen on any subject.* No one would say that. *We* don't talk, one person talks, but not blurbese.

Here's half a sentence (the whole sentence would be unhealthy) from a letter to the *Times Literary Supplement: It is imperative that the ahistorical tendencies of the Lacanian model of the constitution of the subject be articulated upon a historically specific account of the evolution of the bourgeois consciousness.* Would you say that again?

Here's a sentence from *Esquire: For the first time our educated liberals no longer believe instinctively in majority rule.* That's a mouthful. But I don't think it would be said to another person. Sentences like that can only be written by someone unaware of an audience; they're announcements over the PA system.

Here's a sentence from *Time: Most people find great works of art oppressive, since such works invariably center on the nature of human destiny, and that destiny is tragic. Oppressive* and *invariably* are off the mark. What is *tragic?* What is *destiny?*

Here's a sentence by a feminist, Ellen Willis: *A woman cannot hope to find a man who is free of sexist attitudes, nor can she make a man give up his privileges by arguing.* Willis apparently thinks that half the human race is *sexist.*

Here's a history professor at Princeton in *The New York Review: It now seems probable that the population bomb will not explode after all, and that the number of human beings in the world will stabilize at about double the current figure of four billion.* Why this seems probable is not explained.

Here's Jimmy Carter in his 1980 State of the Union address: *I know the limits of moral suasion.* That should be *Moral suasion has limits.* Why did he say it as he did?

In these samples of pushy assertion, who is being fooled—the writer or the audience? Luther said *Pecca fortiter*—sin big—but he didn't mean *that* big. The writer and the audience should be alerted to the big, bad statement by its impersonal, *official tone.*

Advertising has had such a corrupting influence on language that people forget what they sound like. A careful writer insists on sounding like herself instead of an ad, and avoids overassertion, so that what she wants to say has a chance of being heard. She will speak modestly, avoiding overkill adverbs like *phenomenally, absurdly, definitely, undoubtedly, demonstrably, truly, infinitely, endlessly, absolutely, positively, significantly, importantly, meaningfully.* She will try to avoid superlatives—*most, best, finest, worst.* She won't exaggerate—*run to the nearest, it's a must, it's imperative.* She'll try to be reasonable after she says *The reason is* or *This is because.*

Then what can a poor girl do? She can look for assertions that don't require stimulation. She can simplify without oversimplifying. She can figure out what *she* would say and hear herself saying it. Berryman's advice is always apt: "Write as short as you can, in order, of what matters." But if it is true, as Lord Acton said, that "few things matter and nothing matters very much," it would then be true that there's not much to write about, and if one must write short, there's very little to write. The writer's job, though, is to *make* things matter. Nothing matters in itself; it can only be said to matter. Either the subject has to matter to the writer or the writing does, if they're going to matter to others. You need an attitude, a tone. You matter, not the subject. Subjects don't have predicates, you do. Cicero maintained that the easiest letter to write was the one that dealt with nothing.

You needn't ever get *involved* in the subject or be serious or sincere. Belief limits your thinking. In his opening sonnet Sir Philip Sidney writes, "Fool, said my Muse to me, look in thy heart and write!" He went on to write 107 more sonnets. Surgeons have opened millions of hearts and have never found a sonnet. Those sonnets must have been in Sir Philip's tongue. White man speak with forked tongue and so do black, yellow, and red man.

To express yourself forcefully you must commit some offense against the truth, which is deep and silent. Man is an abyss, but you talk about him, don't you? You can't tell the truth in a sentence; no sentence can say it all. You need a period for a sentence, and there are none in the universal flux. You have to make them up.

Dr. Johnson said, "In all pointed sentences some degree of accuracy must be sacrificed to conciseness." When Lord Acton said, "Few things matter," he meant that few things matter to him. When Lincoln said, "As I would not be a slave so I would not be a master," he was not telling what he would do if he had to be one or the other. Bertrand Russell spoke of his *unbearable* pity for mankind, and bore it for ninety-seven years. Learning to write is learning to cut. If you're timid you have a disadvantage. To write swiftly and clearly requires a touch of arrogance.

For the sake of discourse, people allow each other to make the most surprising assertions. If you're a student or some other nobody, naturally you're not allowed to say anything, but you should look forward to graduation when things will be better. The unforgivable sin in a writer is timidity. Blustering is unacceptable only because it's timidity turned inside out.

If you are too careful, you'll find it hard to assert anything, for your tentative assertions will be smothered by misgivings and afterthoughts. Don't let these silence you. What you put down isn't the final word, it's only a report on your thinking. Whatever is proposed implies its contradiction. If you say *Pigs is pigs* you imply pigs is not pigs, or you wouldn't have had to say they were. You say things because there is so much more to say. Try to get your thoughts down as they come, and don't worry about conclusions, answers, and solutions.

Here's a handful of famous quotations. Decide whether they were worth saying: *Each man kills the thing he loves. Those who can, do; those who can't, teach. All good books are alike. The critic who is modest is lost. Let any man speak long enough, he will get believers. We cannot write well or truly but what we write with gusto. When the heart's afire, some sparks will fly out of the mouth.*

If you say *Two and two are four*, who listens? If you say *Two and two are five for these reasons*, everyone listens. When you write you paint. If you liked things the way they are you wouldn't be writing about them. So assert away. You can assert anything if you explain or defend it a little or say it in a *pleasing* way. The trick is to be personal and assertive without sounding like a bully. In short, no mumbling, but no mumbo jumbo either.

Pleasing Sound

Good sentences are like musical phrases; each has a form or logic of its own. No one knows what makes a melody shapely and pleasing, and no one knows what makes a sentence shapely and pleasing. The musical phrase may appeal because it's like a good sentence, or the sentence may appeal because it sounds like music. Music has melody, harmony, and rhythm, and so does speech. Of the three, melody is the most elusive. Writers who have no feeling for melody are said to have no ear. Having no ear is not so great a handicap for the writer as for the musician, but is a handicap nevertheless. A study of good models, that is, reading aloud and imitating good writers, helps train the ear.

Harmony in writing refers to similarity of sounds, and *rhythm*, to repetition. Rhythm in music is strong and clear; in writing, it is more subtle and complicated. The rhythm of good prose can't be taught; it's never been analyzed, though it is the most significant element in the writing of good stylists. Rhythm comes mainly from the writer's preference for certain kinds of sentences. All of us write sentences in patterns we like, but don't use such distinct and forceful patterns as the heavyweights.

Today we find too many sentences that are rhythmless accumulations of words. They are written quickly and are never tested by the ear. Here are factory-made sentences.

> An important if not critical consideration is whether it is possible to replace one group of men by another within the existing political organization.
>
> In England the critical reception is invariably hostile to American confessional poetry.
>
> There are many aspects of this large problem, all of which are to a certain extent interrelated.
>
> He followed the river through the forest around the great bend into the southern part of the country.

Where were the verbs? If the writer doesn't listen for them, the audience won't either.

Since prose rhythm is ordinarily subtle, when it becomes pronounced it wakes the audience up. You need a reason to wake them up, so you better have something special to say, like: *It is a far far better thing I do than I have ever done; it is a far far better place I go than I have ever been. We shall fight on the landing grounds, we shall fight in the fields, and in the streets, we shall fight in the hills, we shall never surrender.* Prose that sounds like verse is only to be used when you're swinging for the bleachers. Repetition is so powerful and so easy a device it is overused, especially in speeches.

Repetition is a rhythmic device; the *balancing* of phrases and clauses is a subtle harmonic device. Many sentences contain complementary or antithetical ideas: This blah blah *and* that blah blah, or This blah blah, *but* that blah blah. Like me, you can be addicted to these sentences, but no one will notice since they are so common and natural—so natural they help to excuse repetition: *Brown eyes say Kiss me or I'll kill you, blue eyes say Kiss me or I'll die.* In balancing a sentence you want to balance the number of beats on each side of the break. Compare *Where are you going, my pretty little maid?* with *Where are you going to, my pretty maid?* Clearly, a writer has got to listen to her stuff, and listen to many alternative ways of putting it.

You can repeat once. Do it twice and the audience wonders what you're up to. The adage "Two's company, three's a crowd" also applies to repetition. An occasional *doublet* will pass, defying the risk of wordiness: *reasonable and acceptable, happy and joyous, disturbed and dismayed, share and participate, hide and conceal, awe and majesty.* Triads are riskier: *neither flesh nor fowl nor good red herring, the energy, the faith, the devotion which we bring to this endeavor, fat, fortyish, and foolish.* Lincoln brought it off when he dared to say *of the people, by the people, and for the people.* But notice how he switched from -ate, -ate to *hallow: We cannot consecrate, we cannot dedicate, we cannot hallow this ground.*

When you repeat, the audience assumes either that you're doing it for emphasis or else that the writing has not been properly tightened. That's why you search for needless repetition, drop unnecessary words, rework sentences, and use pronouns. You never use a circumlocution to avoid repetition. You don't say *Nation . . . nation . . . nation* and then switch to *state.* We do shift from the pronoun *one* to *he* after using it once because continuing to use it, as Thurber said, sounds like someone practicing the trombone: *One should not take one's pencil and chew it in one's teeth if one cannot find words to express oneself the way one likes.*

The question arises whether to start a string of sentences with the same word. Sure. A half dozen sentences could begin with *He*, for example. But you'd want variety within the sentences. A string of sentences should not start with an unusual construction, like an adverb, adverb clause, or participial phrase. *After arriving, he unpacked. After shaving, he came down for breakfast. After breakfast, he had his facial.*

Let us now consider some harmonies to be heard in prose. (Did you hear those *s,r,* and *h* sounds? I hope you heard them without noticing.) Harmonies are near-rhyme, assonance, alliteration, and echo words. You can't use rhyme in prose since people believe it's reserved for poetry. You have to guard against jingles: *creation of this nation, refuse to choose, knew it grew.* But would you accept *usual use, makes one wonder,* and *cool pool?* You probably would, unless you were editing.

Assonance, the repetition of vowel sounds, can be clever and subtle. *This is an insipid drink. Change of pace. Even before the green appeared in the leaves.* Alliteration is the repetition of the initial sounds in words. *Patty's Pancake Palace.* The alliteration of vowels is usually unnoticed, but the alliteration of consonants is distracting and objectionable in Formal. *The car can carry the cases. His hotel was hardly a half block away.* Alliteration can be fun, but it's too easy for serious people to get much kick from it. English is thick with consonant sounds (hear those?) and alliteration is sometimes hard to avoid, but you should avoid it.

Echo words imitate noises in the real world: *bang, shriek, splash, murmur, hush, tinkle.* These are among the most powerful words in the language, and the more you use them the livelier your writing will be. Almost as lively are those words that *suggest* the actions in their sound—*rush, pull, open, grip, drop, kick, call, look.* Any word referring to movement—*lift, drag, up, over, back*—and any word referring to sound—sound is caused by movement—animates the writing. Language that makes no reference to what lives and moves is dull. Good writing, like all good art, produces effects in the body, and produces them more easily through the ear than the eye.

To prove to yourself that hearing is a more important sense than sight, try to say the alphabet backwards by *visualizing* the letters. You can't do it. You can do it by remembering how the letters *sound* when *spoken* forward. In writing, sound is much more important than images. But neither sounds nor images should call attention to themselves, because when they do they lose their effect. The Duchess told Alice: "Take care of the sense, and the sounds will take care of themselves," and that is generally sound advice.

Vividness: Figures of Speech

Figures of speech are daring, imaginative expressions not meant to be taken literally. If on examination your writing seems dull, it's probably lacking the vividness and energy that come from figurative language. Figures are expressions one step further from reality than ordinary language. *Her tears rained down, That's baloney, She laughed like a hyena.* There's no clear distinction between figurative and ordinary language, since all words were originally figurative and were not meant to be taken literally. *Literally* itself is a figure: it means *according to the letter. Taken* is a figure: here it means *mentally conceived. Conceived* is a figure meaning *giving birth to* and so on. Emerson said, "Every word was once a poem." In talking about figures of speech, then, one is not referring to regular figurative uses of language but to specially vivid and conspicuous uses.

Figures of speech have been classified as similes, metaphors, exaggerations, personifications, addresses to the absent, name changes, etc. You're familiar with these devices and have used them all your life, though you may not be able to classify them and call them by their Greek names. Similes, or brief comparisons, are the best-known figures. When we want to speak vividly we turn to similes: *beer flowing like wine, American as apple pie, face like the front of a truck, enough to make a cat laugh, tougher than a two-bit steak, soft as the voice of the adulterer.*

Similes should be avoided in Formal. A simile that has never been heard before attracts attention to itself, away from the subject, and the audience thinks the writer is showing off. Here are examples of what I mean. A trite simile: *The lights on the bridge looked like a diamond necklace.* A forced simile: *The diamond necklace looked like the lights on a bridge.* Trite: *She looked like a million dollars. She looked like a movie star.* Forced: *She looked like Aphrodite. She looked like a tigress.* Trite: *Grinning like the cat that swallowed the canary.* Forced: *Grinning like a boll weevil in deep cotton.* I bet you can't invent similes that you could use in Formal that are neither too hot nor too cold. Try it.

Metaphors, on the other hand, are not only usable but invaluable. They can be vivid and daring, the giving of new names to things and thus a renewing of language, which is the giving of names to things. *He pulled his oar. My hands are clean. She dropped her voice. The words flew.* Effective predicates often depend on strong metaphorical verbs. *The wind stirred. The barometer fell. The skies threatened. The moon climbed.* Such language is packed with metaphor. *Packed* is a metaphor. The wind did not stir, the barometer did not fall, the skies did not threaten, the moon did not climb—they only do so metaphorically.

Metaphors are not an unmixed blessing. In similes one thing is compared to another; in metaphors the two are confused. *Battlefield=field of honor. Sickness=punishment. Woman=rose. Shadow=monster. God=daddy.* Every metaphor misrepresents both the thing being compared and what it's being compared to. *There's a cancer on the presidency. Religion is the opium of the people.* Metaphors allow the mind to invent what never existed: *in a provocative light* (what is a provocative light?), *from the dramatic point of view* (what's that?), *I am a white American male* (am I white? am I American? am I male?). Everything is what it is and not another thing, but humans are poets.

When metaphors are used so often that their original meanings are forgotten, they may be *mixed. That rat's a snake in the grass. These jeans go with where fashion is at.* When dead metaphors are laid beside each other they all pop up like zombies. *The fly in the ointment of the American Dream. We were caught with our pants down and have been playing catch-up ball ever since. The other side of the coin is the tip of the iceberg.*

Metaphors must be used to make writing vivid, but used carefully, so that they are neither dead clichés nor far-fetched and strained. In Formal the writer guards against *overvivid writing.* Many natural idioms and unobjectionable clichés turn lurid when they appear in black ink: *hole in the head, down the drain, smell a rat, up to his ears, beat around the bush, copycat.*

All metaphors must stand inspection. When language becomes unusually forceful, metaphors are in use, and you must check each to see if it can stand the test of being visualized. Can these? *leaned over backwards, wet blanket, wipes his feet on, take the bull by the horns, close the door on, take off my hat to.* Whether the audience would visualize these metaphors depends entirely on the tone of the piece where they appear. Metaphors pose a big problem in Formal, because if you don't use them the writing is dull, and if you do, it may be too vivid. Good metaphors never attract attention; they are not visualized, but felt. Safe metaphors are generally the ones that come to the writer without her looking for them.

Exaggeration is a particular kind of metaphor. *I'm starved. You're better than I am. My check is in the mail.* These exaggerations (hyperboles) are permitted in Formal when the exaggeration is very common or when it is so gross it's clearly a relaxation from the need to speak precisely, rather than a failure to do so. So if you exaggerate, risk a cliché or do it on a grand scale: *big as a house, missed by a mile, golden-tongued, filthy rich.*

Personifications, another figure, are commoner than you think. *Your country needs you. It's a sad day. The plant stood on the table.* Another figure is the address to the absent. *Elvis, what happened?* These addresses are not much used now, since they're thought rather fancy, but they are the basis of prayers. Calling things by new names (metonymy) is a kind of metaphor used in slang and obscenity. Using figures such as *shrinks* (psychiatrists), *suds* (beer), *bread* (money), and *broads* (women) is too exciting for Formal.

Questions directed at the reader, whether rhetorical, phony, or real questions, are also figures of speech. Real questions are good questions that don't have answers, and are avoided by writers who have the answers. Rhetorical questions have answers everyone is supposed to know. Phony questions, such as teachers and journalists are always asking, have answers you're about to be given. *What can you do with leftover spinach? How long should a girl wait? How can we tell a noun from a verb?* I've asked a few phony questions, but I'm not Formal.

In short, the best figures are those that seem natural and unforced. But just as you sometimes have to tell a joke, you sometimes have to use a certain figure despite the risks. Figures of speech are seasoning; you have to use them, but lightly. Formal people are literal minded, and hate what's literary. It's said that grammar is the grave of letters.

Specificity: Names, Quotes, and Anecdotes

Good style is not grand, abstract, big words or big thoughts, but clear and specific. Details do the job. Never trust the teller; trust the tale. Shakespeare is tops because he said nothing and let his characters do the talking. The philosopher Sartre even goes so far as to say, "Evil is the substitution of the abstract for the concrete." (An evil thing to say.) Goethe kept rocks on his desk to remind himself to stay away from abstractions. He also said, "Thinking is more interesting than knowing, but less interesting than looking." Make your readers look. Focus right away on the small, the particular, the visible, to get the reader looking and listening. Flaubert told Maupassant to learn to write by describing a horse in such a way as to distinguish it from all other horses. If you're writing a movie review don't start by telling the plot or delivering your verdict; start with a scene or some lines of dialogue. If you don't see and hear what you're writing about and present it clearly, your audience will wave good-bye as you rise up into the clouds.

An easy trick of style is dropping names. When you use a name you flatter the audience, as if saying to them *You know about him* or *You know about this*. Even if they don't know, they're flattered because you assumed they did. But if you mention many names they haven't heard of, they will feel accused of ignorance and resent your showing off. Professional writers drop names automatically, and figure that if they don't have two or three names per paragraph the writing will be dull. Names are often put in bold print. Audiences want to know about what they know about, and will continue to follow with interest whatever Jacqueline Onassis and Elizabeth Taylor are doing. Did those names wake you up? If not, newer can be found.

An allusion is an even more pleasant flattery, implying that the audience is sharp enough to catch an indirect or remote reference. To mention Watergate is to refer, to mention it twenty years from now will be to allude. Allusions are private language like slang and jargon, and stroke the audience. Much of the appeal of soap operas, formula novels, and literary criticism is allusive.

Quotations please by being references or allusions and by saying something useful. *The Koran says. Bob Dylan says.* When you have a good quotation, squeeze it in. To quote, you have to have one. You get it not from a dictionary of quotations—these will seem artificial—but from your own notebooks, in which you enter sayings you love. Such notebooks, called *commonplace books,* are seldom kept nowadays, but not keeping one shows little foresight in anyone interested in writing. Commonplaces should especially be collected in the areas of one's interest; they're not just a stockpile of quotations, but a fountain of ideas. A writer uses quotes to refer to authority, to flatter the audience, and to help the argument. In view of these strong reasons to quote, one wonders why more is not done. If you don't fall in love with writing that begs to be quoted, you're not likely to become quotable yourself. Isaac Disraeli said, "Those who never quote, in return are seldom quoted." You say you've never heard of Isaac Disraeli? Nine words have made him immortal. Let's see you become immortal in nine words or less.

Akin to the quotation is the *anecdote* that illustrates your point. Anecdotes can be about the famous or about you. They needn't be funny, and if they aren't, guard against introducing them as if they were. Don't be shy about telling personal stories. Every speaker knows that the moment she says *I* the audience wakes up. If she keeps saying *I I I* the audience falls asleep. If you're discussing hot dogs you can talk about your worst, your best, your ideal hot dog. You can talk forever about you and the hot dog, but you can't change the subject to you.

The audience is temporarily interested in you, perhaps more than in what you're saying. That's why personal style, revealing you, is so important. The audience wants your number in order to interpret what you're saying. But skillful writers, like skillful teachers, mystify their audience about themselves. Audiences love to label you—gonzo, dipso, psycho, homo, pinko. Tantalize them with your target, but if they hit you, you deserve it.

Those who write for a living know how important it is to make the writing lively. The quick way to do this is to jazz up the diction, making everything sound more glamorous than it is. The better way is to dramatize the material. Drama is struggle; people struggle, so introduce people. Make ideas important by giving them to people, real or fictitious. Say what they think.

A writer is someone in whom the first, second, and third persons get confused, since they're all in her head. But real live people aren't. Of course writers edit and invent quotations, report nonexistent stories, and write fact-based novels. They're making hay while the sun shines.

Wit and Irony

Few enterprises are riskier than a serious discussion of wit, but I have to do it. I have to warn you not to be witty. Whenever you're tempted to try something clever or funny, remember how serious the world is, think of those long faces out there—you're going to amuse them? They will think you're trying to be funny. Only funny men and homely women get to be funny. Is the Pope funny? Is Walter Cronkite funny?

Also, writing wittily is too hard, because every witty remark you make brings things to a halt. You can't write a paragraph with remarks, you can only write a paragraph with a paragraph. If you say *Power over men is what men and women want*, what comes next? If you say *A hen is an egg's way of making another egg*, where do you go from there? In wit you compress thought, in writing you expand it.

To be witty is to be familiar, and Formal is not familiar. You're not even allowed to be witty in the footnotes. One spark of wit in almost everything that's written—market analyses, research papers, political speeches, psychological studies, editorials, dissertations—one spark sends the whole thing up. Impropriety is the soul of wit, propriety the soul of persuasion. J.S. Mill said, "Opinions contrary to those commonly received can only obtain a hearing by studied moderation of language and the most cautious avoidance of offence." You can attract attention by audacity but you won't obtain a *hearing*. When Shaw said that his desire to exterminate the rich was equaled only by his detestation of the poor, it's unlikely that anyone was moved to share his wealth.

Humor smiles, wit grins and shows its teeth. Humorists exaggerate: *My kids made sixty pounds of dirty laundry over the weekend and the washing machine went berserk and attacked the dog.* Wit hits the nail on the head: *The trouble with living at home is they treat you like one of the family.* Both wit and humor are based on the truth, humor on truths that are worth being given an artistic treatment, and wit on truths that cut and stab.

To attack is the motive of wit. As Bacon says, "Anger makes dull men witty, but it keeps them poor." Only you can decide whether to be witty and poor or stupid and rich. Maybe it's best to have just enough wit to hide it. You write to persuade, not to be shot down in flames. The truth hurts. People laugh it off. Groucho said he was genuinely surprised that he made people laugh, because all he did was tell the truth. Writers quickly discover that when they tell the truth people laugh and when they tell jokes people frown, and that's why truths and jokes are so seldom written. So curb your attempts to be witty until you are a big shot, when it will be too late.

If, in spite of my warnings you still want to be witty, go, and my blessings go with you. Wit is after all our only defense against seriousness, and far too many things of this world are taken seriously—war, money, seduction, Formal English. As Gertrude Stein wisely said, "We are not serious because we are serious." As you go off on your hopeless mission, I will whisper to you the secret of being witty.

Where there's good writing wit is nearby. A good writer is one who says the unexpected. A successful writer *pretends* to say the unexpected. A witty writer says what is *very* unexpected. You become witty by first becoming an expert on what is expected. Wit depends on the *paradox*, or saying things *outside* the normal way. *Nothing succeeds like excess. I am a victim of an intact home. Did you take a bath? No, is one missing? I'm not afraid of work, I can lie down next to it and fall asleep. Take away the miniskirt and what have you got? I now bid you a welcome adieu.* To be a wit you find a *dox*, an old thought or saying, some cliché, and make it your doxy by suddenly taking it in a new way. Turn things upside down. Rename the Seven Dwarfs.

To write wittily you have to love words and love to play with them, which is natural among good writers. The *pun* is a miniature paradox, a discovery of a new way to use a word. *The teenagers are revolting. That conductor knows the score: he goes for baroque. Stop beating around the Freudian bush and get down to sexual morays.*

Puns are inexcusable in Formal because they are distracting and unserious. Puns are inexcusable in Informal because the others didn't think of them first. Puns are at their best and therefore their worst (our wurst is the best) when both meanings that are jumbled in the word fit the context, when the pun is quickly flashed, and when the words are not strained as in a *tur de force.*

In paradoxes and puns, new meanings are revealed. In irony, the sly form of wit, new and often rich meanings are suggested. *He said he was not a crook. Bob's a good team player.* Writers are tempted to use irony because it allows them to say things without being held accountable, and because it compliments the audience's cleverness. Rilke: *What will you do, God, when I die?*

In speaking, the audience is easily tipped off to irony by the speaker's voice and expression, but in writing irony is much harder to convey. The danger in irony is not that it is devious and evasive but that it isn't perceived. Also, too much irony, too many secret meanings, are mere self-indulgence on the writer's part, if not downright wackiness. Only expert writers find the ironic tone, and even then many of their ironies are missed. Readers have gone through the many volumes of Gibbons's *Decline and Fall* without noticing its irony. After five hundred years people still cannot decide if Machiavelli is ironic. They argue about whether Jesus was ever ironic. Are these verses by Kingsley Amis ironic? *Women are really much nicer than men: No wonder we like them.*

The reason irony is missed when it is there and found when it isn't is that life itself is ironic, full of hidden meanings and contradictions. The perfectly ironic tone is therefore no tone at all, or the tone of the truth. Writers have an easier time of it if they take a point of view and sound a particular tone, rather than try to honestly reflect life's ironies. You will always be under pressure to take a basically tragic or comic point of view, though your position may be that life is neither tragic nor comic.

Life is said to be a tragedy for those who feel and a comedy for those who think. You will find almost everyone requiring you to be tragic. God loves a joke, it's said, but apparently everyone else is afraid to laugh. Maybe God's joke, like a German joke, is not a laughing matter. "Thou art too damn jolly," says Captain Ahab. But "Measure the size of a man's understanding by his mirth," says Dr. Johnson.

Heavy irony has a tone easily discerned. When it's harsh and biting, it's called *sarcasm*. *This is good tom tom music for glue sniffers.* Twain: *Our Heavenly Father invented man because He was disappointed in the monkey.* Wilde: *Prayer must never be answered; if it is it ceases to be prayer and becomes a correspondence.* Sarcasm can be clever and dignified, but audiences find it too potent for Formal, and they get plenty of it at home.

Elegance

In writing, showy elegance is using big words; true elegance is leaving words out. Showy elegance is a thousand-dollar wristwatch; true elegance is a nurse's Timex or no watch at all. The elegant writer does not show off much. She would rather die than use jargon, and is embarrassed to have to explain a word. She never feels she has to instruct her audience, but addresses them as if they already knew as much or about as much as she. She says as little as she can as well as she can. She knows that the attempt to be exhaustive exhausts the reader, that saying only what is important pleases him. So she cuts and cuts: if she can give the impression she is spare with words, quiet, oblique in manner, she will get credit for being clever without having to say anything clever. If a writer has only one way to write, let it be elegant. A classy person can talk to anyone.

Of course, many audiences are impressed by *special language*. But large audiences are not. And using it corrupts the writer's thought. Precious style says precious little to precious few. There are telltale signs that a writer is coming on—using *shall*, using *which* in place of *that*, leaving *that* and *who* in where they could be omitted, saying *we we we* like the little pig, and using lots of qualifications, subjunctives, absolutes, and passives. Let's run through a few of these usages that mark showy elegance.

Shall versus will. *Shall* is now used only in first-person questions. *Shall we have lunch? Shall we dance?* Any other use of *shall* is only a literary quotation. *They shall not pass. We shall overcome.* *Shall* is thought to be emphatic—*collection shall be made*—but it isn't. It isn't elegant either, though the English still use it.

Which versus that. In American usage there is a distinction between *which* and *that*. *That* is used to start off clauses that *define* what they refer to. I just used it for the clause *that define what they refer to*. *Which* is used to start off clauses that do not define what they refer to. *That* is not preceded by a comma; *which* is preceded by a comma, since it introduces a new idea. A comma *pins* on new ideas. *Here is the dog that bit me.* No comma. *Here is the dog, comma, which seems to want to bite me. Look at this dress that I've never worn. Look at* this *dress, which I've never worn.* In speech, *that* usually replaces *which.* In writing, *which* is called on to reinforce the comma sounds. Since *which* seldom appears in speech, it's overused by people who associate it with writing and mistakenly think it's elegant. I've used *which* only a few times in these lessons, which you can check. *Which* is always a bit suspect, since it is so often used to tack afterthoughts onto a sentence. Some people think that if you use *that* a couple of times in a sentence that you should switch over to *which,* but that's not necessary. I used *that* four times in the previous sentence and nothing terrible happened to me that I know of. Elegant people, by the way, are not embarrassed by their words and therefore do not resort to synonyms to avoid repetition.

Dropping the relative pronoun. When should you leave the relative pronoun *that* or *who* in? Do you say *Here's the chair that I bought* or *Here's the chair I bought? Ask the girl whom you prefer* or *Ask the girl you prefer?* Omitting the relative pronoun used to be a mark of Informal, but it is omitted so often now in Formal you only have to write it in the places where you'd have to say it. Do not use it to be elegant: use it or omit it as your ear decides, according to the rhythm of the sentence. Here's a test: which of the following do you like best? *I hope that I have proved that he did it. I hope that I have proved he did it. I hope I have proved he did it. I hope I have proved that he did it.* The best of these versions seems to me to be the last one. By using the *that* you can sometimes emphasize the clause it starts.

The relative pronoun *that* refers to persons as well as things. *He's the man that I met. Who* can only be used for persons. You can't say *I think it was the bank who sent it back.* But you can use *whose* to refer to things. *This is the book whose cover is loose.* Wherever you can substitute *whose* for *of which,* an ugly phrase, do so. Similarly, don't say *that which,* say *what.* By all means drop the pronoun when you have a *preposition plus which.* Say *Here's the glass I drank from,* not *Here's the glass from which I drank.* Fix this one yourself: *You need to have something about which to write.*

We versus I. A writer should not say *we* when she means *I,* if she wants to say what she means. If she clearly means *we women* or *we Republicans* she can say *we.* If she vaguely means *I and all the wonderful people like me,* she should not say *we.* Sloppy use of *we* is sloppy thinking. "Still we live meanly, like ants," says Thoreau. Do you live like an ant? It's never elegant to say *we* instead of *I,* or to avoid talking about yourself in cases where you are relevant to the argument.

Using the subjunctive. First I had better remind you of what the subjunctive is. It's a special way of using the *being* verbs and the dropping of the *s* from third person singular verbs. *I ask that the report* be *distributed. I wish Christmas* were *here. The contract provides that each party* pay *half. God* damn *it.* This special subjunctive is not much used now, but it's not dead, and still very lively in proverbial expressions like *So* be *it* and Come *hell or high water,* and in resolutions and commands. *She demanded that he* offer *an apology.* In Formal, the subjunctive is used more often than in Informal: *I insist that you* be *on time, I insist that you* are *on time. If I* were *president, I'd talk straight, If I* was *president, I'd talk straight.* I recommend that the subjunctive be used. You'd avoid old-fashioned and showy uses, such as *I hope that he* be *punished,* and *Would that he* were *behind bars, lest he* do *more harm.*

Similar to the subjunctive, as an old-fashioned, literary form, is the *absolute.* An absolute is a noun linked with a participle. It has no grammatical connection to the rest of the sentence, which is why it's an absolute. *The bus having come, we got on board. The case was lost, the lawyer being to blame.* Since the absolute construction is disappearing but not yet gone, it's effective to use.

The *present perfect tense* is being wiped out of overuse of the simple past, so you should use the present perfect every chance you get. *I ate, I have eaten. They wanted it, They have wanted it. Carol said no, Carol has said no.* Important nuances are conveyed by the present perfect. But don't use it after a past tense question, as in *Did you do it?* Say *Yes, I did it,* not *Yes, I have done it.* When someone asks you a question, reply in his language. *When do you leave?* Say *I leave tomorrow,* not *I will leave* or *I am leaving.*

Elegant people avoid using *if* to start off noun clauses. Instead of *He asked me if I'd come* they say *He asked me whether I'd come.* A little note of elegance they try to keep secret is the use of *so* instead of *as* after negatives. *This piece is not* so *large as that.*

As elegant people always seem attentive, listening, so does elegant writing have an open-minded, alert tone, a tone of conversing rather than lecturing. Elegance depends as much on what you refrain from saying as on what you say. Instead of wondering whether an adverb or transitional expression goes better at the start or the middle of a sentence, be really elegant and leave it out. The word *elegant* means *choice*, and the writer's work lies in choosing as much as in finding. Though some people like to have fingers wagged in their face or like a complete massage, most people prefer the light touch.

Five-Finger Exercises

The poet Brecht said: "We must write for the people in the language of kings." To make your language a little more kingly or queenly, and to make sure you're not circumscribed as you write by the few *kinds* of sentences you're used to hearing, you might want to do this drill. Write ten or twenty sentences each using:

1. introductory subordinate clauses (*Because I love her,* I'll stop smoking.)
2. introductory participial phrases (*Succumbing to her pleas,* I promised to stop.)
3. trailing participial phrases (I cheated, *realizing that a woman is only a woman but a good cigar is a smoke.*)
4. long appositives (She still married me, *the only one of her suitors who dared to smoke.*)
5. passive voice (My cigarettes *are* mysteriously *being spirited away.*)
6. subjunctives (If I *were* single again I could light up.)
7. absolutes (*The long torture over,* I'm no longer addicted.)

Musicians practice all day long, but writers don't; they work seriously, as if to make every word publishable. They're always performing—for themselves. But they'd do well to loosen up—to extemporize, experiment, play with variations, write dialogue for the bedroom, courtroom, locker room, dining room, boardroom. A fun exercise is to work on the One-Two Punch: *An eye for an eye and a tooth for a tooth, The last shall be first and the first shall be last, Do men gather grapes of thorns, or figs of thistles? Prison holds people who should never have been put there and those who should never be let out, Americans drink red wine too warm and white wine too cold.* When you say something well, follow it up.

Pleasing Listeners

What is written just to be read seldom works when used as a speech; *speeches have to be specially written*. Even on Formal occasions, a speech can include informalities in wordiness, repetition, and vividness that you might not get by with in writing. Many smart people have neglected the differences between speeches and other kinds of writing and have failed as speakers. In writing style, less is usually more; in speeches, less is usually a loss. The Gettysburg Address is a great poem, but not a good speech. The tighter, more closely argued a speech is, the less chance it has of succeeding. Lawyers know this and go for hours making their so-called summations. Speakers are supposed to be expansive, allowing the audience to enjoy the honor and treat of being addressed.

In writing, it's the middle that's important, in speaking it's the beginning and the end that are important. The opening of a speech requires the greatest care, for it sets the tone and fixes the relationship between speaker and audience. A speech should end strongly, with a daring thought or conclusion, question, joke, warning, prophecy, or call to action.

Since more freedom is allowed to speakers and fewer demands made on them for instruction, one might conclude that it's easier to write good speeches than pieces meant for the printer. It is. Lesser skills are required in composing speeches, but they are hardly negligible. Special skills are needed not just in composing but in delivering speeches, and everyone should acquire these skills. Everyone should have lessons in speaking as well as in writing. The two subjects are one.

I'll not try to substitute for a course in speaking, but will remind you of how to deliver a speech, for that is part of rhetoric. The traits admired in writers are those admired in speakers. Tact and consideration work with listeners as with readers. In writing, the problem of tone has to be solved, and finding the tone proves to the audience you're interested in them and in the subject. The speaker must also strike the right tone. But her job is easier, since her voice can sound the tone more effectively than words can ever do. It's said of dogs, horses, and children, that they learn much more from your tone than from your words. A speaker would be foolish not to exploit the resources of the voice. The tone of candor and sincerity, so difficult to convey through the artificiality of print, is easily imitated by any speaker. The most powerful trick in all of rhetoric, the sudden change in voice volume, is unavailable to the poor writer who has to make do with punctuation marks.

As the writer must avoid words that bluster or squeak, so must the speaker avoid shouting or mumbling. As the writer has to face up to the possibility that another human being might actually read her stuff, so the speaker must look her audience in the eye. She does not look at her feet or heaven or the back of the room. She's talking to people, not to a room. Like the writer, she has to remember she's a person talking to other people. Of course this makes her vulnerable. But she's used to it; she's done it all her life.

Most inexperienced speakers go like machines, delivering the speech too fast and at the same rate. The sound of one person's voice, however beautiful it may be, grows tiresome. The excitement, rhythm, give-and-take of conversation are lost. The speaker should compensate for the loss by changing pace and emphasis. She controls pace, volume, and pitch, and creates excitement by these devices alone, no matter what is being said. She guards against ending each sentence on the same tone. A speech given in a foreign language can be better, that is, more closely listened to, than a speech given drearily in one's own language.

The tricks of Formal speaking are easy to learn, tricks like speaking very slowly, like gesturing with the hands, chopping with one hand, pointing with the index finger, and opening or raising the arms. It's hard to do too much gesturing, though it's easy to repeat the same gesture too often. Another important device is the significant pause before important words, or speaking the words after the pause—*softly*. In speaking, pauses are important; they help slow the pace, and must not be filled up with *ers*, *ahs*, and *uhs*.

These audible pauses are no problem if one reads a speech or recites it from memory. But neither of these ways of delivering a speech is as effective as speaking from notes or an outline. What makes speech exciting is the impression that it is being made as one listens. "What really exists is not things made but things in the making," says William James. (And that is why it is so important to capture the authentic tone of living speech in whatever you write.)

If a speech is memorized, there's always the danger of forgetting the lines or leaving hunks of it out. Energy spent remembering the lines would be better spent in delivering them with understanding. With memorized speeches, the speaker often forgets what the words say, and sounds like an actor doing Shakespeare without understanding a word. If the speech is obviously being read, the audience feels cheated. When big shots read a speech, everyone knows it's someone else's. Nowadays, with high lecterns and tele-prompters, speakers get away with a lot of reading. You can read your speech if you've rehearsed it well and don't have to look at it too often. The better way is to use an outline that shows the beginning of each sentence or key phrases in the speech. Move your finger down the outline to keep your place as you go. Every speech should be thoroughly practiced before a mirror and before a friend. (If you listen to yourself on tape you may become discouraged.)

Let your posture be natural and your gestures and voice be fairly natural. You needn't worry about pronunciation, since no one cares about that anymore. Loudspeakers are so common that whenever they're missing, the speaker takes pains to make sure she can be heard. The ideal of fine elocution is dead, and precise pronunciation and beautiful voices are resented by audiences, who think the speaker is putting on airs.

The audience listens to the start of the speech, because they want to find out about you. They listen for the end, because they get tired of being spoken to. Don't skimp or botch either. It's good to open with extemporaneous remarks, or ones that seem to be so. Before starting, wait for quiet, count to five, and begin. The ending should be built up so that even the sleepiest member of the audience knows you're in the homestretch. Don't tell a joke unless you're a joker, or unless everyone is, or unless the joke has to be told. Jokes are fiction; anecdotes are true. You can always tell an anecdote.

You should be nervous, for that helps you do a better job. Only a little experience is needed to remove stage fright. If you're terrified, seek practice in speaking, because such insecurity will hurt you in many aspects of your life. Just as the inability to write is overcome by thinking of your audience and what you want to tell them, so the inability to speak is overcome by thinking of your audience and what you want to tell them. If you think only about yourself, sooner or later you'll have to pay somebody to listen.

Revision Quiz

Here are some sentences you would not want to use in Formal. Find the fault (or faults) in each and then revise the sentence so that it will be more effective. My revisions will follow.

1. Sis wrote she was sick on her last postcard.
2. Before we get into all that, let me tell you a little story.
3. I walked and the bus never showed up.
4. He wrote me letters repeatedly, or rather, continually.
5. I hesitate to contemplate the termination of our association.
6. I jogged from Missouri City, Texas, to Texas City, Missouri, during National Radish Week.
7. Neither he nor her are going steady with anybody.
8. Why do we intellectuals always marry homely women?
9. Do not bend, fold, spindle, or mutilate this card.
10. He drinks because he's a Macaroon.
11. At the present time I have not received the widget which I had ordered to be sent.
12. I shall always believe that if I was married, I should be happy.
13. She tore off her feathered boa, whirled around, shook her chestnut tresses, and hissed, "Take back your emeralds, Count Rupert!"
14. By examination of the x rays, the best treatment can be decided on by your doctor.
15. Wearing a designer dress, she utilized the telephone to make an advance reservation for an old fashion barbecue beef dinner at the pint size air condition patio restaurant.
16. Rationalization of company procedures entails the releasing of selected redundant personnel.
17. It is with great relief that I announce that there is no reason in the world to suppose that Chef Wang has actually started a fire out in the kitchen.
18. He is going to be shot because of his courage in speaking up against the government.
19. I hope that I have shown that this committee's responsibility is clear in the matter of failure to repay the loan.
20. Nixon was always very ambitious; he was a very close student of politics; he was greatly stirred by his boyish dream of living in the White House.
21. The long and the short of it is, to defeat Russia in the Olympics can only be done in the following way.
22. Oranges are more or less round, apples are more or less round, but bananas are different.
23. We are presently sending you our shipment with the remainder of the order to be sent later on.
24. Ten people were present in the parlor when Inspector Pudel be-

gan his interrogation of the domestic staff in regard to cook Peggy's knives.

25. My whole family eats weeds and we have no trouble with bleeding gums.

26. When fear creeps in the window, love shoots out the door.

27. In a criminal society criminal lawyers have an easy time getting criminal defendants acquitted.

28. They are a pusillanimous corps of effete snobs and pointyheads.

29. With a good conscience our only sure reward, with history the final judge of our deeds, let us go forth to lead the land we love, asking His blessing and His help, but knowing that here on earth God's work must truly be our own.

30. Many a crown of wisdom is but the golden chamberpot of Success.

My Revisions

1. *Sis wrote she was sick on her last postcard.*
   Formally, you can't say Sis. The phrase *on her last postcard* is misplaced.
   Revised: *My sister wrote on her last postcard that she was sick.*

2. *Before we get into all that, let me tell you a little story.*
   The tone is not just chatty but apologetic. What's the matter with *all that* and why is the story *little?*
   Revised: *Before I talk about that, I'd like to tell this story.*

3. *I walked and the bus never showed up.*
   The relationship of the two ideas is unclear. *Showed up* is Informal.
   Revised: *I'm glad I walked since the bus never came.*

4. *He wrote me letters repeatedly, or rather, continually.*
   The writer should decide which word is best and not offer alternatives.
   Revised: *He wrote me letters continually.*

5. *I hesitate to contemplate the termination of our association.*
   Stuffy diction, and two jingles.
   Revised: *I do not like to think of your leaving us.*

6. *I jogged from Missouri City, Texas, to Texas City, Missouri, during National Radish Week.*
   Anticlimax.
   Revised: *During National Radish Week I jogged, etc.*

7. *Neither he nor her are going steady with anybody.*
   Three mistakes. *He nor her* should be *he nor she. Neither he*

nor she should be followed by a singular verb. *Anybody* should be *anyone*. *Going steady* is Informal, but precise and brief enough to graduate to Formal.
Revised: *Neither he nor she is going steady with anyone.*

8. *Why do we intellectuals always marry homely women?*
Rhetorical questions like this one backfire. And who is *we?*
Revised: *Many intellectuals marry homely women, and I've asked myself why.*

9. *Do not bend, fold, spindle, or mutilate this card.*
Lists are tedious. No one knows *spindle*, so cut it. *Mutilate* has inappropriate connotations of sacrilege.
Revised: *Please do not fold or damage this card.*

10. *He drinks because he's a Macaroon.*
Faulty reasoning about cause. If you feel you have to talk about why he drinks, say something like *He's a Macaroon, and Macaroons are notorious for their drinking,* or more suggestively, *He's a Macaroon who loves to drink.*

11. *At the present time I have not received the widget which I had ordered to be sent.*
Wordiness and a jingle—*widget which.*
Revised: *I have not received the widget I ordered.*

12. *I shall always believe that if I was married, I should be happy.*
Three verbs, three mistakes. *Shall* and *should* are affected. *Was* is not Formal enough, and should be the subjunctive *were.*
Revised: *I will always believe that if I were married I would be happy.*

13. *She tore off her feathered boa, whirled around, shook her chestnut tresses, and hissed, "Take back your emeralds, Count Rupert!"*
Too rich. The words are acceptable, considered separately, with the possible exception of *tresses,* but together they distract from the excitement of the events.
Revised: *Pulling off her boa, she whirled around and hissed, "Take back your emeralds!"*

14. *By examination of the x rays, the best treatment can be decided on by your doctor.*
By examination of should be *By examining,* since the gerund is more forceful than the noun. The passive voice is used unnecessarily and makes the opening phrase dangle.
Revised: *By examining the x rays, your doctor can decide on the best treatment.*

15. *Wearing a designer dress, she utilized the telephone to make an advance reservation for an old fashion barbecue beef dinner at the pint size air condition patio restaurant.*

Here we have nouns masquerading as adjectives. *Utilized the telephone* is fancy and nouny for *called*. What does her dress have to do with anything? Get rid of it.

Revised: *She called to reserve an old-fashioned barbecued beef dinner at the small, air-conditioned patio restaurant.*

16. *Rationalization of company procedures entails the releasing of selected redundant personnel.*

    The diction is *too* euphemistic, and doesn't do the job it wants to do. It also suffers from nounitis.

    Revised: *The company has to let some people go.*

17. *It is with great relief that I announce that there is no reason in the world to suppose that Chef Wang has actually started a fire out in the kitchen.*

    Wordiness here. *It is, there is, in the world, actually, that that that.* General pomposity.

    Revised: *You will be relieved to know that the kitchen is not on fire.*

18. *He is going to be shot because of his courage in speaking up against the government.*

    This loose sentence fizzles. Change to emphatic.

    Revised: *Because he courageously spoke against the government, he will be shot.*

19. *I hope that I have shown that this committee's responsibility is clear in this matter of failure to repay the loan.*

    Ugly sound in *I hope that I have shown that this.* Also, the nouns smother the verb.

    Revised: *The loan has not been repaid, and the committee is responsible.*

20. *Nixon was always very ambitious; he was a very close student of politics; he was greatly stirred by his boyish dream of living in the White House.*

    Needless qualifiers, *very, greatly.* Clichés, *close student, boyish dream.* Circumlocution, *living in the White House.* Try to combine clauses starting with the same subject.

    Revised: *A student of politics and ambitious even as a boy, Nixon dreamed of being President.*

21. *The long and the short of it is, to defeat Russia in the Olympics can only be done in the following way.*

    The long and the short of it is an Informal stall. The infinitive phrase *to defeat Russia* can't be the subject of a passive verb. You probably didn't know that rule, but you don't have to, since it's a logical one.

    Revised: *Russia can only be defeated in the Olympics in this way.*

22. *Oranges are more or less round, apples are more or less round, but bananas are different.*

Nothing wrong with this except it's boring. Comparisons are tedious and should be justified.

Revised: *Thank goodness bananas are not round like apples, oranges, and all those other fruits.*

23. *We are presently sending you your shipment with the remainder of the order to be sent later on.*
   Wordiness. Vagueness. Dangling, trailing *with* phrase.

   Revised: *We are sending you half your order now and will send you the rest as soon as we can.*

24. *Ten people were present in the parlor when Inspector Pudel began his interrogation of the domestic staff in regard to cook Peggy's knives.*
   Alliteration of *p*s. Wordiness. Extra details.

   Revised: *Ten servants were seated in the parlor when Inspector Pudel began to question them about the cook's knives.*

25. *My whole family eats weeds and we have no trouble with bleeding gums.*
   Logic. The *and* merely *suggests* a causal connection between two events.

   Revised: *After my family started to eat weeds, all of our trouble with bleeding gums stopped.*

26. *When fear creeps in the window, love shoots out the door.*
   Too lively for Formal.

   Revised: *When love begins to fear, love dies.*

27. *In a criminal society criminal lawyers have an easy time getting criminal defendants acquitted.*
   Too assertive. The audience might doubt that society is criminal.

   Revised: *In a criminal society criminal lawyers would have an easy time getting criminal defendants acquitted.*

28. *They are a pusillanimous corps of effete snobs and pointyheads.*
   Probable faults in diction. *Pusillanimous* (cowardly) and *effete* (worn out) are not known to an audience that uses the hateful term *pointyheads*, but that audience might like the sound of them anyway. *Corps* is vague. The stylistic objection to the sentence is that it's mere description.

   Revised: *These intellectuals can no longer rise to the occasion.*

29. *With a good conscience our only sure reward, with history the final judge of our deeds, let us go forth to lead the land we love, asking His blessing and His help, but knowing that here on earth God's work must truly be our own.*
   Two dangling *with* phrases. *Let us go forth* is a literary cliché. *To lead the land we love*—alliteration. *Truly* is meaningless. These words of John F. Kennedy, preceding assassination attempts on Castro and the secret war in Vietnam, are sanctimonious.

   Revised: *I can't.*

30. *Many a crown of wisdom is but the golden chamberpot of Success.*

This sentence by Mark Twain cannot be improved. But you couldn't use this sentence in Formal because you can't talk about chamberpots. That make you mad? Good, it's a way to get smart.

The End

I'm sure you did well on the revision quiz. It's not hard to find the faults in someone else's sentences. Revising the sentences is hard. I made it look easy, but it takes awhile to learn. Some of my sentences could stand improvement, but I've had it with this book. Getting something down that's halfway decent is the most tiring work—though never tiresome. Writing beautifully? Forget it.

Somerset Maugham said, "To write simply is as difficult as to be good." This Game of English is wickedly hard. But if it was easy, it wouldn't be worth playing. And it is worth playing, for its real and its symbolic stakes. The symbolic stakes are worldly success. The real stakes are improvements in one's understanding.

Keats said that fine writing is next to fine doing. He didn't say it was right behind it. People sense that the two are somehow associated, and that's why they admire and want to imitate those who express themselves well. Since ancient times teachers have asserted that talking and writing well is essentially a moral matter, rather than a matter of being clever. Good expression does seem to require courtesy, patience, self-knowledge, and courage.

Can people be taught to express themselves well? That's a good question. I don't know. If you could teach them to be good, you could teach them to talk and write well. But then, if they were good, would they have much to say? Walter Bagehot said, "The reason so few good books are written is that so few people that can write know anything."

Unless you're good, in the old sense of the word, you're not likely to win satisfying victories in the Game. The Game is fairly honest, and in the long run cheaters never prosper. If you speak with the tongues of angels, advertisers, politicians, professors, louts, and harpies, when do *you* get to talk?

So speak up—let the others take their turn at listening.

Index